To Adventure Guides throughout the world, in every Workplace setting – disciple makers and transformation agents:

Be strong in the Lord, and in the power of His might; for He is able to do exceedingly abundantly more with you than you can ask or think; according to the power that works in you.

the Map Maker's Guide

A Study in Workplace Disciple Making and Community Transformation

ROB STREETMAN

INLIGHT CONSULTING

Encouraging, Edifying and Equipping Workplace Leaders for Community Transformation

Douglasville, Georgia

Published by inLight Consulting, Inc.
Rob Streetman, President
Douglasville, Georgia
ISBN 978-0-9962274-1-4

The Map Maker's Guide

Contents

Your Assignment 7

Preface 9

Introduction 13

Section One – Preparation

Map 1 – The Workplace Mission 19

Map 2 – Searching Out the Matter 27

Map 3 – Renewing the Mind 35

Map 4 – The Adventures of Our Life in Christ 41

Map 5 – The Fear of the LORD 51

Section Two – Surrendering to His Purpose

Map 6 – The Purposes of God 61

Map 7 – The Church He is Building – Vision 67

Map 8 – Intimacy with God 73

Map 9 – The Gospel of the Kingdom 79

Map 10 – Desires and Assignments 85

Map 11 – Surrendering to His Purpose 91

Section Three – Sacrificing for His Plan

Map 12 – Counting the Cost – Our Investment 97

Map 13 – Suffering for the Kingdom 103

Map 14 – Chaos Navigation 111

Map 15 – The One Another Fellowship 119

Map 16 – Who is Serving Who? 125

Map 17 – Our Identity in Christ 131

Map 18 – Disciple Making God's Way 137

Map 19 – Workplace Ministry Formation 145

Section Four – Submitting to His Power

Map 20 – The Life that Glorifies Our Father in Heaven 153

Map 21 – The Power of His Life 159

Map 22 – The Power of Abiding 167

Map 23 – The Power of Prayer 173

Map 24 – The Power of Unity 181

Map 25 – God's Mighty Force 187

Map 26 – The Church He is Building – Model 195

Epilogue – For Your Assignment 201

Bibliography 205

Recommended Reading 206

The Map Maker's Guide

Your Assignment

And Jesus came and spoke to them, saying, "All authority has been given to Me in heaven and on earth. Go therefore and make disciples of all the nations, baptizing them in the name of the Father and of the Son and of the Holy Spirit, teaching them to observe all things that I have commanded you; and lo, I am with you always, even to the end of the age." Matthew 28:18-20

The Great Commission is not evangelism, and it is not teaching – it is something more. The Great Commission was not given to Seminary students – it was given to everyone. The Great Commission is not even a program for church growth. The Great Commission is SO MUCH MORE!

The Great Commission is our Co-mission! It is the mission we have been called to share with the One who has been given all authority in heaven and on earth. Think about that for a minute. What mission could be more important and more exciting? Let's get this right, right here at the beginning:

Our Lord, Jesus Christ, intends for the Great Commission to be our lifestyle and our life's assignment!

If you have come to *The Map Maker's Guide* by way of *The Map Maker* then you know your assignment: God has positioned you with authority and influence, as an instrument of righteousness, for His kingdom and glory. You have been prepared to lead others through the same adventure you have enjoyed. The Great Commission is a mission we take with others.

Paul, a disciple of Jesus Christ, put it this way to one of those he had discipled:

You therefore, my son, be strong in the grace that is in Christ Jesus. And the things that you have heard from me among many witnesses, commit these to faithful men who will be able to teach others also. 2Timothy 2:1-2

If you have not had the opportunity to read *The Map Maker*, then I encourage you to do so. It is available in multiple formats through www.themapmakerbook.com. *Part 1 – Somebody's Adventure* is also available, free of charge, at the same site. I encourage you to share the parable as the Lord leads you.

However you have come to *The Map Maker's Guide,* my prayer is that you will use it to maximum advantage for the kingdom of God. As you will discover, it consists of 26 turn-key lessons that can be taught in one hour sessions. Each lesson contains everything the leader needs to disciple others through an adventure that leads to joyful, Spirit-filled ministry.

Humbly yours and forever His,

Rob

The Map Maker's Guide

Preface

Our Desire

Delight yourself in the Lord, and He will give you the desires of your heart. Psalm 37:4

inLight Consulting – our ministry to Leaders in the Workplace – was birth out of an extended wrestling with God over my future vocational life. After 25 years in the Information Technology business, He decided it was time for me to do something else. Not knowing what the something else was, I vehemently resisted. He was persistent and long-suffering. I love Him for that. I finally relented.

The conversation at my surrender went something like this:

"Okay God, I give up. What do you want me to do?"

"What is the desire of your heart?"

I turned to my heart and asked, "What is your desire?"

"To help Christian Leaders find joyful, Spirit-filled ministry", was its reply.

"That's it", said my Father, "That's my purpose for the next season of your life."

And so began an adventure – a new season in my life. For each of the next thirty days, the Lord had a word for me about this new adventure. One in particular has become the framework for this guide.

**To find joyful Spirit-filled ministry, Christian Leaders must surrender to God's
purpose, sacrifice for God's plan, and submit to God's power.**

This requirement has been the story of my life for the last nine plus years. I can tell you from experience that surrender, sacrifice and submission are well worth the reward of finding Him in His purpose, plan and power. I would do it all again. I might do some things differently, but the transaction (so to speak) has been greatly weighted in my favor.

I am sure your adventure will be different from mine. We serve a dynamic, "don't box me in", God. Like most adventures, there will be a mixture of excitement and fear. I pray that you will find much more of the former. I promise that you will learn how to deal with the latter.

It is the glory of God to hide a matter, and the glory of kings to search out a matter (Proverbs 25:2). Jesus spoke in parables "because it has been given to you to know the mysteries of the kingdom of heaven…" (Matthew 13:11). This guide will lead you on a treasure hunt, in search of the mysteries of the kingdom of God. You will be encouraged to be faithful stewards of the treasures you discover (1Corinthians 4:1-2). If you seek the knowledge of God with your whole heart, I guarantee that He will fill your adventure with sweet anticipation; and a wonder that will not disappoint.

Finding joyful, Spirit-filled ministry has been God's desire for you since before the beginning of time. This guide is a product of that desire. There are no coincidences for God's children. That you have begun reading this guide at this time in your life, during this time in history, is the result of innumerable miracles. God has orchestrated events that you might discover the desire He has deposited in you. He fully intends to give you the desire of your heart – for His kingdom, His name and His glory.

Our Mission

Let your light so shine before men so that when they see your good works, they will glorify your Father in heaven. Matthew 5:16

When inLight Consulting was birth, I had no idea that Workplace Ministry existed. I assumed our mission field would be leaders within church organizations. God had a different plan in mind. Through a series of circumstances only He could have orchestrated, He established our mission to the Workplace.

The mission of inLight Consulting is to encourage, edify and equip Leaders in the Workplace to become disciple makers and transformation agents in their communities.

God is a good communicator. He always chooses His words carefully. Here's what we've come to understand about His mission for us:

Encourage: To put courage in. Our enemies have used fear to inhibit God's work in the Workplace. Courage is not the absence of fear, but God's grace to face and defeat that fear, and His enemies.

Edify: To build up with the truth, beginning with a strong foundation. The truth makes men free. A man made free by the truth is a mighty weapon in the hand of God.

Equip: To repair something or someone God's intended use (the nets in Matthew 4:21; the saints in Ephesians 4:12). God is healing individual brokenness and corporate division in response to His Son's prayer (John 17:20-23).

Leader in the Workplace: A Christian that has been given influence in the Workplace. The Workplace includes business, education, government, media, arts/entertainment, family and religion – the "Seven Mountains of Culture". Those "given influence" are not just the top layers of an organization. For example, most teachers have influence over thirty children and their families. Influence can be with customers, employees, partners, students, patients, congregants, etc.

Disciple Makers: Making disciples is the Biblical prescription for joining God in His story and ultimate purpose of restoring all that was lost in the Garden.

Transformation Agents: The Biblical prescription for our maturation in Christ is found in Romans 12:2 and 2Corinthians 3:18. Transformation that begins with the individual will eventually impact family, fellowship and community.

My intention in sharing our mission is two-fold. First, this guide has been developed to serve God out of the mission He has given to inLight Consulting. Our prayer and confidence is that it will accomplish that mission in your life and in the lives of those over whom God has given you influence. You will also discover that the truths found in this guide apply to areas beyond the Workplace. Through it, you will also find joyful, Spirit-filled ministry in marriage, parenting, recreation, etc. – in every environment where you are doing God's work.

Secondly, I hope you appreciate the breadth and depth of God's offering in this guide. He has not been caught by surprise at the decline of the church. He has been preparing a people and giving them influence – in large and small settings – to be His makers of disciples and His agents of transformation. Follow this guide and you will discover a deeper intimacy with Him and a broader impact for Him. He expects a return on His investment in your life and vocation. His eye is roaming to and fro about the Earth, looking for the one in whom He can show Himself strong; the one that is loyal to Him (2Chronicles 16:9). He is looking for you.

Our Appreciation

Beholding Him as in a mirror, we are being transformed from glory to glory into the very image of Christ; and this by the Holy Spirit. 2Corinthians 3:18

When I first understood that our mission field would be the Workplace, I thought God had entrusted me with a brand new ministry. I've been naïve before, and probably will be again. It didn't take long to figure out that there were hundreds of Workplace ministries in America, and around the world. After a brief moment of disappointment, I soon realized how blessed I am that so many have gone before.

Two Workplace ministers that have particularly influenced the formation of inLight Consulting are Os Hillman and Lance Wallnau. My first Workplace Ministry conference was hosted by Os' Marketplace Leaders Ministries. Many of you may recognize Os from his devotional, *Today God is First* (referenced extensively in this guide). Lance has spoken into my life at these conferences and through his 7M University resources. I am eternally grateful for their influence and mentoring.

You cannot be a disciple maker if you are not being made one yourself. I have been blessed throughout my life by men of God, carefully position to lead me to Christ and encourage me to spend time in His presence. Most recently, this has been my dear friend, John Brown. John has discipled many disciple makers in the ways of God and the keys of His kingdom. Much of the truth you will find in this guide was delivered through this faithful and patient servant.

Some adventures are harder than others. Leaving the securities of corporate America to start a "faith ministry" has been a struggle and a challenge. It is my humble opinion that no other man has been so blessed by his family and friends. Their prayers have protected, their words have encouraged, and their example of life lived in Christ has been used by God to draw me deeper into His kingdom. My wife, Beth, has been particularly patient and long-suffering. We have faced this adventure together. We could not have done it without her commitment to our King; and, secondly, to the fool for Christ that loves her more than he can express in words.

The Map Maker's Guide

Introduction

Study Guide Overview

> *Work out your own salvation with fear and trembling; for God is in you to will and do to His good pleasure.* Philippians 2:12-13

> *Do not fear, for it is the Father's good pleasure to give you the kingdom.* Luke 12:32

The purpose of this guide is to equip you, as a Leader in the Workplace, to lead others into joyful, Spirit-filled ministry. Ministry is what we do when we participate in God's work. Ministry that is joyful is not necessarily easy ministry. It may not even be fun ministry. Joyful ministry is ministry filled with joy in the Lord. The joy of the Lord will be your strength to endure when ministry is difficult and something less than fun. Spirit-filled ministry is manifested by the power of God through the fruit and gifts of the Spirit.

To find joyful, Spirit-filled ministry, you must surrender to God's purpose, sacrifice for His plan and submit to His power. These three general steps, along with some preparation, form the framework for this guide. Here's an introductory comment about each one:

> The **Preparation s**ection will introduce the spiritual foundation for the curriculum, explore how we intend to search out the truth as stewards of the mysteries, and challenge the reader with a few of those mysteries.

> Before the foundations of the earth, God deposited a desire in the heart of every Marketplace Leader. **Surrendering to His Purpose** creates an atmosphere for hearing and believing the living word of God; and sharing in His heart's desires for the kingdom.

> The Lord reveals enough of His plan for the Marketplace Leader to count the cost and ask, "Is **Sacrificing for His Plan** something I am willing to do?" This is THE decisive moment – what William Blackaby called "the crisis of faith".

> Christians participate in God's work as vessels of the Father, Son and Holy Spirit. He is the Potter; we are the clay. We become useful vessels by **Submitting to His Power** – being transformed so that we may be used as agents of transformation.

While each of the lessons in this guide has been written to stand on its own, the greatest impact will occur for those that progress through the guide as it is written. The process is more important than you may realize at this time. Resist the urge to skip unfamiliar or unpleasant lessons. Allow at least one week for each lesson to process you and your group. The truth will make you free.

We recommend using this guide in a group setting, but it will also be effective for the Marketplace Leader who wants to go deeper on their own. In either case, **be sure at least three people are praying for you; and one of these is encouraging you through to completion.**

Approaches to Making Disciples

The Map Maker's Guide is, by design, more challenging than the disciple making resources you may have been exposed to of late. Adventures are something "less than" when they are not challenging. The gospel message, and its impact, must not be weakened in this study. Trust the LORD with the resource you have been given.

As you will see in the section on format, there is a comprehensive approach to the lessons. Each part has been carefully developed and constructed for maximum kingdom impact. However, it is important for the leader of this study to be flexible in their presentation of the material.

Please note that I am talking flexibility, not compromise. The best approach: Come prepared, but flexible. Flexible for what? Flexible for the Holy Spirit to guide the meeting, and the overall study. This will require your preparation before the meeting – particularly getting your heart in the place where you can sense the Holy Spirit's guidance. You will likely find this is easier as you move through the study.

You will also notice that I have not provided discussion questions. It is my conviction that discussing the truth with others, right after a lesson, is a distraction. It is better for each person to first discuss the truth they have heard with the Holy Spirit. Encourage your group to discuss what they hear with you and each other outside the meeting. This will encourage community.

It would be beneficial for everyone in your study group to have a copy of *The Map Maker's Guide*. However, I do not want resource cost to stand in the way of you making disciples. Therefore, you have my permission to copy each lesson for those in your group that cannot afford to invest in a book. I suggest you hand these copies out after you have taught the lesson.

Finally, a word about accountability. Holding someone accountable, after the fact, is not as powerful as encouraging them in the beginning. It is the Holy Spirit's responsibility to draw and convict. Your role is to encourage and assist. So, you do what you do best and let Him do the rest.

Lesson Format

> *And we desire that each one of you show the same diligence to the full assurance of hope until the end, that you do not become sluggish, but imitate those who through faith and patience inherit the promises.* Hebrews 6:11-12

Each lesson in the Adventure Guide is formatted in the same way. Each section plays an important part in the discipling process. Maximize your time and effort by immersing yourself in each one.

Spiritual Exercise

The spiritual exercise is intended to be an activity requiring effort, carried out to sustain or improve health and fitness… of our spirits. The purpose is to follow our spirits in turning our hearts and minds to God. Changing your physical position may help (e.g., kneeling or standing). There is a prayer offered, but you should supplement it with your own confession, thanksgiving and requests.

Introduction

The introduction is intended to get you thinking about the lesson, particularly in regard to *The Map Maker's Guide* as a whole, the section you are in, and any related lessons.

Definition

It is no coincidence that the Hebrew and Greek languages were developed to record the Old and New Testament. They are the creation of God for the expression of the kingdom. Hidden in their words are depths and richness of meaning that cannot be expressed in the English language. One of the easiest and most rewarding ways to search out the mysteries of the kingdom is to understand the full meaning of the most important words. One or more words related to the lesson will be highlighted here.

Searching Out the Matter

My intention for this, the main section of each the lesson, is to lean heavily on passages of Scripture. I have attempted, successfully in more cases than others, to keep my commentary to a minimum. My responsibility as a disciple maker is to lead you to our Teachers: Jesus Christ and the Holy Spirit. I cannot overstate the importance of you hearing from Them. This is covered in more depth in the Preparation section.

I have experienced the Lord speaking through various translations of the Holy Bible. However, I have found that the best translations for searching out the mysteries are those that follow word-for-word methodologies, as they are less subjective to the translator's doctrinal biases. These include the King James Version, the New King James Version, the New American Standard Bible and Young's Literal Translation. These versions and more can be found on a website that I use extensively: www.blueletterbible.org.

All Scripture references, except those noted, are from the New King James Version (Thomas Nelson, Inc.). Footnotes and headings have been excluded.

Conclusion

As you might expect, the conclusion contains a summary of the lesson and/or a few concluding remarks. I have also attempted, in the **Application** subsection, to encourage you to do something with the truths you have discovered in the lesson. Let me encourage you here to ask God what He would have you do.

Lastly, the conclusion contains a **Reckoning**. As with the **Spiritual Exercise**, the importance of this section cannot be measured by its size. You will learn early in the Adventure Guide that reckoning is one of God's ways for renewing our minds. The truths you will find in this section have the potential to empower you in this adventure. Some will be more impactful that others. With God's help, you will recognize the ones He has particularly chosen for this season of your life. Hang on to them; and speak them often to yourself.

Assignment

You will not be graded on the assignments. They serve a more important purpose: To help you stay engaged with your Teachers. Keep this in mind as you are determining which to pursue. I encourage you to have someone hold you accountable in this discipline.

There is one assignment that appears in each lesson:

> Review your notes and the Scripture passages from this week's module. Share the ones that are most meaningful to someone you are discipling.

This is important for at least two reasons: First, sharing with someone else will strengthen your own understanding. Second, as a leader, the Great Commission applies to you. Making disciples is one of your primary responsibilities. My hope is that these lessons enable the development of that work in your life.

Devotion

The devotion included with each lesson is optional reading. They provide a related and additional perspective. The Lord has encouraged me through them. I pray that they will encourage you, as well.

Descriptive Changes

You may notice two notational differences between this guide and The Map Maker book. First, there is the replacement of "Marketplace" with "Workplace". This change has been made to help avoid a growing confusion with the terms. People hear "marketplace" and they think "business". I constantly have to explain that the meaning to inLight Consulting is "where people work".

Secondly, I have attempted to remove all references to "America", "American church" and "Western church". The truths of The Map Maker span countries, continents and hemispheres. Hopefully, these changes will remove any confusion and encourage leaders in all segments of the workplace – and in all parts of the world – to make disciples and transform their spheres of influence.

The Map Maker's Guide

Section One - Preparation

"What preparation could I possibly need?" was Somebody's next objection. "I'm important. I'm good at what I do. I know how to make friends and influence people. I'm a leader in my community."

"Yes, Somebody, you are," said the Map Maker, "But no one has taken one of My adventures without first being prepared. You'll be glad you took the time. Trust Me. After all, I am the Map Maker and these are My maps.

Now pay attention because this is the first lesson of your preparation: Not only are these my maps, but this is My adventure."

The Lord has been orchestrating events and preparing leaders in the marketplace for such a time as this. He will invite them, unite them, and anoint them for the witness of His kingdom. Even leaders must be prepared prior to their venturing out into a new adventure.

This section introduces the purpose, framework and methodology of the curriculum. Searching out the truth, and how we handle it, will be explored. The faithful adventurer will discover the truth's transforming power as it challenges a number of existing paradigms.

The Map Maker's Guide

Map 1 - The Workplace Mission

Spiritual Exercise

For where two or three are gathered together in My name, I am there in the midst of them. John 18:20

Gathering together "in My name" means we are here for His agenda and His concerns. Take a moment to lay down your expectations for this time of study, and turn your attention to Him. Not only will He be in our midst, but He will have something to say. Our surrender positions us to hear and recognize His voice.

Prayer

Father God, we have gathered together to hear from Your Son. We proclaim that we are here for Him and His agenda. We recognize that the One through Whom all things were made is in our midst. We bow before You and Him. We give our full attention to being together in His name – Jesus, the Anointed One, the Holy Son of God. Guide us in our discussion and open our hearts to Your desires. In Christ's name. Amen.

Introduction

Most people spend most of their waking hours in the Workplace. It is the place where we engage people in commerce and conversation, and where we find community and cooperation. The Workplace is the place where ideas, philosophies and worldviews are expressed, discussed and debated. The Workplace is where we live.

There is Another that lives there. He created the Workplace; and He intends to abide and reign there. Where God's people go, there also goes God. It is inaccurate to call the Workplace "secular", unless the Workplace is "void of God". Ah, but that might be our problem. Perhaps we – even Christians – have decided that God does not desire to be in the Workplace.

In this module, we will explore God's desire for the Workplace. We will learn that He has given influence and authority to Christians in the Workplace for this critical season. We will discover a model for Workplace Ministry that will encourage them to become disciple-making transformation agents in their spheres of influence.

Definition

Marketplace (aka, Workplace) Ministry: Typically refers to evangelism or other Christian activities that are targeted towards the secular workplace, as opposed to homes, churches, or specialized venues (e.g. crusades). It can also refer to particular parachurch organizations that focus on such ministry. The term probably entered circulation in the 1980s, though groups with similar emphases (e.g. the Christian Business Men's Fellowship) have been around much longer.

The term "Marketplace Ministry" does include 'evangelism'. However it is much broader than that. It speaks to the fact that any Christian can fulfill their desire to serve God in the workplace. This can assuage a lot of guilt in those that want to "go into fulltime ministry" as they realize they are already in "fulltime" ministry. *Source: Wikipedia, the Free Encyclopedia (electronic)*

Map 1 - The Workplace Mission

The terms "marketplace" and "workplace" are interchangeable. We have chosen the latter; believing it to be more descriptive of "where people work". In either case, it is important to recognize that workplace ministry is as old as the Christian faith.

> *Wherever He entered, into villages, cities, or the country, they laid the sick in the marketplaces, and begged Him that they might just touch the hem of His garment. And as many as touched Him were made well.* Matthew 6:56

> *Now while Paul waited for them at Athens, his spirit was provoked within him when he saw that the city was given over to idols. Therefore he reasoned in the synagogue with the Jews and with the Gentile worshipers, and in the marketplace daily with those who happened to be there.* Acts 17:16-17

Searching Out the Matter
(All Scripture references, but those noted, are NKJV; Thomas Nelson, Inc.; footnotes and headings excluded)

Two-Fold Chaos

We are in the midst of the most culturally significant time in the history of this world – and in the church that resides here. Consider the chaos that has gripped society – moral failure in every arena, the splintering of the family, economic depression, etc. This chaos will affect every single person on the planet – including those in the Body of Christ.

Chaos can be a good thing. The chaos of persecution dispersed Christians from Israel in the 1st Century. The United States of America became a superpower out of the chaos of WWII. By God's mercy, the chaos we are experiencing will turn many from their idols. But where will they turn?

In many places, the church has become a subculture to the world around it. We have failed our Lord's desire for us to be in it, but not of it. We should not be surprised that we are suffering along with them; the same chaos has now taken hold of the church: Moral failure, the splintering of family and fellowship, economic depression, etc.

Consequently, the children of God in many nations of the world are experiencing a "double chaos"; a chaos of society and a chaos of the church. This "two-fold chaos" will test our faith and shake our foundations. Perhaps this chaos is God's mercy for the church. Perhaps He is trying to get our attention. Perhaps He wants more for us.

Broken and In Need

The church, through conformity to the world, has lost much of its influence; and is becoming culturally insignificant. Consider these statistics – gathered from Christian denominations and ministries over the last 15 years:

- Only 20% of Americans regularly attend church.

- Every year more than 4000 churches close their doors, compared to just over 1000 church starts.

- 88% of the young adults raised in evangelical fellowships leave the church before the end of their freshman year in college.

- The abortion and divorce rates in the church are as high as in the world.

- In a 2007 Barna Survey, it was discovered that 54% of non-Christian young people (ages 16 – 29) believe that a lot of Christians are hypocritical; only 26% believe a lot have good values and principles; and only 9% as people you can trust.

Map 1 - The Workplace Mission

- Jesus has been praying for over 2000 years that we would be united; yet there are over 30,000 denominations, just in the United States.

- World Christian Trends research from 2001 reveals that the church in America is spending $1,550,000 per baptism. In India, the figure is $9803.

These are just a few of the many indicators that point to the church's decline. Many are calling for revival, renewal and restoration. We need something more. We need transformation.

God's Response

God has not been caught by surprise; nor has He given up on us. He has been preparing a people for such a time as this!! Who are these people? Who will God use to lead the next spiritual awakening in the church? Who best understands, and embraces, the dynamics of change? Take a look at what some influential leaders have to say.

> *I believe one of the next great moves of God is going to be through the believers in the workplace.*
> Dr. Billy Graham, Evangelist

> *God is marshalling his people in the workplace as never before in history. God is up to something. The next spiritual awakening could take place in the marketplace.* Henry Blackaby, Pastor and Author

> *Indeed, as with 1st century Christianity, it all begins in the marketplace, where the disciples of Jesus daily rub shoulders with the lost.* Bill McCartney, Founder: Promise Keepers

> *The work of the church is what is done between Sundays when the church is scattered all over the metropolitan area where it is located - in homes, schools, offices, on construction jobs, in market places.* Dick Halverson, Pastor, U.S. Senate Chaplain

> *In today's global community, the greatest channel of distribution for 'salt and light' is the business community.* Bill Pollard, Chairman, ServiceMaster

> *Spirituality in the workplace is exploding.* Laura Nash, Business Ethicist, Harvard University

> *God has begun an evangelism movement in the workplace that has the potential to transform our society as we know it.* Franklin Graham, Founder: Samaritan's Purse

God has positioned leaders in the Workplace – investing influence and authority in them – to lead the spiritual transformation of their families, fellowships and other spheres of influence. He has called them to an adventure of disciple-making and transformation.

Who are the most influential people in your community? Are you one of these people? Will you answer the call?

Who is a Leader in the Workplace?

A Leader in the Workplace is a Christian in business, education, government, medicine, etc. that has God-given influence, authority and resources for advancing His kingdom, bringing glory to His name, and unifying the Body of Christ.

These individuals have been providentially chosen to lead the spiritual transformation of their spheres of influence. They understand and embrace the dynamics of change needed in a transformation agent; and, as one of the most influential leaders in their communities, they are positioned to be disciple makers.

It is important to recognize that God-given influence is not reserved for those at the highest levels of an organization. For example, most teachers have influence over thirty children and their families. The potential

Map 1 - The Workplace Mission

for kingdom impact through their influence is tremendous. Furthermore, the most mature Christian in the boardroom is the one that carries the most kingdom influence and authority for everyone in attendance.

The Advantage of Workplace Ministry

There are currently 30,000+ registered denominations in the U.S. Many sprang up out of divisiveness and one-upmanship. How might Christ overcome the pride and weakness of man to create the church He has in mind?

It is important to recognize the fellowships to whom God has connected us. That begins with family and the fellowships we gather with on a regular basis. But it also extends into the places where we spend most of our waking hours. In the Workplace, spheres of influence are potential fellowships.

There are at least three reasons why the Workplace has become the church's best hope for revival, renewal and restoration.

1. Leaders in the Workplace embrace change, and the chaos it may cause, as an opportunity to improve their spheres of influence (2Corinthians 3:18).
2. Leaders in the Workplace are doers. 20% of the people doing 80% of the work does not happen in Workplace. Like Jesus, they expect everyone to be a doer (Matthew 7:24-27).
3. Leaders in the Workplace place a high value on cooperation. They understand the power of synergistic effort (Ephesians 4:16); and they do not tolerate divisiveness (1Corinthians 1:10).

If you have a sphere of influence in the Workplace, then you have been called for this critical season. God has invested more in you than you (or anyone else) can see at this moment. He desires to prepare you for your kingdom assignment in the Workplace. As this graphic demonstrates, it is important to recognize that Christians are at different levels of maturity in their walk with God.

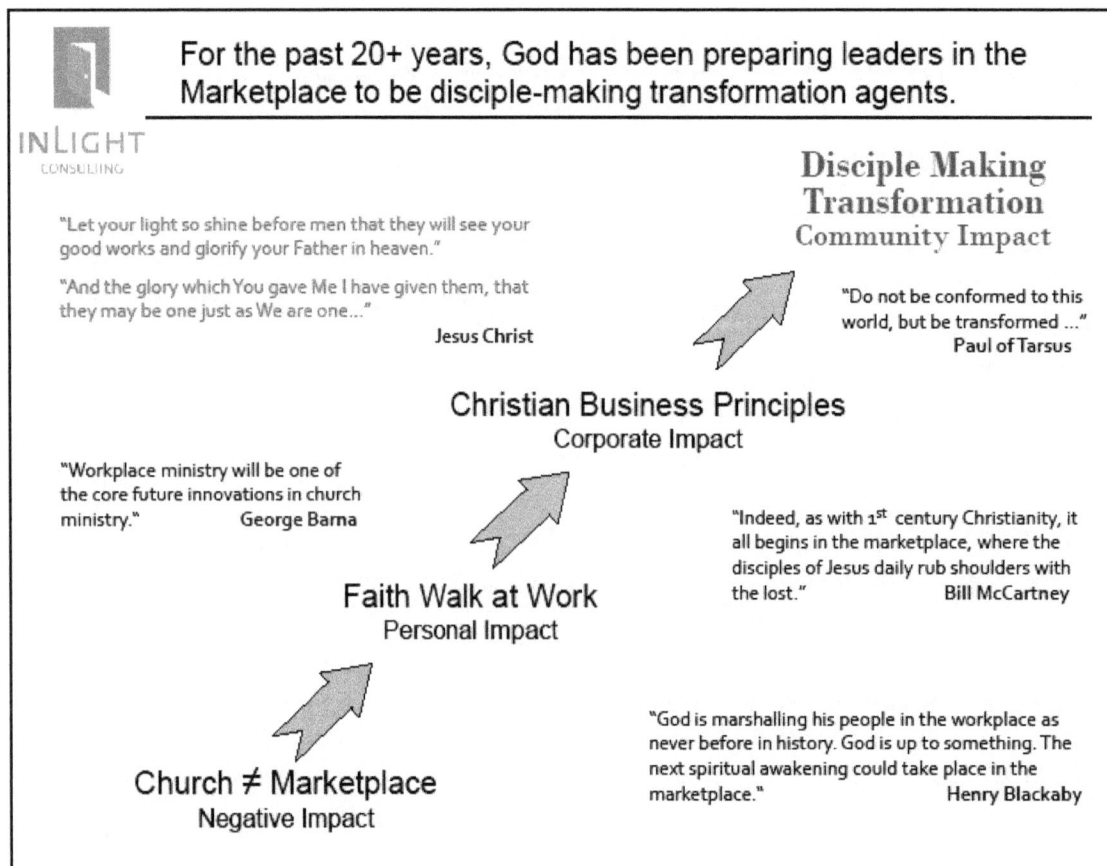

22

Map 1 - The Workplace Mission

No matter where you are on the Workplace Ministry maturity curve, God is calling you to more. His divine power has given to us all things that pertain to life and godliness, through the knowledge of Him who called us by glory and virtue (2Peter 1:3). We must lay hold of that for which Jesus laid hold of us; and work out our own salvation with fear and trembling, for it is God working in us to will and do to His good pleasure; which is to give us the kingdom (Philippians 3:12, 2:12-13; Luke 12:32).

IMPORTANT NOTE: I am not attacking denominations or doctrines, but the spirit of divisiveness that has used them to interfere with our Lord's prayer for unity (John 17:20-23). Workplace Ministry is simply an opportunity to find unity where the "church" is not so confined. Furthermore, I am not suggesting that individuals leave their organized fellowships and create a type of "Church in the Workplace". This would only increase the problem. Local fellowships are critical to the disciple-making process for every believer.

God's Work is Our Adventure

To be transformation agents, Leaders in the Workplace must themselves be transformed. This is the prescription for maturity in the kingdom of God. Paul refers to it twice:

> But we all, with unveiled face, beholding as in a mirror the glory of the Lord, are being transformed into the same image from glory to glory, just as by the Spirit of the Lord. 2Corinthians 3:18

> And do not be conformed to this world, but be transformed by the renewing of your mind, that you may prove what is that good and acceptable and perfect will of God. Romans 12:2

The Holy Spirit will transform us into the image of Christ, one glory to glory season at a time. So, how do we begin?

> Delight yourself also in the Lord, and He shall give you the desires of your heart. Psalm 37:4

We begin by "being soft" before the Lord and, in that surrendered state, discovering the desire that God has given for this season. After a season of transformation, the Leader in the Workplace steps out into God's assignment, into Christ's command to:

> Let your light so shine before men, that they may see your good works and glorify your Father in heaven. Matthew 5:16

Notice that the command is not to do good works, but to "let your light so shine". That light is the life of Christ (John 1:4). It takes the transformation of 2Corinthians 3:18 and Romans 12:2 for men to see Him in the work that will bring glory only to our Father in heaven. It is the work of the Holy Spirit, under the discipleship of Jesus Christ, through submitted vessels (i.e., Leaders in the Workplace).

This is "easier said than done". There are many challenges:

- There are battles to be fought against the enemies of the church: Satan, the world and our own carnality (Ephesians 6:12; James 4:4; Romans 8:7);

- Transformation requires surrender, sacrifice and submission (1Peter 5:6);

- Leadership must be "for", not "over" – in Christ-like service (John 13:14).

It is for this reason that the adventure must be taken in community. Jesus went with His twelve, and sent them out in pairs. Paul never went on a missionary journey alone. We all need those we are discipling, and those that would disciple us. We need prayer coverage, as well. For many years now, I've had at least three people praying for God's protection and guidance for me.

Map 1 - The Workplace Mission

Making a Kingdom Difference

With God, all things are possible. By discipling those within their sphere of influence, Leaders in the Workplace can make a difference for the kingdom. They will be made into leaders that...

- Recognize the investment God has made in them – and the power He has toward them;
- Surrender to God's purpose for this season in their lives;
- Are transformed from glory to glory into the very image of Christ;
- Let their light (Christ's life) shine for our Father's glory;
- Passionately pursue relationship with the Bridegroom and the Bride;
- Search out the mysteries and good news of the Kingdom;
- Disciple those that God has (and will) send into their sphere of influence;
- Experience joyful, Spirit-filled ministry; while...
- Lead the transformation of their communities.

Before the foundations of the earth, God deposited a desire in the heart of every Leader in the Workplace. He has been orchestrating events to reveal and establish the identity, gifts and spheres of influence needed to accomplish that desire. The Lord will accomplish His commission to make disciples by drawing others into the Workplace Leaders' sphere of influence. Disciple making as a lifestyle will replace the program mentality that has failed the church. As the darkness grows darker, God's light will shine ever brighter through supernatural works that transform communities. God will be glorified and His kingdom will be established for all to see!

Conclusion

We live in perilous times; for our families, for our spheres of influence, and for the church. God has allowed – perhaps even orchestrated – the chaos we now live in, to create an opportunity for disciple making and transformation. He is doing a new thing – because a new thing is needed. He is moving in the Workplace; positioning and commissioning His children to lead a spiritual awakening and restoration movement.

The timing of this movement is providential. We must begin now and proceed quickly. The Lord desires to bring spiritual transformation to the church through Leaders in the Workplace. Those that answer God's call will make a kingdom difference in the Workplace.

Application

God is inviting those that are hungry for His presence, hungry to see His glory, and hungry for transformation in their lives, families and spheres of influence. For such a time as this, will you:

1. Let your light shine – for His glory?
2. Do God's work – in His power?
3. Allow God to make disciples through you?
4. Help lead the spiritual transformation of your community?

God is calling – will you go? We would be blessed to partner with you in the discovery of God's purpose, plan and power for joyful, Spirit-filled ministry – ministry specifically established, by God, for you!

Map 1 - The Workplace Mission

Whether you desire to leverage this guide or not, you must now consider yourself on notice that God did not invest in you unwisely, or without an expectation of return. Trust Him to show you the desire of your heart. Begin the adventure!

Reckoning

God has a kingdom purpose for me.

Assignment

1. Review your notes and the Scripture passages from this week's module. Share the ones that are most meaningful to someone in your spheres of influence.

2. Prayerfully consider the opportunity of this adventure with God. It is not for the faint-hearted, but for the courageous. It is not for the fearless, but for the humble. Trust God, do good, dwell on His promises, taste and see that the Lord is good (Psalm 37:3). Write down your thoughts and response to God.

Devotion

Strategic Alliances in God's Kingdom
Marketplace Ministry Tips (Chapel Hill News and Views) by Rob Streetman

Strategic alliances, partnerships and mergers are common business practices. Their intent is to create synergistic business relationships; where the whole is greater than the sum of the parts. Such arrangements can have significant impact on a market; even on an entire industry. One could argue that the key to the dominance of American business has been our ability to work together for the common good.

It could also be said that our decline has been the result of an insidious infestation of selfish, independent, and divisive motivations. We have lost the ideals represented by the morals and ethics of the common good. Capitalism is suffering from a self-inflicted disease.

I am hopeful that there are at least a few captains of industry working on the cure. I admit that it is far beyond my education and training. In fact, some might suggest that I keep out of the conversation until I am better qualified to offer a solution; and I agree with them. Therefore, let me offer a solution from Someone with far more wisdom.

> [Jesus prayed] Father, I pray that they all may be one, as You, Father, are in Me, and I in You; that they also may be one in Us, that the world may believe that You sent Me. And the glory which You gave Me I have given them, that they may be one just as We are one. John 17:21-22

Christian businesses have the opportunity to participate in the Father's answer to His Son's prayer by overcoming the fears and failings of our current business culture, and intentionally seeking the glory of God in relationship with each other. In so doing, the glory of God will be manifested in their work. This is the great hope of Marketplace Ministry.

Marketplace Ministry Tip: Seek out business relationships with God's higher purpose in mind. Find a group of peer professionals that can help you grow spiritually as a Marketplace Leader.

The Map Maker's Guide

Map 2 - Searching Out the Matter

Spiritual Exercise

There are many promises for the man, woman and child that will put their trust in God. Here are a few.

> *As for God, His way is perfect;*
> *The word of the LORD is proven;*
> *He is a shield to all who trust in Him. 2Samuel 22:31*

> *Trust in the LORD, and do good;*
> *Dwell in the land, and feed on His faithfulness.*
> *Delight yourself also in the LORD,*
> *And He shall give you the desires of your heart.*
> *Commit your way to the LORD,*
> *Trust also in Him,*
> *And He shall bring it to pass.*
> *He shall bring forth your righteousness as the light,*
> *And your justice as the noonday. Psalm 37:3-6*

> *The LORD is good, A stronghold in the day of trouble;*
> *And He knows those who trust in Him. Nahum 1:7*

As we will see in this study, searching out the mysteries of the kingdom will require the grace to trust Him more. Let's turn our hearts to the one that supplies that grace.

Prayer

Father God, we come to you now encouraged by your promises. We thank you and praise you for the provision You have made for us – the grace to trust You and lay hold of that for which Christ Jesus laid hold of us. We surrender to the working of the truth of Your word – to make us free. In Jesus' name; Amen.

Introduction

The availability of Christian resources in America is astounding. I dare say something has been written or recorded about every circumstance and situation that challenges every man, woman and child in this country. ChristianBook.com has over 500,000 products. I don't know how they keep up with all the books, tapes and study guides. Furthermore, there must be thousands of TV stations, and tens-of-thousands of radio stations, all broadcast for the sake of the Gospel of Jesus Christ. Who can imagine the number of websites dedicated to the application of God's word?

Jesus said, "And you shall know the truth, and the truth shall make you free." (John 8:32) So why is the church in America so bound? Why has she become as captive as the world in some of the most obvious sin – abortion, divorce, pride, greed, etc.?

Speaking from my own experience as a church leader, I believe it is our ignorance of Him, and the neglect of our heart's desire to know Him, that has left us prisoners to the deception of Satan, the world and our flesh. Our enemies know that knowledge is power; that this is particularly true in the kingdom of God. They will fight

Map 2 - Searching Out the Matter

us tooth and nail to keep the knowledge of God hidden from His children and the world. The agents of deception are all around us.

> *And Jesus answered and said to them: "Take heed that no one deceives you."* Matthew 24:4

> *If anyone among you thinks he is religious, and does not bridle his tongue but deceives his own heart, this one's religion is useless.* James 1:26

> *So the great dragon was cast out, that serpent of old, called the Devil and Satan, who deceives the whole world; he was cast to the earth, and his angels were cast out with him.* Revelation 12:9

This adventure is not for the passive, nor the faint of heart. We must fight for the truth that will make us free. Praise God, we have been given weapons for the battle.

> *For the weapons of our warfare are not carnal but mighty in God for pulling down strongholds, [5] casting down arguments and every high thing that exalts itself against the knowledge of God, bringing every thought into captivity to the obedience of Christ, and being ready to punish all disobedience when your obedience is fulfilled.* 2Corinthians 10:4-6

Throughout this study, we will uncover many weapons for our warfare. Let us desire and determine to use them!! But first, they must be discovered.

In this map, we will begin the incredible adventure of searching out the vast mysteries of God's kingdom. We will be challenged to venture out into the "higher than" thoughts and ways of God. And we will discover the keys to a safe and successful journey.

Definition

Truth (*aletheia*): Objectively, signifying "the reality lying at the basis of an appearance; the manifested, veritable essence of a matter" (Romans 9:1; 2Corinthians 11:10). Used especially of Christian doctrine, for example in Galatians 2:5 where "the truth of the Gospel" denotes the "true" teaching of the Gospel, in contrast to perversions of it. The word has an absolute force in John 14:6; 17:17; 18:37, 38. In Ephesians 4:21, where the RV, "even as truth is in Jesus," gives the correct rendering, the meaning is not merely ethical "truth," but "truth" in all its fullness and scope, as embodied in Him. He was the perfect expression of the truth; this is virtually equivalent to His statement in John 14:6. *Vine's Expository Dictionary*

Mystery (*mystērion*): Hidden thing, secret, mystery; generally mysteries, religious secrets, confided only to the initiated and not to ordinary mortals; a hidden or secret thing, not obvious to the understanding; a hidden purpose or counsel; the secret will of God; the secret counsels which govern God in dealing with the righteous, which are hidden from ungodly and wicked men but plain to the godly. *Blue Letter Bible Outline of Biblical Usage*

Searching Out the Matter
(All Scripture references, but those noted, are NKJV; Thomas Nelson, Inc.; headings and footnotes excluded)

Our adventure into joyful, Spirit-filled ministry will be filled with "searching out the matter". Most have yet to discover that this searching is God's way for our coming to know Him and His doctrine.

> *It is the glory of God to conceal a matter,*
> *But the glory of kings is to search out a matter.* Proverbs 25:2

> *And He said to them, "To you it has been given to know the mystery of the kingdom of God; but to those who are outside, all things come in parables, so that*
> *' Seeing they may see and not perceive,*
> *And hearing they may hear and not understand;*

Map 2 - Searching Out the Matter

Lest they should turn,
And their sins be forgiven them.'" Mark 4:11-12

So, what are these matters and mysteries that have been hidden for our discovery?

For My thoughts are not your thoughts,
Nor are your ways My ways," says the Lord.
For as the heavens are higher than the earth,
So are My ways higher than your ways,
And My thoughts than your thoughts. Isaiah 55:8-9

These matters and mysteries are the thoughts and ways of God that can only be measured by the vastness of the universe. The farthest galaxy from Earth is over 13 billion light years away!! This should give us some idea of the magnitude of our Father's invitation.

And what are we to do with the mysteries of the kingdom? Consider the following verses:

Whoever transgresses and does not abide in the doctrine of Christ does not have God. He who abides in the doctrine of Christ has both the Father and the Son. If anyone comes to you and does not bring this doctrine, do not receive him into your house nor greet him; for he who greets him shares in his evil deeds. 2John 1:9-11

Let a man so consider us, as servants of Christ and stewards of the mysteries of God. Moreover it is required in stewards that one be found faithful. 1Corinthians 4:1-2

The children of God are commanded to abide in, and be stewards of, the mysteries of God. A good steward does not limit his understanding to a portion of the Master's property. He seeks out what is good and profitable in it. In his faithfulness, he leverages what he finds – to the Master's benefit.

The Doctrine of Christ
The Vast Estate of God's Mystery

Whoever transgresses and does not abide in the doctrine of Christ does not have God. He who abides in the doctrine of Christ has both the Father and the Son.
2John 9

For *as* the heavens are higher than the earth, So are My ways higher than your ways, And My thoughts than your thoughts.
Proverbs 25:2

And He said to them, "To you it has been given to know the mystery of the kingdom of God...
Mark 4:11

Let a man so consider us, as servants of Christ and stewards of the mysteries of God.
1Corinthians 4:1

The Invitation of God

It is the glory of God to conceal a matter, But the glory of kings is to search out a matter.
Proverbs 25:2

Doctrines of Man
Confined to the House?

Map 2 - Searching Out the Matter

And so God invites us outside the boundaries of the doctrines of man to explore the vast estate of His mysteries – what the Bible calls "the doctrine of Christ".

Searching Safely

It is our responsibility – to ourselves, our families, and everyone in our spheres of influence – to carefully avoid the deception of false doctrine (i.e., leaving the safety of the Master's property). The Master has defined the "property lines" by His word. Men have done their best, by their doctrines, to define those boundaries. We must have a cautious respect of the doctrines of man, but not allow them to bind us from searching further. There is much to explore, if we are to be good stewards. We can do this safely, trusting God to protect us from wandering off the property, if the motivations of our hearts are aligned with His.

1. Our hearts are pure and rightly motivated. Those that find themselves "out of bounds" are usually motivated by self-aggrandizement and self-sufficiency. The prayer of Psalm 139:23-24 is a great protection.

2. We recognize that we have been wrong before, and might be wrong again. Most of us would have fought over some "truth" that we once held, which over time turned out to be something less than we thought. The humble heart is the heart to which God reveals His mysteries.

3. We look to the Spirit and Christ Jesus to be our teachers. We must be careful to remember than men are only vessels and instruments of the truth. Our ears must be tuned to the voice of God.

4. Our hearts are bent toward unity – not dismissing someone even when we know they are wrong. One of my favorite teachers has a habit of saying, "It may not mean what I say it means, but it must mean something. You put meaning to it; but, please don't discard me in your disagreement." God is more interested in our relationships than in our defense of the truth. The truth can defend itself.

NOTE: I hope and pray that these things are true of me and this study. I would greatly appreciate you letting me know if you see or sense anything contrary to these points. You will be doing me a great personal service.

We can venture out "safely"; and this is how we will search out the matters of God in this study. The purpose of our stewardship is too amazing and critical to ignore:

> To me, who am less than the least of all the saints, this grace was given, that I should preach among the Gentiles the unsearchable riches of Christ, and to make all see what is the fellowship of the mystery, which from the beginning of the ages has been hidden in God who created all things through Jesus Christ; to the intent that now the manifold wisdom of God might be made known by the church to the principalities and powers in the heavenly places, according to the eternal purpose which He accomplished in Christ Jesus our Lord, in whom we have boldness and access with confidence through faith in Him. Ephesians 3:8-12

God's eternal purpose is for His manifold wisdom to be made known BY THE CHURCH. That's us!! In Christ Jesus our Lord, we have boldness and confident access, through faith in Him, to know and make known the mysteries of God.

Becoming Faithful Stewards

God would not command our stewardship without making a way for us, in accordance with His great plans. T. Austin-Sparks said, "Let us all pray every day that we shall not only hear the Scriptures expounded, but that a great act of God shall be done in us whereby our spiritual eyes are opened to see and know the Lord." Isn't that what we all want?

> For the word of God is living and powerful, and sharper than any two-edged sword, piercing even to the division of soul and spirit, and of joints and marrow, and is a discerner of the thoughts and intents of the heart. Hebrews 4:12

Map 2 - Searching Out the Matter

The word of God is described as a double edged sword. It cuts bone from marrow, soul from spirit, etc. It is heavy; and sometimes just plain difficult to receive – to make it a part of our life. But, the good news is that it doesn't have to be overwhelming. The Holy Spirit has laid out for us the keys for discovering and receiving the truth. In this day, it is important that we understand these keys, and teach them to everyone in our spheres of influence that will listen.

The first key is our hunger and thirst for righteousness.

> *Blessed are those who hunger and thirst for righteousness, for they shall be filled.* Matthew 5:6

The natural mind would say, "Blessed are the righteous." But it is those who are hungry and thirsty who are blessed. Righteousness comes – and the truth with it – when we recognize our emptiness and respond out of a deep need. As we prepare to read, or hear, the Scriptures, let us confess our need and proclaim our desire to know the Lord and His truth.

The second key comes to us in a warning – failing to receive a love of the truth.

> *The coming of the lawless one is according to the working of Satan, with all power, signs, and lying wonders, and with all unrighteous deception among those who perish, because they did not receive the love of the truth, that they might be saved.* 2Thessalonians 2:9,10

This passage is taken out of Paul's exhortation regarding the Great Apostasy. Those without a love of the truth are at great risk of falling away from the faith. It is important to note that the love of the truth is something that is given. It is not earned, but it must be received.

While each key is truly important to our entering and receiving the mysteries, **the third key** is the most critical. Jesus shared it while answering those that marveled at, yet questioned, His teaching.

> *If anyone is willing to do His will, he will know of the teaching (or doctrine), whether it is of God or whether I speak from Myself.* John 7:17 (NASB)

To know the source and reality of the truth, we must be willing to respond in obedience to that truth. As someone has said, "We must come with a proceeding 'Amen'." This is distinctly more than a willingness to consider the truth. It is to accept it by faith – trusting God for the outcome – even before we begin searching.

Key number four is the beginning of our response to the truth – entering into it.

> *Woe to you lawyers! For you have taken away the key of knowledge. You did not enter in yourselves, and those who were entering in you hindered.* Luke 11:52

When the truth comes, we must respond by "entering in". To understand this key step, consider two things that we might "enter into". One is a contract. In a contract, we commit ourselves to the conditions of our agreement – our preceding "Amen".

Second, let's assume our contract grants us access to the Vast Estate of God's Mysteries; to be stewards there. Upon "entering into" the contact, we are allowed to "enter in" and live on the estate. "Entering in" is committing to, and abiding in, the mysteries of God!

As we discussed earlier, the faithful steward does more than hear about the mysteries of God – they do something with them. This leads us to **the fifth key** for entering and receiving the mysteries of God: Being "doers of the word".

> *But be doers of the word, and not hearers only, deceiving yourselves. For if anyone is a hearer of the word and not a doer, he is like a man observing his natural face in a mirror; for he observes himself, goes away, and immediately forgets what kind of man he was. But he who looks into the perfect law of liberty and continues in it, and is not a forgetful hearer but a doer of the work, this one will be blessed in what he does.* James 1:22-25

Map 2 - Searching Out the Matter

We must do something with what we have been given. Otherwise, we risk losing it and deceiving ourselves; even forgetting who we are in Christ.

Conclusion

It is God's intention for every one of His children to search out the mysteries of His kingdom – and do something with them. To do otherwise is to risk deception and falling away. There are many motives and excuses for settling for less. Every one of them is from our enemies – intended for our destruction.

Because Jesus is the truth and the truth is in Him, searching out the mysteries of God results in our finding Him. Many are afraid they will wander, or be lead, "out of bounds" – into heresy. Those with a humble and hungry heart should not fear in this way.

Our Loving Father knows we are like children. We need His help in our searching. He takes our hand and leads us into the vast estate of His thoughts and ways. He has provided the keys that enable and encourage us to search out the matters of His mysteries.

Application

As Leaders in the Workplace, we are called to lead others into the vast mysteries of God. This is a primary responsibility of "making disciples… teaching them to observe all that I have commanded you." No one can lead where they will not go themselves. Those that lead well, go before the ones they are leading.

Leaders in the Workplace are in the best position to lead the children of God into the full expression of His mysteries – from hearing to doing. They are where most spend most of their waking hours, out where the doing is done. God has established every Christian Leader in the Workplace for this purpose, in this very critical season.

Go, therefore, and explore!!

Reckoning

Christ, by His Spirit, will make us faithful stewards of the mysteries of God (Mark 1:17; 1Corinthians 4:1-2).

Assignment

1. Review your notes and the Scripture passages from this week's module. What were the most challenging concepts about the truth of God? What do you think the Holy Spirit is trying to teach you in this regard? Share this with someone in your spheres of influence.

2. Ask the Lord for the grace to practice the steps of knowing and receiving the truth:

    i. A hunger and thirst for righteousness.
    ii. A love of the truth.
    iii. Courage and discipline to come with your "Amen" first.
    iv. Enter into the truth you are given.
    v. Becoming a doer of the word and work.
3. Go deeper into the truth – by exploring this week's devotion.

Devotion

The "And" of Searching in Community
From Rob Streetman, The inLight Adventure Blog

Map 2 - Searching Out the Matter

There was a time in my life when I would pass over sections of Scripture because they were beyond my understanding. At the time, I didn't understand how serious God was about our being faithful stewards of the mysteries of His kingdom. I didn't realize that there were things hidden for me to search out. I also wasn't aware that He had a "way" of searching that would open up the mysteries of His word. I call this way: The "and" of searching in community.

I discovered this way through a contrast of meetings that providentially happened within a week of each other. In the first meeting, I saw – even felt – the tension rise in the room when the teacher introduced the topic of baptism. At least half the participants moved to the edge of their chairs waiting, it seemed, to hear the teacher say something that they did not agree with. I am convinced that their ears were closed to hearing, and the Spirit was grieved.

The second meeting was a blessed contrast. As with the first, there were people from various denominations. I am sure that each had a different understanding of the topic: Communion. But their hearts were softer towards God word, and each other. They were not looking to be right. They just wanted to know the truth; and knew they didn't know it all.

The scripture that was introduced was Jesus' claim (in John Chapter 6), to be the bread of life that must be consumed by those that desire to have eternal life. It was asked, "What did Jesus mean when He said:

> … Most assuredly, I say to you, unless you eat the flesh of the Son of Man and drink His blood, you have no life in you. Whoever eats My flesh and drinks My blood has eternal life, and I will raise him up at the last day. For My flesh is food indeed, and My blood is drink indeed. He who eats My flesh and drinks My blood abides in Me, and I in him. John 6:53-56

After some consideration, one brother said he wasn't sure, but thought it meant "so and so" to him. The next jumped in and said, "And it means… to me." A third, "And it seems to be saying…"

To be honest, I can't remember what any of them said about the meaning – because the Holy Spirit was focusing me on the "and" of their hearts. At no time during the conversation was "no" or "or" used. No one corrected or disagreed with the others. It was truly amazing; so amazing that I almost missed the most amazing thing:

In the midst of searching out the matter in loving community, this passage – that had so long been a mystery to me – was given meaning, somewhere deep in my heart. I couldn't explain what I understood (that came later), but I knew something that I had not known before. The word – that word – became alive for me.

In reflection, I was reminded of Paul's encouragement to the church in Rome:

> For I say, through the grace given to me, to everyone who is among you, not to think of himself more highly than he ought to think, but to think soberly, as God has dealt to each one a measure of faith. For as we have many members in one body, but all the members do not have the same function, so we, being many, are one body in Christ, and individually members of one another. Be kindly affectionate to one another with brotherly love, in honor giving preference to one another… Be of the same mind toward one another. Do not set your mind on high things, but associate with the humble. Do not be wise in your own opinion. Repay no one evil for evil. Have regard for good things in the sight of all men. If it is possible, as much as depends on you, live peaceably with all men. Romans 12:3-5, 10, 16-18

Since that day – at least three years ago – I have not been in a meeting of kindred minds and hearts where I did not hear a word from the Lord. Where two or three are gathered <u>in His name</u>, He is there (and He has something to say).

I pray that He gives you a heart to hear the mysteries of His kingdom. I pray the blessing of community on all your future meetings.

The Map Maker's Guide

Map 3 - Renewing the Mind

Spiritual Exercise

> *Go therefore and make disciples of all the nations... teaching them to observe all things that I have commanded you...* Matthew 28:19-20

> *And the things that you have heard from me among many witnesses, commit these to faithful men who will be able to teach others also.* 2Timothy 2:2

As we turn to the Lord, consider again that His ways are the best ways. He has invited us to participate in His Father's story as disciples that make disciples. Our "teaching them to observe" is more than "instructing them to obey". Teaching must include demonstrating. Observe means "to attend to carefully, take care of, to guard". Disciples that make disciples are stewards of Christ's commandments, committing them to faithful men and women. This is the church's Great Commission. It is a high calling. We need His mercy and grace.

Prayer

Heavenly Father, in Christ Name, and by Your Spirit, we commit ourselves to be disciples that you can use to make disciples. We believe that Your word will make us free, and transform our communities for Your Name's sake. Have mercy on us, Father God. We need your help. Amen.

Introduction

> *Most assuredly, I say to you, he who believes in Me, the works that I do he will do also; and greater works than these he will do, because I go to My Father.* John 14:12

> *For we are His workmanship, created in Christ Jesus for good works, which God prepared beforehand that we should walk in them.* Ephesians 2:10

> *Let your light so shine before men, that they may see your good works and glorify your Father in heaven.* Matthew 5:16

> *Now to Him who is able to do exceedingly abundantly above all that we ask or think, according to the power that works in us, to Him be glory in the church by Christ Jesus to all generations, forever and ever. Amen.* Ephesians 3:20-21

These and many verses like them speak of the greater-than life that God has made possible for His children. So, where are the "greater works"? What must we do to walk in them? Is there a key that opens the door that leads to the life Christ promised in John 14:12?

In this module we will explore such a key: The Renewing of the Mind. As we search out this matter, God will give us revelation and understanding for the role reckoning plays in bridging the gap between hearing the word of God and walking in His good works.

Definition

Reckon (*logizomai*): To reckon, count, compute, calculate, count over, to take into account, to make an account of; metaph. to pass to one's account, to impute; a thing is reckoned as or to be something,

Map 3 - Renewing the Mind

i.e. as availing for or equivalent to something, as having the like force and weight; to number among, reckon with; to reckon inward, count up or weigh the reasons, to deliberate; to consider, take into account, weigh, meditate on; to suppose, deem, judge; to determine, purpose, decide.

Special Footnote: This word deals with reality. If I reckon (logizomai) that my bank book has $25 in it, it has $25 in it. Otherwise I am deceiving myself. This word refers more to fact than supposition or opinion. *Outline of Biblical Usage,www.BlueLetterBible.org*

Searching Out the Matter
(All Scripture references, but those noted, are NKJV; Thomas Nelson, Inc.; footnotes and headings excluded)

Faithful Stewards of the Mysteries

> *It is the glory of God to conceal a matter,*
> *But the glory of kings is to search out a matter.* Proverbs 25:2

> *And the disciples came and said to Him, "Why do You speak to them in parables?" He answered and said to them, "Because it has been given to you to know the mysteries of the kingdom of heaven, but to them it has not been given.* Matthew 13:10-11

In both the Old and New Testament, God made it clear that He had concealed matters that His disciples should be searching out. Why? Because He is a father; and like all fathers, He has treasures that are only for His children. He pleasures in the joy we express in the seeking and the finding (think Easter egg hunt, or treasure in the field).

We are not only invited to search out the mysteries, we are required to be faithful stewards of them.

> *Let a man so consider us, as servants of Christ and stewards of the mysteries of God. Moreover it is required in stewards that one be found faithful.* 1Corinthians 4:1-2

It is important to consider what it means to be a faithful steward. It is not enough that the steward knows there is a fertile field. He must plow and plant it. And once the crop has come up, he must harvest and sell it. In other words, he must do something with what has been given him to steward.

What are these great mysteries of Scripture? Which come to mind for you? Is it abiding in Christ? Or, being crucified with Him? How about "greater is He that is in me"? Casting out demons? Raising the dead? These and many more are the mysteries of God – promised and commanded by Christ.

There is a power associated with the mysteries of God that we have read and heard about, but few have experienced. Our Heavenly Father wants much, much more for His children! He has given us a Word that is powerful and purposeful. The faithful steward is God's agent and vessel for powerful manifestations of that Word. This is, indeed, a high calling and responsibility.

Regrettably, we have been more hearers than doers.

Doers of the Work

There is no lack of good preaching and teaching in the American church. Information overload has come to the church. What little time we allocate to spiritual matters is primarily invested in hearing and reading. Is it any wonder that we have forgotten who we are in Christ and the great exploits He intends for us to do?

> *But be doers of the word, and not hearers only, deceiving yourselves. For if anyone is a hearer of the word and not a doer, he is like a man observing his natural face in a mirror; for he observes himself, goes away, and immediately forgets what kind of man he was. But he who looks into the perfect law of liberty and continues in it, and is not a forgetful hearer but a doer of the work, this one will be blessed in what he does.* James 1:21-25

Map 3 - Renewing the Mind

However we come around to it, we must begin to be doers of the truths we hear. Otherwise, we will continue to be deceived and forgetful of who we are. This is a death spiral for our souls! Deception begets deception; and forgetfulness begets forgetfulness.

James follows this warning with a more sobering one.

> *What does it profit, my brethren, if someone says he has faith but does not have works? Can faith save him? Thus also faith by itself, if it does not have works, is dead. Was not Abraham our father justified by works when he offered Isaac his son on the altar? Do you see that faith was working together with his works, and by works faith was made perfect? For as the body without the spirit is dead, so faith without works is dead also.* James 2:14-26 (select verses)

The penalty of dead faith is devastating to the individual that carries it around. To God, it is a terrible stench (think road kill). Thankfully, God has given us all we need for godliness and abundant living. We don't have to live our lives in deception, forgetfulness and dead faith. God has made a way!

Bridging the Gap

God has given us a way out of this devastating predicament. He has given us a key that bridges the gap from hearing to doing; from the hearing of faith to the work of faith; and from deception and forgetfulness to prosperous work. The Holy Spirit called it *logizomai*; and used it 41 times in the New Testament. Here are a few examples:

> *Likewise you also, <u>reckon</u> yourselves to be dead indeed to sin, but alive to God in Christ Jesus our Lord.* Romans 6:11

> *For I <u>consider</u> that the sufferings of this present time are not worthy to be compared with the glory which shall be revealed in us.* Romans 8:18

> *When I was a child, I spoke as a child, I understood as a child, I <u>thought</u> as a child; but when I became a man, I put away childish things.* 1Corinthians 13:11

> *Finally, brethren, whatever things are true, whatever things are noble, whatever things are just, whatever things are pure, whatever things are lovely, whatever things are of good report, if there is any virtue and if there is anything praiseworthy—<u>meditate</u> on these things.* Philippians 4:8

Reckon is an accounting term, meaning to record something in a journal. Spiritual reckoning is the process of making true for me what God says is true – balancing my mind with His. It is laying hold of (or accessing) the mind of Christ.

Before we go on, it should be noted that reckoning is not a positive reinforcement technique. It is more than the power of positive thinking... because the power is not in our thinking, but in the thing we are thinking about: The word of God.

The Power of the Word

The mysteries of God are found in the word of God, both in the written form we call The Holy Bible and in the spoken form that comes to us in our intimate relationship with God. This word is a great and mighty treasure, a catalyst for the work of God.

> *For the word of God is living and powerful, and sharper than any two-edged sword, piercing even to the division of soul and spirit, and of joints and marrow, and is a discerner of the thoughts and intents of the heart.* Hebrews 4:12

> *So shall My word be that goes forth from My mouth;*
> *It shall not return to Me void,*

Map 3 - Renewing the Mind

But it shall accomplish what I please,
And it shall prosper in the thing for which I sent it. Isaiah 55:11

These verses remind us that the power for reckoning is not limited by mental ability or the strength of will. It is not limited by age, nor even by spiritual maturity. No, the word of God has all the power it needs – within itself – to accomplish the reckoning.

Reckoning's Purpose in the Process of Faith

To understand the purpose and power of reckoning, let's take a walk through the process of faith and see how the great empowering mysteries of God can be worked out in our lives.

Before there is faith, there must be the hearing of the word of God.

So then faith comes by hearing, and hearing by the word of God. Romans 10:17

Hearing is predicated on our willingness to surrender our hearts to what God says (i.e., His will).

For with the heart one believes unto righteousness, and with the mouth confession is made unto salvation. Romans 10:10

For assuredly, I say to you, whoever says to this mountain, 'Be removed and be cast into the sea,' and does not doubt in his heart, but believes that those things he says will be done, he will have whatever he says. Mark 11:23

As we can see in these verses, faith is a function of the heart. Therefore, we can say that the word of God finds its resting place in the heart of the believer. But how does it get from the heart to the mind, and from there out to our hands, feet and mouth – the instruments of the good work we are to walk in? Consider this:

I beseech you therefore, brethren, by the mercies of God, that you present your bodies a living sacrifice, holy, acceptable to God, which is your reasonable service. And do not be conformed to this world, but be transformed by the renewing of your mind, that you may prove what is that good and acceptable and perfect will of God. For I say, through the grace given to me, to everyone who is among you, not to think of himself more highly than he ought to think, but to think soberly, as God has dealt to each one a measure of faith. Romans 12:1-3

To prove (or complete)... the will of God, we must first allow God's will (i.e.,what He has said) to renew our minds. This is where reckoning comes in. In reckoning the word that has been heard and believed, the mind is renewed – by that word and the measure of faith that comes with it.

But we all, with unveiled face, beholding as in a mirror the glory of the Lord, are being transformed into the same image from glory to glory, just as by the Spirit of the Lord. 2Corinthians 3:18

The transformation that comes by the renewing of the mind is into the very same image as the glory of the Lord. That image is none other than the One that only does what the Father is doing – the very thing that is His will; the will that was heard in His word. We must do the same in response to the word of the Father, Son and Holy Spirit.

Therefore, my beloved, as you have always obeyed, not as in my presence only, but now much more in my absence, work out your own salvation with fear and trembling; for it is God who works in you both to will and to do for His good pleasure. Philippians 2:12-16

It is important to note that the willing and doing is God's work. Rather than waste energy trying to do His work, we should focus our attention on the responsibility we have been given: Making sure our hearts are surrendered, exercising the measure of faith we have been given, reckoning what He says to be true, and walking in the work He is doing.

Map 3 - Renewing the Mind

If we will work out our salvation with fear and trembling, He will do His part to bring the supernatural life of Christ out of us; and we will be a blessing to Him and to the world around us. We will experience the "greater than" life.

> *He who believes in Me, as the Scripture has said, out of his heart will flow rivers of living water.*
> John 7:38

A Word about Repentance

As the mysteries of God are reckoned in our mind, the Holy Spirit uses them to expose thoughts and ways that are contrary to the higher ways and thoughts of God. Our first response should be confession and repentance from our old and carnal way of thinking, to the way and/or thought given by the Lord. This is a simple, yet powerful, step in the process of transformation.

Conclusion

Spiritual reckoning is the process of making true for me what God says is true – balancing my journal with His. Reckoning also means to "meditate on", "to deliberate" and "to consider". It is a process for laying hold of that for which Christ Jesus laid hold of me (Philippians 3:12). Reckoning is a means of applying a word of faith to the renewing of our minds. This renewal is necessary for the work that ultimately perfects that faith (James 2:22). Therefore, reckoning is a bridge from hearing to doing the greater than things that have been promised.

Application

Consider the "greater than" verses (e.g., John 14:12, Matthew 5:16, Ephesians 3:20). For the Leader in the Workplace, these are an encouragement that what we hear from God is actually possible, through us and through those within our spheres of influence. The word of God becomes powerful when we reckon it to be so and respond by walking in the work He has given us to accomplish for His kingdom. It becomes a spiritual, motivational, and physical force that the violent will use to take the kingdom.

Reckoning

The truth will make me and others free (John 8:32).

Assignment

1. On a 3x5 card, write three or four truths God would have you reckon for this season of your life. This must be done prayerfully, so you will hear the specific truths that He has for you. See the following devotion for the ones God has given me. You will likely have a different set than I, but make no mistake about it: The truths that God has given you to reckon are His grace to empower your unique journey in this adventure.

2. Share your reckonings with someone that will encourage you in them, for the days ahead.

3. Be a disciple maker by helping someone else understand and discover the truths God has for their reckoning.

Map 3 - Renewing the Mind

Devotion

Excerpt from Marketplace Challenges – The Adventure Awaits
From Rob Streetman, The inLight Adventure Blog

Commitment and Reckoning

Every soldier – everyone drafted into the King's army – must determine who they will serve. It will either be the evil alliance – yourself, the world, and Satan – or it will be the King of kings. You simply cannot serve both sides with any success. Double agents are inevitably confused about their allegiance and traitors are quickly exposed. Conversely, commitment to the King brings the hope of victory, faith in the resources of the Kingdom, and the love of the King and His followers.

As you prepare for the days ahead, I encourage you to reckon the truths of the Kingdom into your life. Reckoning is an accounting term, meaning to record something in a journal. Reckoning then is the process of making true for me what God says is true – balancing my journal with His. It is laying hold of that for which Christ Jesus laid hold of me (Philippians 3:12).

Try this simple exercise. On a 3x5 card, write three or four things God would have you reckon to be true about you, for this season of your life. This must be done prayerfully, so you will hear the specific truths that He has for you. You will likely have a different set than I, but let me share them with you as an example and to make the point of their importance:

1. <u>I am a bondservant and steward</u>. I volunteered for this assignment and I will be found faithful to it.
2. <u>I have been crucified with Christ; it is no longer I who live but Christ Who lives in me</u>. I am a dead man. The only life others should see is His. I have no rights, but those He assigns for me.
3. <u>Greater is He that is in me than he that is in the world</u>. There is nothing for me to fear (except the One Who is Greater). I am a fearless overcomer and Kingdom taker.

Let me encourage you again to seek the Lord for your reckonings. Whatever they are, reckon them every morning. Keep them close to you – some place where you will be reminded of them throughout the day. They will keep your mind on the things of Heaven. They will renew your mind. In a supernatural way, they will make you into faithful, obedient followers of the King... violent Kingdom takers.

The Map Maker's Guide

Map 4 - The Adventures of Our Life in Christ

Spiritual Exercise

Rejoice in the Lord always. Again I will say, rejoice! Let your gentleness be known to all men. The Lord is at hand. Be anxious for nothing, but in everything by prayer and supplication, with thanksgiving, let your requests be made known to God; and the peace of God, which surpasses all understanding, will guard your hearts and minds through Christ Jesus. Philippians 4:4-7

During a particularly stressful time in my life (a time that included daily panic attacks), this passage became a recipe for peace and a weapon against the enemy. What Satan intended for evil, God turned to my good. Here's how it works (this prayer is written in a general way; be as specific as you can).

Prayer

Father in Heaven, I rejoice in Your presence. I rejoice in the promise of Your protection and peace in this circumstance! I surrender to the expression of Your gentleness to everyone involved – even those that appear to be my enemies. I know You are with me in every trial and tribulation. By Your grace, I refuse to be anxious. Thank You for this opportunity to experience and prove Your love. I pray for Your protection and guidance in this situation. I will not be able to persevere without You. I desperately need You. I receive Your peace and I rest in Your protection, through Your Son; in whose name I pray. Amen.

Introduction

… for it is God who works in you both to will and to do for His good pleasure. Philippians 2:13

Do not fear, little flock, for it is your Father's good pleasure to give you the kingdom. Luke 12:32

Commit your way to the Lord,
Trust also in Him,
And He shall bring it to pass.
He shall bring forth your righteousness as the light,
And your justice as the noonday. Psalm 37:5-6

Our God is a process oriented problem solver. All of His creation operates in process: From birth to death; from dead in sin to alive in Christ, from glory to glory, etc. Give Him a problem and He will give you a process to solve it. The Bible is His story – the grand process that He is orchestrating to get back what was lost to Him and mankind in the Garden of Eden (more on this later).

Most of the major topics of Scripture are process oriented. We are to continue and grow in some of them (e.g., faith, hope and love). Others are processes that God uses to mature us (e.g., tribulation, sanctification, transformation, and disciple-making). Even our salvation is a process; not a singular event.

Regrettably, we have become an event-focused people. "If it isn't happening now, it just isn't happening" is our motto. "What have you done for me today?", has become our measure.

Map 4 The Adventures of Our Life in Christ

This degraded perspective has affected our doctrine and our discipline. For example, we are more concerned with the event of a lost soul making a decision than with the processes of sanctification and discipleship. We give more attention to what we can squeeze out of God in 30-minute devotion events than we give to the life He wants to live in and through us every moment of the day.

Recognizing that God operates "in process" will dramatically change our perspective of the life we are to live in Christ. It will impact our relationship with God and with all of His creation. To encourage us in this new way of thinking – and to continue to prepare ourselves for the adventure that lies ahead – we will search out a few of the processes God has instituted for making us His people; on this Earth and in Heaven. We will discover that these processes are truly the adventures of our life in Christ.

Definition

Adventure: An undertaking usually involving danger and unknown risks; the encountering of risks; an exciting or remarkable experience. *www.merriam-webster.com*

Transformed (*metamorphoō*): To change into another form; of Christ's transfiguration; of believers, the obligation being to undergo a complete change which, under the power of God, will find expression in character and conduct. *Vine's Expository Dictionary*

Greek Verb Tenses: For those that have a love of the truth, searching out the Scriptures can be a most exciting and rewarding treasure hunt. One way to better understand the meaning of a particular verse is to explore the verb tenses used. Here are a few that we will consider:

> **Aorist Tense** – The aorist is a "simple occurrence" or "summary occurrence" – a completed event – most often translated into the English past tense (e.g., "Jesus <u>wept</u>.").

> **Present Tense** – The present tense denotes continuous or progressive action. It shows 'action in progress' or 'a state of persistence.' (e.g., "...<u>reckon</u> yourselves to be dead indeed to sin but alive to God in Christ Jesus our Lord.").

> **Future Tense** – The future tense corresponds to the English future, and indicates the certain or contemplated occurrence of an event which has not yet occurred (e.g., ... we shall be saved by His life.).

Verb tenses can be found using the tools provided in www.blueletterbible.org.

Searching Out the Matter
(All Scripture references, but those noted, are NKJV; Thomas Nelson, Inc.; footnotes excluded)

Transformation

As we learned in Map 1, to be transformation agents, Leaders in the Workplace must themselves be transformed. Following the discovery of the desire God has placed in our hearts for this season (Psalm 37:4), a period of transformation is necessary to prepare us for the good work associated with that desire (Matthew 5:16). This Biblical prescription for spiritual maturity is found in 2Corinthians 3:18.

> *But we all, with unveiled face, beholding as in a mirror the glory of the Lord, are being transformed into the same image from glory to glory, just as by the Spirit of the Lord.* 2Corinthians 3:18

As you can see in the following graphic, transformation is like climbing a mountain. It is a process that occurs as we behold the glory of Christ (in prayer and meditation, in Bible study, in other believers, etc.) and allow the Holy Spirit to transform us from one level of glory to another. This new level of glory is simply a condition where more of the glory that Christ has given us can be seen; and more of His character is getting out of us onto others.

Map 4 The Adventures of Our Life in Christ

INLIGHT
CONSULTING

God is calling Marketplace Leaders to an adventure that will transform them and those in their spheres of influence.

Let your light so shine before men, that they may see your good works and glorify your Father in heaven.
Matthew 5:16

New Glory Level

And the glory which You gave Me I have given them, that they may be one just as We are one: I in them, and You in Me; that they may be made perfect in one, and that the world may know that You have sent Me, and have loved them as You have loved Me.
John 17:22-23

But we all, with unveiled face, beholding as in a mirror the glory of the Lord, are being transformed into the same image from glory to glory, just as by the Spirit of the Lord.
2Corinthians 3:18

Old Glory Level

Delight yourself also in the LORD, and He shall give you the desires of your heart.
Psalm 37:4

It is interesting to note that the Greek word for transformed – *metamorphoo* – is only found in two other places in the New Testament. Another is in Paul's letter to the Romans:

> *And do not be conformed to this world, but be transformed by the renewing of your mind, that you may prove what is that good and acceptable and perfect will of God.* Romans 12:2

The transformation process involves the renewal of our minds, and a move away from conformity to the world. As we learned in Map 3, reckoning the truths of God for ourselves is one way that we can participate with the Holy Spirit's work. Beholding the glory of the Lord is another. In both cases, our transformation is evidenced by the increased manifestation of that glory.

Understanding God's intention in the transformation process may already be stretching your paradigm of the normal Christian life (that's a good thing). It may seem too fantastic to be possible; but, it doesn't stop there. Let's look at the third occurrence of *metamorphoo* - found in Matthew 17:

> *Now after six days Jesus took Peter, James, and John his brother, led them up on a high mountain by themselves; and He was transfigured before them. His face shone like the sun, and His clothes became as white as the light.* Matthew 17:1-2

Do you see it? Jesus was *metamorphoo-ed* on the Mount of *"Metamorphoo"*. Could this be possible for us? Well, I haven't seen too many Christians glowing like Jesus, but it has to make you think, "What's possible?" Perhaps God intends for us to have a greater impact on our surroundings. Consider the following:

> *For we are to God the fragrance of Christ among those who are being saved and among those who are perishing.* 2Corinthians 2:15

Paul is not speaking of super Christians, but of every Christian who ministers out of the transformed life.

Map 4 -The Adventures of Our Life in Christ

One of the most inspiring quotes I have ever read speaks volumes about the potential in those that will lay hold of the truth regarding our transformation:

> *Our deepest fear is not that we are inadequate. Our deepest fear is that we are powerful beyond measure. It is our light, not our darkness that most frightens us. We ask ourselves, who am I to be brilliant, gorgeous, talented, fabulous? Actually, who are you not to be? You are a child of God. Your playing small does not serve the world. There is nothing enlightened about shrinking so that other people won't feel insecure around you. We are all meant to shine, as children do. We were born to make manifest the glory of God that is within us. It's not just in some of us; it's in everyone. And as we let our own light shine, we unconsciously give other people permission to do the same. As we are liberated from our own fear, our presence automatically liberates others. Return to Love*
> by Marianne Williamson, Harper Collins, 1992

Belief/Faith

We've covered the process of faith, as it relates to our reckoning of God's truth, in Map 3. So, just as a point of further edification, let's take a look at the most recognized verse in the Holy Bible.

> *For God so loved the world that He gave His only begotten Son, that whoever believes in Him should not perish but have everlasting life.* John 3:16

Many of us have learned that the believing of John 3:16 is a continual action – believe and keep on believing (a process). A Greek scholar once shared with me that the meaning goes even deeper. After years of study and meditation (he's 80 years old), he understands the verse to mean:

> *For God so loved the world that He gave His only begotten Son, that whoever is believing into Him should not perish but is having everlasting life.*

Believing into Him… is having everlasting life. This is our progressive (and adventurous) life in Christ.

NOTE: "Belief" and "faith" are synonyms, translated from the Greek *pistis*. The Bible makes it clear that faith is a process that begins the most important event: Our initial belief in Jesus Christ.

Salvation

Having come this far, it should be no surprise to learn that salvation is also a process. It has a beginning – justification; and it has an end – glorification. Many understand the middle part to be sanctification. This is not entirely correct. Sanctification is one of the processes of salvation, but it is not <u>the</u> process of salvation. Salvation, as you might expect, is much more.

Salvation (*sōtēria*): Deliverance, preservation, safety, salvation; deliverance from the molestation of enemies; in an ethical sense, that which concludes to the soul's safety or salvation (of Messianic salvation); salvation as the present possession of all true Christians; future salvation, the sum of benefits and blessings which the Christians, redeemed from all earthly ills, will enjoy after the visible return of Christ from heaven in the consummated and eternal kingdom of God.

Outline of Biblical Usage, BlueLetterBible.org

Save (*sōzō*): To save, keep safe and sound, to rescue from danger or destruction; to save one from injury or peril; to save a suffering one from perishing (i.e., one suffering from disease); to make well, heal, restore to health; to preserve one who is in danger of destruction, to save or rescue; to save in the technical biblical sense; to deliver from the penalties of the Messianic judgment; to save from the evils which obstruct the reception of the Messianic deliverance.

Outline of Biblical Usage, BlueLetterBible.org

As you can see, the definition of salvation describes a process – as do the verses below:

Map 4 – The Adventures of Our Life in Christ

For by grace you <u>have been saved</u> (perfect tense) through faith, and that not of yourselves; it is the gift of God, [9] not of works, lest anyone should boast. Ephesians 2:8-9

For the message of the cross is foolishness to those who are perishing, but to us who <u>are being saved</u> (present tense) it is the power of God. 1Corinthians 1:18

For we are to God the fragrance of Christ among those who <u>are being saved</u> (present tense) and among those who are perishing. 2Corinthians 2:15

Much more then, having now been justified (aorist tense) by His blood, we <u>shall be saved</u> (future tense) from wrath through Him. For if when we were enemies we were reconciled (katallassō; aorist tense) to God through the death of His Son, much more, having been reconciled (same), we <u>shall be saved</u> (future tense) by His life. Romans 5:9-11

But he who endures to the end <u>shall be saved</u> (future tense). Matthew 24:13

As followers of Jesus Christ, we "have been saved", we "are being saved" and we "shall be saved". The implications of this are profound. For example, how do you answer the question: "When were you saved?"

It makes you think, doesn't it? That's exactly what the Lord is after – followers that will consider the truth. As we continue in this study, I pray that you will be challenged with many opportunities to consider the truth more deeply.

This perspective on salvation as a process is the perfect opportunity for you to practice what we have covered regarding our adventure into the mysteries of God (Map 2). Review that lesson to be sure you are searching out the matter safely; and you are exercising the five keys to receiving and entering into the truth.

To close out this topic, we should praise God that salvation is a process – because it is a process where God is doing the greatest thing He has ever done for man; and not just in a moment, but in the full length and breadth of our lives. He is continuously and progressively saving us!!

Sanctification

As mentioned earlier, sanctification is one of the processes of our salvation, but not the only one. As a distinct process, it is (in a sense) less than salvation. However, fully understood, sanctification can be appreciated – and therefore appropriated – as a process of God that is much more than we might think or imagine. Consider these definitions:

Sanctification (*hagiasmos*): Separation to God; and, the course of life befitting those so separated; from the root ***hagiazō***.   *Vines Expository Dictionary*

Sanctify (*hagiazō*): To render or acknowledge, or to be venerable or hallow; to separate from profane things and dedicate to God (consecrate things to God, dedicate people to God); to purify (to cleanse externally; to purify by expiation: free from the guilt of sin; to purify internally by renewing of the soul).
                                                                                Outline of Biblical Usage, BlueLetterBible.org

Vine's additionally points out that "to sanctify" is used of:

   (a) the consecration of the Son by the Father (John 10:36);

   (b) the Lord Jesus devoting Himself to the redemption of His people (John 17:19);

   (c) the setting apart of the believer for God (Acts 20:32);

   (d) the effect of the Death of Christ on the believer (Hebrews 10:10);

   (e) separation of the believer from the world - by the Father through the Word (John 17:17, 19);

   (f) the believer who turns from such things as dishonor God and His gospel (2Timothy 2:21).

Map 4 The Adventures of Our Life in Christ

From these definitions, we come to understand that sanctification is the setting apart (or preparation) of things and people intended for God's use (or presence). The important thing here is that it is about God more than it is about us. It reminds me of two admonitions:

> *And I heard another voice from heaven saying, "Come out of her, my people, lest you share in her sins, and lest you receive of her plagues.* Revelation 18:4

> *And with many other words he testified and exhorted them, saying, "Be saved from this perverse generation."* Acts 2:40

In this evil day, we would do well to heed these admonitions; to be set apart for our appearance in the presence of God, and for His intended use of us as His instruments. In so doing, we hasten the day of the Lord's return.

> *Let us be glad and rejoice and give Him glory, for the marriage of the Lamb has come, and His wife has made herself ready. And to her it was granted to be arrayed in fine linen, clean and bright, for the fine linen is the righteous acts of the saints.* Revelation 19:7-8

There is a grand and glorious day when the Bride has made herself ready – set apart, transformed and purified – to co-reign with the King of kings and Lord of lords. It is the Father's desire, the Son's passion, and the Holy Spirit's work that we would – through surrender, sacrifice and submission – make ourselves ready for His return.

The process of sanctification is immensely important in every area of our lives – particularly in the area where we spend most of our waking hours.

Sanctification in the Workplace

Map 4 The Adventures of Our Life in Christ

Undoubtedly, Leaders in the Workplace have become the spiritual leaders of our communities… across all spheres of society. As go the leaders, so goes the Workplace; and so goes our communities. Right or wrong, this is reality in post-Christian America.

Wherever you place yourself on this maturity scale, there is always opportunity to be more impactful for God's kingdom. That is the vision of this study. It is the purpose of our being transformed from glory to glory into the very image of Christ. It should be a comfort to know that God is the Manager of the processes that will mature us into disciple making transformation agents.

Conclusion

For more than 20 years, God has been transforming the hearts and minds of Leaders in the Workplace and sovereignly raising them up within strategic spheres of influence. This is not the first time in American history that God has been merciful and gracious to His people through Leaders in the Workplace. Revivals have been birth from business prayer lunches.

Now is the time for Christian Leaders in the Workplace to ask themselves some important questions: How are we leading? Timidly, or boldly? In assurance of our faith, or with doubt and double-mindedness? With purity of heart, or with a greyish hypocrisy?

Remember, God is a process oriented problem solver; and there is no problem that He cannot solve. As we see in Paul's prayer for the Ephesians, God will move powerfully on your behalf – beginning with the work He is doing in you. Consider the following for yourself.

> Therefore I also, after I heard of your faith in the Lord Jesus and your love for all the saints, do not cease to give thanks for you, making mention of you in my prayers: that the God of our Lord Jesus Christ, the Father of glory, may give to you the spirit of wisdom and revelation in the knowledge of Him, the eyes of your understanding being enlightened; that you may know what is the hope of His calling (His purpose), what are the riches of the glory of His inheritance in the saints (your assignment), and what is the exceeding greatness of His power toward us who believe (His power), according to the working of His mighty power (His plan)… Ephesians 1:15-19

If we are to join Him in the work, we must do things His way. His ways are active, continuous and progressive. His Son is making us. The Holy Spirit is transforming us. These processes are truly the adventures of our life in Christ.

Application

It is really quite simple (though not necessarily easy): As Leaders in the Workplace, we are called to lead those within our spheres of influence into and through the processes God has established for our growth as the Body of Christ. We must recognize that these are processes that take time and attention. We must fight the temptation to be event oriented in our responsibilities to the Master. We must encourage, edify and equip others to do the same.

As Jesus said, "Go and make disciples…".

Reckoning

God is working in us to will and do to His good pleasure (Philippians 2:13).

Map 4 The Adventures of Our Life in Christ

Assignment

1. Review the Bible passages for this week. Study and meditate on those that may have challenged your understanding. Ask the Lord to give meaning to them for you. Share this with someone in your spheres of influence.

2. The Greek word for transformed (2 Corinthians 3:18) and transfigured (Matthew 17:2) are the same. What does this tell you about God's purpose for your life?

3. Ask God to reveal the fears that are prohibiting your transformation and service to Him. Ask Him to reveal the lies behind those fears, and the truths that you can use against them. Lastly, deal with each lie and the fear will fly. Adventure without fear is all excitement.

Devotion

Finding Joyful, Spirit-filled Ministry
From Rob Streetman, The inLight Adventure Blog

The Lord desires that every Marketplace Leader find joyful, Spirit-filled ministry in every area of their life – work, home, church, etc. It is important to note that this includes their ministry in the workplace. This is, after all, the place where they spend the largest portion of their waking hours.

The first step in the journey towards joyful, Spirit-filled ministry is discovering the desire God has placed in your heart for this season of your life (Psalm 37:4). As you surrender to that desire, it becomes a purpose of God that will not be denied Him (Job 42:2).

God has the perfect plan for accomplishing His purpose. That plan is a true adventure. It is complex (by human standards) and involves many other individuals. It is an orchestration in the fullest sense. It's best left to Him; and it's okay not to know the whole plan. God does, however, reveal enough of His plan to allow a counting of the cost. This is one of Christ's commands (Luke 14:28).

Map 4 The Adventures of Our Life in Christ

In counting the cost, we find that God's plan will require a sacrifice. Sacrificing for His plan is the second step of the journey. As Christ said, "And whoever does not bear his cross and come after Me cannot be My disciple." (Luke 14:27) Following Christ requires that the Marketplace Leader take the same road. This is the most decisive moment in the journey – The Marketplace Leader must ask himself, "Will I trust Him enough to agree to sacrifice for a plan I don't understand and cannot control?"

In step three, the Marketplace Leader submits to the power of the Holy Spirit – to work out what doesn't belong and to work in all that is needed for the supernatural work He will do in and through the Leader. Like going through boot camp, the old man is torn down that the Leader might be built up into the image of Christ.

Finally, the Marketplace Leader is prepared to let their light so shine before men that they will see their good work and glorify their Father in Heaven (Matthew 5:16). It is important to note that the "your" in this verse is plural. There are no lone rangers in God's economy. God gives the Marketplace Leader influence for the purpose of discipling others through the process and into the work – a work of unity for His glory.

The Map Maker's Guide

Map 5 - The Fear of the LORD

Spiritual Exercise

The fear of the LORD is the beginning of wisdom; a good understanding have all those who do His commandments. His praise endures forever. Psalm 111:10

The fear of the LORD is the beginning of knowledge, but fools despise wisdom and instruction. Proverbs 1:7

In the fear of the LORD there is strong confidence, and His children will have a place of refuge. Proverbs 14:26

The fear of the LORD leads to life, and he who has it will abide in satisfaction; he will not be visited with evil. Proverbs 19:23

Many of God's kingdom treasures are precipitated on "the fear of the LORD": Wisdom, knowledge, confidence, life, satisfaction, protection from evil, etc. With so much at stake, it is our responsibility – and it is to our advantage – to understand this facet of our relationship with the LORD.

Prayer

Dear LORD, thank you for offering so much in our fear of You. We confess our confusion and neglect of attention in this area of relationship with You. Search us, O God, and know our hearts; try us, and know our anxieties; and see if there is any wicked way in us, and lead us in the way everlasting. We long to walk in victory with You, for Your glory and kingdom. Teach us how to fear You. Thank You for Your attention to our humble prayer. In Christ's name. Amen.

Introduction

As the church has become more seeker-friendly, the "hellfire-and-brimstone" sermons that were once commonly preached have been replaced with a softer, more pleasing message. Consequently, truth regarding the fear of the LORD has been lost. It has become popular to teach that the fear of the LORD is primarily about having reverence, or awe, towards Him. That's not the way Jesus put it to His disciples.

And I say to you, My friends, do not be afraid of those who kill the body, and after that have no more that they can do. But I will show you whom you should fear: Fear Him who, after He has killed, has power to cast into hell; yes, I say to you, fear Him! Luke 12:4-5

As we see in this verse, fear can be good… and bad. There are things and beings we should fear, and those that we should not. Fear can paralyze us, and fear can empower us. The truth of this in the kingdom of God is particularly important, for much is at stake.

Definition

Fear (*yare'*, Hebrew): To fear, revere, be afraid; to stand in awe of, be awed; to be fearful, be dreadful, be feared; to cause astonishment and awe, be held in awe; to inspire reverence or godly fear or awe; to make afraid, terrify. *Outline of Biblical Usage, BlueLetterBible.org*

Map 5 - The Fear of the LORD

Fear (phobos, Greek): Fear, dread, terror; always with this significance in the four Gospels; reverential fear of the LORD, as a controlling motive of the life, in matters spiritual and moral, not a mere "fear" of His power and righteous retribution, but a wholesome dread of displeasing Him, a "fear" which banishes the terror that shrinks from His presence and which influences the disposition and attitude of one whose circumstances are guided by trust in God, through the indwelling Spirit of God. *Vines Expository Dictionary*

Note that the Vines Expository Dictionary determined it was important to point out that "fear, dread and terror" were always the intended meaning in the four Gospels – an interesting invitation for us to search out the matter of fear; and be made free by the truth of it.

Searching Out the Matter
(All Scripture references, but those noted, are NKJV; Thomas Nelson, Inc.; headings and footnotes excluded)

Fear or Cowardice

There are two Greek words that are translated "fear" in the New Testament. The most common (and the one used in the Introduction verse) is *phobos*. *Phobos* means terror, awe and reverence (in that order). You may be surprised to know that *phobos* is not the word used in this often quoted verse:

> *For God has not given us a spirit of fear, but of power and of love and of a sound mind.* 2Timothy 1:7

The Greek word here is *deilia*, which means cowardice. So, you see, the spirit of fear is not the same as the *phobos* of God. It is the drawing back from the enemies of God when challenged about the testimony of our Lord.

As His children, we have power over these enemies. Our drawing back is cowardice – not the fear God intends. Let us turn our hearts to God in proper fear of Him; and ask Him to identify any fear we have of His enemies.

Out with the Bad

During the transformation process, the Holy Spirit will work ungodly fear out of us. Along the way, He will expose fears that inhibit our transformation and our obedience to Christ. All the while, Satan will be attempting to leverage these fears to His advantage. If we will submit to the Holy Spirit's work, what Satan intends for evil, God will turn to good.

Near the end of the transformation process, there will be what some call a strongman – a more powerful demon – that we must overcome before walking out into our assignment. God will allow this strongman to attack us with the fears that will most inhibit our glorifying Him in our new assignment. These will <u>not</u> be more than we can bear. We must courageously face and defeat them. God has given us a number of promises in this regard.

> *Therefore submit to God. Resist the devil and he will flee from you. Draw near to God and He will draw near to you. Cleanse your hands, you sinners; and purify your hearts, you double-minded.* James 4:7-8

The process of transformation includes cleansing and purification, in submission to God, which produces power over the evil one.

> *The angel of the LORD encamps all around those who fear Him, and delivers them.* Psalms 34:7

The agents of Satan are not the only beings hovering around you. Those that have a godly fear of the LORD have His angels encamped around them to assist in their battles.

Map 5 - The Fear of the LORD

For God has not given us a spirit of fear, but of power and of love and of a sound mind. 2Timothy 1:7

We have not been given a spirit of cowardice. As His children, we have power over ungodly fear and cowardice. Our power is the truth of God. When the spirit of fear comes, we must not run from it. God would have us face it, and deal with it!

How do we deal with ungodly fear? It is very simple. I encourage you to memorize – and exercise – the following key to victory over ungodly fear.

> *Behind every ungodly fear there is a lie. Deal with the lie and the fear will fly.*
> *The truth that replaces the lie will become a weapon for you and others.*
> *God will have turned to good, what Satan intended for evil.*

In with the Good

While the Holy Spirit is working ungodly fear out of us, He is developing in us a more righteous fear of the LORD. The Holy Spirit began teaching me about this godly fear through the following verse.

> *Thus says the LORD:*
> *" Heaven is My throne,*
> *And earth is My footstool.*
> *Where is the house that you will build Me?*
> *And where is the place of My rest?*
> *For all those things My hand has made,*
> *And all those things exist,"*
> *Says the LORD.*
> *"But on this one will I look:*
> *On him who is poor and of a contrite spirit,*
> *And who trembles at My word."* Isaiah 66:1-2

The LORD is saying that He doesn't need anything from us. But there is one He will look on. Most are familiar with the requirement of a poor and contrite spirit, but who is the one that trembles at His word? Does that describe our response to His word? Are we seriously considering the consequences of being out of His will?

Continuing with the word to Isaiah, we find God's opinion of the ones that are not poor, contrite and trembling.

> *He who kills a bull is as if he slays a man;*
> *He who sacrifices a lamb, as if he breaks a dog's neck;*
> *He who offers a grain offering, as if he offers swine's blood;*
> *He who burns incense, as if he blesses an idol.* Isaiah 66:3

Do these verses cause me to tremble? Perhaps they should. Those that are described here are not only "out of God's will". Their sacrifices are an abomination to Him. They are out of relationship – a fearful place, indeed!

This fear is not solely an Old Testament concept – as Paul makes clear to the Corinthians.

> *Therefore we make it our aim, whether present or absent, to be well pleasing to Him. For we must all appear before the judgment seat of Christ, that each one may receive the things done in the body, according to what he has done, whether good or bad. Knowing, therefore, the terror of the Lord, we persuade men; but we are well known to God, and I also trust are well known in your consciences.* 2Corinthians 5:9-11

Map 5 - The Fear of the LORD

Paul is making two important points here. First, there is a judgment seat for Christians – not for salvation, but for the works we have done. Second, there is a "terror of the Lord" in this day of the New Covenant. The mention of both concerns together should give us pause.

God does not want us walking around under an overbearing cloud of fear. Remember, there is also His love. We are to consider the mercy and severity of God. Both His love and His fearsomeness are important components of our relationship with Him.

How Should We Fear Him?

There are at least four types of God-ward fear that we must allow the Holy Spirit to develop in us – and through us into others. They are the fear of:

1. Entering into His presence in an unworthy manner

   Therefore whoever eats this bread or drinks this cup of the Lord in an unworthy manner will be guilty of the body and blood of the Lord. But let a man examine himself, and so let him eat of the bread and drink of the cup. For he who eats and drinks in an unworthy manner eats and drinks judgment to himself, not discerning the Lord's body. For this reason many are weak and sick among you, and many sleep. 1Corinthians 11:27-30

   Communion is a sacrament – a sacred meeting with the Lord. Paul's warns that there are consequences for entering the Lord's presence in an unworthy manner. What is the manner worthy of the King of kings and the Lord of lords?

   Pursue peace with all people, and holiness, without which no one will see the Lord...
   Hebrews 12:14

   Therefore, having these promises, beloved, let us cleanse ourselves from all filthiness of the flesh and spirit, perfecting holiness in the fear of God. 2Corinthians 7:1

   We will not see the Lord if we are not pursuing holiness – the holiness which is perfected in the fear of the LORD. Many have mistaken the encouragement of Hebrews 10:19 ("having boldness to enter the Holiest by the blood of Jesus") as license to enter the presence of God and Christ in an unworthy manner. Careful examination of this passage reveals that our drawing near must be "with a true heart... sprinkled from an evil conscience".

   This may seem too difficult; even impossible. Keep in mind that our Heavenly Father and Christ desire our communion. They have made a way, but it must be Their way. The fear of the LORD does not prevent our approaching. It enables it!

2. Becoming His enemy

   Because the carnal mind is enmity against God; for it is not subject to the law of God, nor indeed can be. Romans 8:7

   Do not love the world or the things in the world. If anyone loves the world, the love of the Father is not in him. 1John 2:15

   Adulterers and adulteresses! Do you not know that friendship with the world is enmity with God? Whoever therefore wants to be a friend of the world makes himself an enemy of God. James 4:4

   The world is an alluring place. Even Christians are seduced by its offerings. We are not given a new mind when we are reborn. Our carnal minds must be renewed. It is sobering to realize that the desire to be a friend with the world makes us an enemy of God.

3. Inhibiting His work in our lives

Map 5 - The Fear of the LORD

See that you do not refuse Him who speaks. For if they did not escape who refused Him who spoke on earth, much more shall we not escape if we turn away from Him who speaks from heaven… Therefore, since we are receiving a kingdom which cannot be shaken, let us have grace, by which we may serve God acceptably with reverence and godly fear. For our God is a consuming fire. Hebrews 12:25, 28-29

Therefore, my beloved, as you have always obeyed, not as in my presence only, but now much more in my absence, work out your own salvation with fear and trembling; for it is God who works in you both to will and to do for His good pleasure. Philippians 2:12-13

Our freedom to choose does not vanish when we become followers of Jesus Christ. We can refuse the voice of God and choose not to serve Him. We can resist His will and His work in us. We have been warned that He is a God of justice; and encouraged that He is a God of love. We participate in the work He does in us, and through us, with fear and trembling.

4. Falling into apostasy

Let no one deceive you by any means; for that Day will not come unless the falling away comes first… 2Thessalonians 2:3

Now the Spirit expressly says that in latter times some will depart from the faith, giving heed to deceiving spirits and doctrines of demons… 1Timothy 4:1

The coming of the lawless one is according to the working of Satan, with all power, signs, and lying wonders, and with all unrighteous deception among those who perish, because they did not receive the love of the truth, that they might be saved. 2Thessalonians 2:9-10

For if we sin willfully after we have received the knowledge of the truth, there no longer remains a sacrifice for sins, but a certain fearful expectation of judgment, and fiery indignation which will devour the adversaries. It is a fearful thing to fall into the hands of the living God. Hebrews 10:26-27, 31

As much as we would like to believe otherwise, there are those that can and will fall away from the faith. This is not what some call "back-sliding". It is the full loss of someone's salvation. As the writer of Hebrews has said, "It is a fearful thing…"

What we must keep in mind is that fear can be a good thing. It can discourage us from sin. It can drive us to God and Jesus Christ. It motivates us to enter Their presence in a way that is honoring for Them and beneficial for us.

Love and Fear

It has become popular to teach from 2Timothy 1:7 and 1John 4:18 that God has removed fear from His children – including our fear of Him. We've dealt with the 2Timothy verse, previously in this study. Let's consider the 1John verse in context.

No one has seen God at any time. If we love one another, God abides in us, and His love has been perfected in us. And we have known and believed the love that God has for us. God is love, and he who abides in love abides in God, and God in him. Love has been perfected among us in this: that we may have boldness in the day of judgment; because as He is, so are we in this world. There is no fear in love; but perfect love casts out fear, because fear involves torment. But he who fears has not been made perfect in love. 1John 4:12,16-18

First, it is <u>perfect</u> love that casts out fear (v. 18). Verse 12 explains that this perfect love comes from loving one another. Do we qualify, or are we merely on the way? I confess that I am still working this out myself. However, it is clear from these and previously sited verses that love and fear are a part of our relationship with God. I propose that the fear of the LORD leads us to the perfect love that casts out all fear (another Kingdom

Map 5 - The Fear of the LORD

process). God is love (v. 16). When we are perfected in Him, there will be no need for fear. In the meantime, let's take a look at…

Developing the Fear of the LORD

Oh, fear the LORD, you His saints!
There is no want to those who fear Him.
The young lions lack and suffer hunger;
But those who seek the LORD shall not lack any good thing.
Come, you children, listen to me;
I will teach you the fear of the LORD.
Who is the man who desires life,
And loves many days, that he may see good?
Keep your tongue from evil,
And your lips from speaking deceit.
Depart from evil and do good;
Seek peace and pursue it. Psalm 34:9-14

Verses 13 and 14 are the King David's instruction for finding the fear of the LORD. Read them again. If you're like me, it's not what you expected. But what good news! There is a discipline that we can follow that will develop, in each of us, the fear of the LORD.

Like his father before him, Solomon sought to explain how someone might come to understand the fear of the LORD.

My son, if you receive my words,
And treasure my commands within you,
So that you incline your ear to wisdom,
And apply your heart to understanding;
Yes, if you cry out for discernment,
And lift up your voice for understanding,
If you seek her as silver,
And search for her as for hidden treasures;
Then you will understand the fear of the LORD,
And find the knowledge of God. Proverb 2:1-5

The heart zealous for wisdom, understanding and discernment will understand the fear of the LORD. Of course, these things are easier said than done. In fact, they cannot be done without the empowering grace of God, the counsel of the Holy Spirit and the life of Christ within us. Praise God!! All we need has been given!!

For everyone who asks receives, and he who seeks finds, and to him who knocks it will be opened. Luke 11:10

Jesus said, "Follow me and I will make you…" This includes the development of the appropriate fear of the LORD. It is possible to walk in the fear of the LORD.

Conclusion

As we battle the enemies of our God, we will face many fears. Fear is one of our enemies' most powerful weapons. God created us with the capacity to fear, but not for the purposes of the enemy. In fact, He has made it clear that His children have nothing to fear in the enemy. We are to be more than conquerors in Christ Jesus.

But there is a fear – the fear of the LORD – which we must allow the Holy Spirit to cultivate in our lives. That fear is the beginning of wisdom, provision, protection, and many more of His promises. In many cases, it is

Map 5 - The Fear of the LORD

terror and trembling (Philippians 2:12). It is the humble, fearful Christian that dares to enter into the presence of God. It is the fear of knowing that we are the temple of the Living God – who is a consuming fire(Hebrews 12:28-29).

The fear of the LORD is grounded in love and is therefore a mystery and a treasure. It is for our good. It empowers and makes us free – free to do the same for those we disciple. As a mystery and a treasure, the fear of the LORD must be searched out, and shared with others. Be encouraged that you will find what you are looking for. Encourage others and your courage will be multiplied.

Application

Ask, seek and knock. Have you ever thought to ask the Father to give you the fear of the LORD? Have you ever sought it out? Have you knocked at the door with a fearful expectation that the One Who shines brighter than the Sun will answer? As we prepare ourselves for this adventure, now is the time to start.

Reckoning

The LORD is to be feared.

Assignment

1. Review your notes and the Scripture passages from this week's module. Share the ones that are most meaningful to you, with someone else. The truth will make them free.

2. What are the things or beings of which you have an ungodly fear? Can you identify the lie behind your fear? Deal with the lie and the fear will fly; and the truth you find will make you free.

3. Seek God for the holy fear that leads to wisdom, protection, fruitfulness, etc.

4. This is the last lesson in the preparation section of The Mapmaker's Guide. You should review the previous lessons to ensure you have prepared yourself as much as God will allow.

Devotion

Wrestling With God
TGIF Today God Is First Volume 1 by Os Hillman

"So Jacob was left alone, and a man wrestled with him till daybreak." - Genesis 32:24

All that Jacob had lived for was coming down to one event - his reunion with Esau. More than 20 years had passed since Jacob had manipulated his father's blessing away from his brother Esau. During these years God had been changing Jacob from a controller and manipulator to a man who was learning to trust God. He was now ready to meet Esau. However, he was fearful that Esau might take revenge on him and his family for his past sin, so he sent a gift ahead, while he retreated and sought mercy from God.

As an angel appeared to Jacob, he realized the only hope he had was in God. Only if God blessed him would he survive this ordeal. In the past, Jacob would have sought to solve his problem his way. Now, he wanted only God's way. He wanted Him so badly that he wouldn't let go of the angel. He was striving with God, but it was the right kind of striving. Jacob was striving to have all God's blessing on his life. He was seeking God with all that he had. "When the man saw that he could not overpower him, he touched the socket of Jacob's hip so that his hip was wrenched as he wrestled with the man" (Gen. 32:25). The only way to overcome the strong will of this man was to physically immobilize him. The angel touched the socket of Jacob's hip. It was painful; it broke him. This was the final stage of removing the old nature from Jacob. It was the place of complete

Map 5 - The Fear of the LORD

brokenness and surrender. No longer would Jacob walk in his own strength. He would now have to lean on a cane, symbolic of his leaning on God alone.

What does God have to do in our lives to remove the controlling and manipulative nature that so often is part of a workplace believer's life? Perhaps it will require a time of immobilizing, loss of a job, loss of income, loss of health, loss of a close relationship. These are His methods of preparation. Your new nature will not be complete until you've stopped striving with God through your own self-efforts. If God is taking you through this process, be encouraged; it is because of the inheritance He has prepared for you. However, the inheritance can only be received when God brings us to total dependence on Him.

Reprinted by permission from the author. Os Hillman is an international speaker and author of more than 10 books on workplace calling. To learn more, visit http://www.MarketplaceLeaders.org.

The Map Maker's Guide

Section Two - Surrendering to His Purpose

The Map Maker led Somebody by the hand out of the Preparation Room, down the hall, and past the Map Room ("Again?", thought Somebody). They stopped at a door beautifully engraved with one large and powerful looking word. That word was **PURPOSE**.

Standing outside the room, the Map Maker explained, "The room you are about to enter is filled with people like yourself. They are Somebodies who are looking for the purpose of their adventure. You will discover that you have much in common with them."

Before the foundations of the earth, God deposited desires in the heart of every Leader in the Workplace. He has been orchestrating events to reveal and establish the identity, gifts and spheres of influence needed to accomplish them. Surrendering to His purpose creates an atmosphere for hearing and believing the living word of God; and sharing in His heart's desire for the Bride.

The purpose of this section is to encourage Workplace Leaders to put aside their agendas and position themselves to hear, understand and surrender to God's general and specific purposes for this season of their lives. This is not about figuring it out. It's about humbling oneself and searching for the desire that He has placed in them; trusting that their specific desire will supplement His eternal purposes.

The Map Maker's Guide

Map 6 - The Purposes of God

Spiritual Exercise

> *Jesus answered them and said, "My doctrine is not Mine, but His who sent Me. If anyone wills to do His will, he shall know concerning the doctrine, whether it is from God or whether I speak on My own authority.* John 7:16-17

The one who is willing to obey His Master's command before he hears it is the one who will understand what the Master is saying. In contrast, the one who comes to only hear, and not obey, deceives himself – even forgetting what kind of man he was (i.e., the Master's faithful servant).

> *But be doers of the word, and not hearers only, deceiving yourselves. For if anyone is a hearer of the word and not a doer, he is like a man observing his natural face in a mirror; for he observes himself, goes away, and immediately forgets what kind of man he was.* James 1:22-24

As we position ourselves before the Master, let's commit ourselves to obedience; bringing our "amen" first; to be doers of His word.

Prayer

Amen, Father, amen. We bring a heart that desires to obey. We surrender our will to Yours. Give us ears to hear and hearts to respond. In the name of Jesus Christ our Lord.

Introduction

Finding purpose in life is one of man's greatest pursuits. It is a part of our DNA. Regrettably, we seek to find purpose in many of the wrong places. Don't misunderstand; it's not necessarily because all these places are wrong. Many are quite noble – work, family, church, service to others. God wants to give us purpose in all these areas.

The challenge is discerning from where, or whom, our purposes in life originate; for that thing or person will then govern the motivations and measures for our success. If our purposes center on our work, then we will become performance driven and prideful. If they begin with our relationships, we will become controlling and self-indulgent. Even service toward others – if it is the source of our purpose – will result in people-pleasing codependence.

For our purposes to be right and virtuous, they must originate in the One that has ordained and orchestrated them. They must be understood and pursued in the context of His greater purposes. This section of our adventure toward joyful, Spirit-filled ministry is focused on this critical first step – Surrendering to His Purposes.

This is a worthy saying: Your purpose is not to be found in a place or activity, but in a Person. Only God is the source of the purposes that are good, praiseworthy and worthwhile. Therefore, it is critical that we discover God's purposes for each season of our lives.

Map 6 - The Purposes of God

Definition

Purpose (*prosthesis*): A setting forth of a thing, placing of it in view, the showbread ("bread of faces", in the tabernacle, showing the offer and necessity of fellowship with God). *Outline of Biblical Usage, BlueLetterBible.org*

Searching Out the Matter
(All Scripture references, but those noted, are NKJV; Thomas Nelson, Inc.; footnotes excluded)

Adjusting Our Focus

Most of our teaching about the "original sin" centers on what Mankind lost in Adam and Eve's rebellion. We ruminate and regret our own reduced state.

"Woe is me! I have to toil for my living."

"Woe is me! I have to labor in childbirth."

But, what about God? Have you ever considered what God lost in the Garden of Eden? Shouldn't we be concerned about His loss? As with anyone else we love, shouldn't we be interested in Him getting it back? After all, He is the Master of the kingdom we call home – the place of our stewardship to the King. It just might be that Him getting back what belongs to Him is the best thing that could happen to us.

Our understanding of God's loss is vital to our pursuit of His purposes for our lives; for a few very good reasons:

1. His ultimate purpose is to restore what He lost in our rebellion.
2. His purposes for us are secondary to His purposes for Himself and His kingdom.
3. It is within the context of His greatest purposes that we discover and understand the general and specific purposes for each season of our lives.

Most importantly, we are living in His story; and focusing on His story from His perspective will keep us humble and give Him pleasure.

Restoring that which was Lost

The Bible may be the only book written that is not spoiled by reading the end of the story first. In fact, it is encouraging and edifying to know what God is after; because we know that He will get whatever it is.

In the conclusion of His story, in the book of the Revelation, we discover what He has been up to since that fateful day in the Garden of Eden: Nothing less that the complete restoration of what He lost in Mankind's rebellion.

> *Now I saw a new heaven and a new earth, for the first heaven and the first earth had passed away. Also there was no more sea. Then I, John, saw the holy city, New Jerusalem, coming down out of heaven from God, prepared as a bride adorned for her husband. And I heard a loud voice from heaven saying, "Behold, the tabernacle of God is with men, and He will dwell with them, and they shall be His people. God Himself will be with them and be their God. And God will wipe away every tear from their eyes; there shall be no more death, nor sorrow, nor crying. There shall be no more pain, for the former things have passed away."* Revelation 21:1-4

Oh, what a glorious day! It is the day we long for, when "all things are made new". It is the grand finale of God's great story (at least the part He has revealed). In John's description of this great day, we find a tight synopsis of His restorative purpose. And it's not verse four – as wonderful and well quoted as it has become.

Map 6 - The Purposes of God

The greatest purposes of God are found in verse three – the order reminding us that it is for Him before it is for us:

1. "He will dwell with them" – It was always God's intention to inhabit His people. Jesus spoke of its beginning, "If anyone loves Me, he will keep My word; and My Father will love him, and We will come to him and make Our home with him." (John 14:23) This is the spiritual reality of that which will be physically manifested in the New Jerusalem.

   God will restore the habitation He intended to have with His people.

2. "They shall be His people" – We can only imagine the depths of intimacy God had with Adam and Eve in the Garden – and His loss in their rebellion. God sent Jesus to make a way for the restoration of His relationship with us. Jesus prayed the will of the Father back to Him in John 17:

   And this is eternal life, that they may know You, the only true God, and Jesus Christ whom You have sent. v. 3

   … that they all may be one, as You, Father, are in Me, and I in You; that they also may be one in Us. v. 21

   God will fully restore the intimate relationship He intended to have with His children.

3. "God Himself will be… their God" – The third thing God lost in the Garden was His reign in the hearts of His people. Before they disobeyed God's command regarding the Tree of the Knowledge of Good and Evil, Adam and Eve determined that they were better suited to make decisions for themselves. They determined to be their own kings. They rebelled against God in a futile attempt to become like Him.

   God will fully restore His reign in the hearts of His subjects.

In the coming weeks we will look deeper into each of these great and mighty purposes, and explore their impact on the general and specific purposes that God has given us for this season of our lives. For now, please consider a few more encouragements regarding the role of purpose in the discovery of joyful, Spirit-filled ministry.

Ultimate, General and Seasonal Purposes

In addition to the three ultimate purposes found in God's restoration story, there are what we might call general purposes. These include the purposes that every Christian has been given (e.g., to be salt and light); and the purposes that are given to large groups of Christians. For example, all pastors are called to shepherd the flock that has been given to them. Some general purposes may span seasons, but not continue for a person's entire lifetime (e.g., pastor, mother).

There is a desire in each of our hearts to pursue the ultimate and general purposes of God. Each of us has a desire for God to get back what He lost in Mankind's rebellion. We each have a desire to obey everyone of God's and Christ's commandments. It is good to think of these as "foundational desires" in the sense that they are central to our walk with the Lord. We must dedicate ourselves to a lifetime of discovering these desires in our own hearts, and surrendering to them.

Seasonal desires are different. These are desires that God has put in a particular person, or persons, for a particular season. God often gives the same desire to a group of individuals in order to draw them together for a community purpose. However, the seasonal desire for the group is still more specific than those that I am calling ultimate and general.

Why is this important? When you ask your heart (or someone else's), "What is your desire?", the initial response will often be a general desire. For example, "I want to love God and people more." Or, "I want to

Map 6 - The Purposes of God

glorify God in all I do." These are good answers, but they are not specific to the person or the season. They, along with many other general desires, are for everyone at all times.

What we are looking for is something like, "I want to build a company that glorifies God in the telecommunications industry." Specific desires may also identify themselves as a burden. For example, to get prayer back in school or save children from slave trafficking. These are the desires that God turns into assignments.

Two closing points here: First, not everyone I have asked has been able to articulate a seasonal desire. I have not decided for myself if this is because they haven't been given one, or they are not ready to find it. This leads me to my second point.

It is critical that we pursue our seasonal desires on the foundation of God's three ultimate purposes, as well as the general desires He has given us for obedience to His word. God's orchestration and timing are perfect. We should not become discouraged – or judge another – when a seasonal desire is not obvious. As disciple makers, we must patiently and lovingly encourage others to explore and surrender to all the desires that God has placed in their hearts.

Letting Go of Our Purposes

> *And we know that all things work together for good to those who love God, to those who are the called according to His purpose.* Romans 8:28

> *I know that You can do everything, and that no purpose of Yours can be withheld from You.* Job 42:2

These two promises can be a powerful encouragement for those that are surrendered to God's purposes. All things work together for their good, and the purposes they are walking in will be fulfilled.

However, for these promises to be ours, our purposes must be His. Discovering God's purpose for a particular season of our lives begins by wiping the slate clean, even putting aside the things we "know" God is calling us to do. This is an intentional "letting go". It is an offering to God. It is surrender to God's purposes.

The immediate result of our surrender is the liberty to hear God without presumption; knowing that what we hear is God speaking. Additionally, there are three long term benefits:

1. The continued affirmation of the call. We are never found guessing about the Lord's purpose for our lives.

2. The enhanced ability to see all God is doing to manifest His purpose. God wants us to be full participates in the work He is accomplishing in and around us.

3. God rewards our surrender with a deeper understanding of His heart – something beyond "blind faith".

Together, these benefits are a part of the "spirit of wisdom and revelation" found in Paul's first prayer for the Ephesians (Ephesians 1:15-21).

This understanding includes the positioning of our purpose in His bigger picture. When the going gets tough, we can rest in the fact that God is in control, and we can put our faith in His promises – like those found in Psalm 37.

> *Commit your way to the Lord,*
> *Trust also in Him,*
> *And He shall bring it to pass.*

Map 6 - The Purposes of God

He shall bring forth your righteousness as the light,
And your justice as the noonday. Psalm 37:5-6

The steps of a good man are ordered by the Lord,
And He delights in his way.
Though he fall, he shall not be utterly cast down;
For the Lord upholds him with His hand. Psalm 37:23-24

Purpose or Plan?

The purposes of God and the plans of God are not the same thing, but they can be easily confused. In the simplest terms, purpose is <u>what</u> God would have you do, and plan is <u>how</u> He will accomplish His purpose with and through you. It is important to keep the purpose and the plan separate, but synchronized – continually testing the plan against the purpose. The purpose is a spiritually safer place because it requires surrender – an intentionally weak position; whereas the plan requires effort and decision – two things we can subconsciously subvert from God.

We will talk more about the plan in the future. For now it's good to know that God usually reveals enough of the plan for us to discover the sacrifice and trust that will be required. Jesus' command to "count the cost" becomes real to many for the first time, when God begins to reveal His plan.

Be Careful in Your Approach

Man's ways of discovering God's will for our lives have infected the church. For example, a well-known Christian author wrote the following:

> *"God has created every person with a purpose. But not everyone discovers what that purpose is. To find out, get to know yourself – your strengths and weaknesses. Look at your opportunities. Examine where God has put you. Then seek His counsel. He will give you a vision for your life."*

The author seems to suggest that finding God's purpose begins with seeking to know yourself. A much more profitable approach would be seeking to know God's counsel first. We can do this by humbly recognizing the limits of our knowledge and understanding; and pursuing His wisdom in the "delight" that is soft as clay in the Potter's hands (Psalm 37:4). Again, this is an exercise in surrender – putting us in a place to both hear His voice and find Him in the adventure.

Conclusion

The purposes of God will not be denied Him (Job 42:2). All things work together for good to those that are called to His purpose (Romans 8:28). If we are working for His purposes, it will be all good for us. If we are not, then we are probably working against Him. We would do well to know the purposes of God – ultimate, general and specific. That will be the focus of the remainder of this section. For now, be forewarned that His purposes will run against those of our carnal nature.

Application

People look to Leaders in the Workplace for vision and purpose. This is a characteristic of the "natural born leader" – a flattering and encouraging title. But there is more for God's people. Step into the purposes of God, and you will become a supernatural leader! Now that's something to get excited about!

Reckoning

God is restoring what was lost in the Garden.

Map 6 - The Purposes of God

Assignment

The most important thing about this exercise is spending time with God – asking Him questions that He is eager to answer. It is about fellowship with the One that has been orchestrating events and processes to bring you (and those around you) into this season. There are no coincidences for God's children; and He does not intend for His children to be blind to His purposes.

1. Review the Bible passages for this week. Share at least one of the concepts with someone you know.

2. Each day this week, ask the Lord to show you the purposes you have assumed. Set these aside.

3. Intentionally surrender to the general purposes He has for all Christians. I suggest you do this verbally (e.g., "Father God, I surrender to living for Your glory."). Others include:

    1. Loving Him with all your heart, mind, soul and strength;
    2. Agreeing with Jesus for Unity;
    3. Disciple-making; and,
    4. Anything else He brings to your attention.

4. Ask God to show you the desire/burden He wants to share with you. Ask Him to break your heart for what breaks His.

Devotion

From Os Hillman TGIF: Discovering Your Purpose

If you are going to discover how God wants to use your life and work, you must know why you were created. If you start trying to determine your purpose in life before understanding why you were created, you will inevitably get hung up on the things you do as the basis for fulfillment in your life, which will only lead to frustration and disappointment.

First and foremost, God created you to know Him and to have an intimate relationship with Him. In fact, God says that if a man is going to boast about anything in life, "boast about this: that he understands and knows me" (Jer. 9:24). Mankind's relationship with God was lost in the Garden when Adam and Eve sinned. Jesus' death on the cross, however, allows us to restore this relationship with God and to have an intimate fellowship with Him. The apostle Paul came to understand this when he said, "I gave up all that inferior stuff so I could know Christ personally, experience his resurrection power, be a partner in his suffering, and go all the way with him to death itself" (Phil. 3:10, THE MESSAGE).

Establishing this relationship with God is vital to understanding your purpose. If you don't have this relationship with God, you will seek to fulfill your purpose out of wrong motives; such as fear, insecurity, pride, money, relationships, guilt, or unresolved anger. God's desire is for you to be motivated out of love for Him and to desire to worship Him in all that you do. As you develop your relationship with God, He will begin to reveal His purpose for your life. "For I know the plans I have for you, declares the Lord" (Jer. 29:11).

Reprinted by permission from the author. Os Hillman is an international speaker and author of more than 10 books on workplace calling. To learn more, visit http://www.MarketplaceLeaders.org.

The Map Maker's Guide

Map 7 - The Church He is Building - Vision

`Spiritual Exercise

Therefore I also, ... making mention of you in my prayers: that the God of our Lord Jesus Christ, the Father of glory, may give to you the spirit of wisdom and revelation in the knowledge of Him, the eyes of your understanding being enlightened; that you may know what is the hope of His calling, what are the riches of the glory of His inheritance in the saints, and what is the exceeding greatness of His power toward us who believe, according to the working of His mighty power... Ephesians 1:15-19

Prayer

Father God, we believe in Your Son and we love His Body on Earth and in Heaven. Thank you for the gifts of faith and fellowship. We humbly pray that You would give us the spirit of wisdom and revelation in the knowledge of You and your Son Jesus. We are blind without Your enlightenment. Enlighten the eyes of our understanding that we may know the hope of Your calling, our value as Your inheritance, and the power You have towards us for Your kingdom purposes. Have mercy and be gracious to us, O God. In the name of Jesus Christ, our Lord. Amen.

Introduction

The rebellion of Adam and Eve was devastating to mankind, and costly to God. The Creator lost His reign in the hearts of mankind; He lost His relationship with them; and He lost His habitation among them. This all happened in the first three chapters of Genesis. The rest of the Bible is the story of Him getting it all back – culminated in the last three chapters of The Revelation. It is a beautiful story of love, rescue and restoration.

In this lesson, we will search out one of the God's great losses – His habitation with and in His children. We will discover that there is a part for us to play and a blessing that comes from pursuing the restoration of His habitation. Moreover, we will see that God's habitation is found in a plurality of people (more than 85% of the "you" pronouns in the New Testament are plural). There are no lone-rangers in the kingdom of God. We were made for community.

Definition

Church (*ekklesia*): From *ek*, "out of," and *klesis*, "a calling", was used among the Greeks of a body of citizens "gathered" to discuss the affairs of State; a gathering of citizens called out from their homes; an assembly. *Vine's Expository Dictionary*

The *ekklesia* are "the called out ones". When Jesus was here on Earth, the Romans were the superpower kingdom. As such, they set out to transform the nations under their rule by sending an assembly of Roman leaders, chosen from each segment of culture (e.g., business, arts, philosophy, government), to infuse or force Roman culture into the native country. We see this in the New Testament, where the Jewish government was a puppet to the Romans. For example, the Sanhedrin could not kill Jesus without Pilate's approval. This group of transformation leaders was called the *ekklesia*.

Map 7 - The Church He is Building - Vision

Searching Out the Matter
(All Scripture references, but those noted, are NKJV; Thomas Nelson, Inc.; footnotes excluded)

God's Habitation

The New Testament refers to God's habitation as the Body of Christ, the Church, and the Bride of Christ. Here are a few verses that speak to the wonderful mystery of His habitation.

> *Jesus answered and said to him, "If anyone loves Me, he will keep My word; and My Father will love him, and We will come to him and make Our home with him. John 14:23*

The reward for every faithful follower of Jesus Christ is the habitation of both Him and His Father.

> *And what agreement has the temple of God with idols? For you are the temple of the living God. As God has said, "I will dwell in them, and walk among them. I will be their God, and they shall be My people." 2Corinthians 6:16*

The indwelling of the Father is a sign of His ownership. His Son paid the price for our salvation that His Father would be in us and all around us. It is important to note here that the "you" in this verse is plural.

> *For this reason I bow my knees to the Father of our Lord Jesus Christ, from whom the whole family in heaven and earth is named, that He would grant you, according to the riches of His glory, to be strengthened with might through His Spirit in the inner man, [17] that Christ may dwell in your hearts through faith; that you, being rooted and grounded in love, may be able to comprehend with all the saints what is the width and length and depth and height—to know the love of Christ which passes knowledge; that you may be filled with all the fullness of God. Ephesians 3:14-19*

This is high heavenly language; the language of mystery. Stop for a moment and let the last phrase sink in: …that you may be filled with <u>all the fullness of God</u>. Let us be diligent to lay hold of that for which Jesus laid hold of us. Let us surrender to the Father's habitation.

> *Therefore, my beloved, as you have always obeyed, not as in my presence only, but now much more in my absence, work out your own salvation with fear and trembling; for it is God who works in you both to will and to do for His good pleasure. Philippians 2:12-13*

The work of God is an internal work. He is working from the inside out.

> *Behold, I stand at the door and knock. If anyone hears My voice and opens the door, I will come in to him and dine with him, and he with Me. Revelation 3:20*

It is His desire to come in and abide. He is knocking and He desires to remain. Truly, the Triune God has taken up residence within each of His people, and in us corporately. The Father, Son and Holy Spirit, in wisdom and might, have come to abide in us. The kingdom of God has come in the vessels of born again believers.

Pause for a moment and consider this mystery (since you are to be a faithful steward of it). Ask God to give you a vision and a confidence of this reality. He did for me. Like me, you may not be able to explain it to others, but you will carry it with you for the rest of your life.

By coming to spiritually dwell in us, God has begun restoring His habitation in His people. That work will culminate in the physical manifestation we find at the end of His story. He has blessed us with a wonderful description of His completed work:

> *And I heard, as it were, the voice of a great multitude, as the sound of many waters and as the sound of mighty thunderings, saying, "Alleluia! For the Lord God Omnipotent reigns! Let us be glad and rejoice and give Him glory, for the marriage of the Lamb has come, and His wife has*

Map 7 - The Church He is Building - Vision

made herself ready." And to her it was granted to be arrayed in fine linen, clean and bright, for the fine linen is the righteous acts of the saints. Revelation 19:6-8

Now I saw a new heaven and a new earth, for the first heaven and the first earth had passed away. Also there was no more sea. Then I, John, saw the holy city, New Jerusalem, coming down out of heaven from God, prepared as a bride adorned for her husband. And I heard a loud voice from heaven saying, "Behold, the tabernacle of God is with men, and He will dwell with them, and they shall be His people. God Himself will be with them and be their God. Revelation 21:1-3

In His sovereign providence, God will complete the work of restoring His habitation. His purposes will not be denied Him. In the meantime, we have the awesome privilege and responsibility to participate in this restorative work. As with any adventure, the more we know about the journey, the better prepared we will be to participate in its purpose. Jesus said that He would build His church. It begs the question, "What does that building look like?"

The *Ekklesia* of Christ

The Roman *ekklesia* was not a sub-culture group, trying to be like the Jews. They were a counter-culture group, sent to transform the Jewish culture into that of the Roman Empire. It is important to recognize that Jesus' chose this word to describe the kingdom He came to build. The disciples would have understood exactly what Jesus had in mind: A counter-culture kingdom that would transform the kingdoms around it.

As we know from history, both *ekklesias* rubbed native society the wrong way. Jewish uprisings were constant and eventually led to the Roman destruction of Jerusalem and the Temple. It was (and is) no different for the *ekklesia* of Christ.

Our King intends to establish His kingdom by transforming the native culture through His "called out ones". From its formation, the true Church has stood against both the pagan world and the religious culture; and it has been persecuted. The Romans eventually crucified thousands of Christians; and we know the Jews played their part in the persecution of the early church.

This should not deter us. We must become "the called out ones". We must deny ourselves, take up our cross, and follow Him.

> *Therefore let us go forth to Him, outside the camp, bearing His reproach. For here we have no continuing city, but we seek the one to come. Hebrews 13:13-14*

What Christ began, He will complete. He will build His church. He has called us out to participate in the work with Him. But, what will that church look like? We have vision for its completion; namely, the Bride and the New Jerusalem. But, is there something more tangible that will guide our participation with Him? How will He build His church? Amazingly, He will build it through the very people He has come to inhabit.

Christ not only died for our sins and was resurrected that we might have life, but He gave us gifts that we might be edified (aka, built up, made) into His church.

> *And He Himself gave some to be apostles, some prophets, some evangelists, and some pastors and teachers, for the equipping of the saints for the work of ministry, for the edifying of the body of Christ, till we all come to the unity of the faith and of the knowledge of the Son of God, to a perfect man, to the measure of the stature of the fullness of Christ; that we should no longer be children, tossed to and fro and carried about with every wind of doctrine, by the trickery of men, in the cunning craftiness of deceitful plotting, but, speaking the truth in love, may grow up in all things into Him who is the head—Christ—from whom the whole body, joined and knit together by what every joint supplies, according to the effective working by which every part does its share, causes growth of the body for the edifying of itself in love. Ephesians 4:11-16*

Map 7 - The Church He is Building - Vision

This is the church that Christ envisioned – the church that would be His Bride. We are to be that church, for the LORD's habitation. This is our destiny. Every follower of Jesus Christ has a desire in their heart for the church described in this passage:

- Equipped; meaning to be fixed for its intended use (like a bone or net).

- Unity of both faith and knowledge; even unto perfection that is measured by the full stature of Christ.

- No longer deceived.

- Able to speak the truth in love.

- Maturing in **all** things.

- Knit tightly together; like a hug instead of a handshake, or a beautiful tapestry.

- Effectively working; the Greek here is *energeo*; the energy of ministry.

- Every part doing its share; no 20% doing 80% of the work.

- A fellowship building itself up in love.

Are you having the same thought I'm having? How is this possible? We are so far from this; I can't imagine how we will get there! The work required is more than we can think or imagine. For over 2000 years, we have proven, over and over again, what a mess we can make of it.

Praise God, it is not up to us. In fact, things are moving along in spite of our efforts. Even in this day of apparent decline, we can be encouraged that He has not been caught by surprise.

The Advantage of Workplace Ministry

There are currently 30,000+ registered denominations in the U.S. Many of these sprang out of divisiveness and one-upmanship. How might Christ overcome the pride and weakness of man to create the church He has in mind?

It is important to recognize all the fellowships to which God has connected us. That includes the ones God has created in the places where we spend most of our waking hours. God has not given the Workplace over to His enemies. His kingdom has come and must be established there. His Son is using the Workplace to build His church – through leaders He has planted there.

Building the Kingdom is about cooperation, not competition. Interestingly, this is a fundamental Workplace principle. In the Workplace, a follower of Jesus Christ can pursue fellowship with the brethren without the constraints of doctrine and denomination; and work in unity for the glory of the Father without engaging in divisive sectarianism. In the process, God will honor our agreement with His Son's prayer for unity by showing up in the work. And others will be drawn to Him there.

Conclusion

Denominations, and other groups that form around the doctrines of man, are not evil in themselves. Our battle is not against flesh and blood. However, it is time for us to become fierce in our fight against the spirit of divisiveness that has used our rebelliousness to interfere with God's purposes – particularly His purpose in creating a habitation for Himself.

Ministry in the Workplace is simply an opportunity to find unity where the "church" is not so confined. This is not a call for individuals to leave their current fellowships and create a type of "Workplace Church". This would only increase the problem. Local fellowships are critical to the disciple-making process for every

Map 7 - The Church He is Building - Vision

believer. Nevertheless, we must surrender to God's purpose for habitation wherever we have influence; particularly in those places where He is building.

Application

For many, Christ's vision for the church has not been seen, much less experienced. They may not know or believe it is possible. God has given you a vision and a desire for the church He is building in your sphere of influence. It is time to start sharing it.

Reckoning

Christ is building His church in the Workplace.

Assignment

1. Review your notes and the Scripture passages from this week's module. Share the ones that are most meaningful to someone in your spheres of influence.

2. How do you define church? Do you believe that your organized church fellowship should provide for every area of Christian life? What if your paradigm was such that your activities in the institution were but a subset of "doing church" God's way? What if there was more?

3. Why do we call our congregations, denominations and institutions "churches"? How is this potentially confusing to those inside and outside the *ekklesia*?

4. Use the tool provided on our website to begin identifying your Sphere of Influence. It can be found at:

   http://www.inlightconsulting.com/SmallGroupStudy/AdventureGuideBibleStudySeries_SphereofInfluenceTool.pdf.

Devotion

The Power of Community

From Rob Streetman, Marketplace Ministry Tip, Chapel Hill News and Views Magazine

"No man is an island." English writer John Donne made this assertion in 1624. It is a truth that has stood the test of time. No man (or woman) can survive, separate from the human collective. This has been proven by science, and witnessed day by day in our own lives. We cannot live an abundant life without others. So, why do we try?

First, we try to live in isolation because we are taught that being independent is a sign of maturity. We are taught to stand on our own two feet. It is the strong man and woman that don't need anyone (e.g., John Wayne). We are encouraged to be the captain of our own ship, failing to realize that everyone else is being taught the same. Of course, the truth of the matter is we find more abundant life when we live in community. Ironically (and this is a huge point), the true sign of maturity is becoming dependable – while continuing to depend on others. The Jewish community is so successful in business because this is their way of life.

Secondly, relationships are hard work. Ask anyone that has taken on a business partner. It is difficult to have a partnership when ships don't normally have two captains – unless those captains discover how to work together. As an Enterprise Architect at SunTrust Banks, I was constantly working on teams – and it was incredibly difficult. Why? Because, in that culture, we were motivated by competition, not cooperation. It makes me sad to think back on the loss of productivity in those teams. We could have accomplished so much more in a cooperative culture.

Map 7 - The Church He is Building - Vision

Marketplace Ministry Tip: Identify who God has put in your sphere of influence to share in your marketplace adventure. Consider that He is motivated to assist you in developing strong relationships with others – peers, partners, employees, other businesses (John 17:20-23). The productivity and abundant life you will find is well worth the determination and courage it will take to forge successful relationships.

The Map Maker's Guide

Map 8 - Intimacy With God

Spiritual Exercise

It is impossible to love someone you do not know. It is no coincidence that our primary desire toward God – eternal life – is to know Him and His Son in the most intimate way possible:

> *And this is eternal life, that they may know You, the only true God, and Jesus Christ whom You have sent.* John 17:3

The Greek word that is translated "know" in this verse is used to describe the deepest relationship between two people.

> **Know (*ginōskō*):** Learn to know, come to know, get a knowledge of, perceive, feel; to become known; Jewish idiom for sexual intercourse between a man and a woman. *Outline of Biblical Usage, BlueLetterBible.org*

This is much different from the knowing associated with intellectual and moral understanding (*gnōsis*).

The normal Christian life is a life of growing in relational knowledge of God. How awesome it is to know from the start that the One who has identified Himself as the Truth is encouraging us to an intimate relationship with Himself, and with our Father in heaven!

As we continue in this adventure together, let us commit ourselves to be motivated, sustained and completed by the chief desire of God's heart for us: That we would love Him with all our heart, soul, mind and strength (Mark 12:30). Let us commit ourselves to fight for what has been given and stolen away: To know God; that we might love Him more.

Prayer

Dear Father, it is our heart's desire to love You, Your Son and the Holy Spirit - even more than we ever have before. As we begin this adventure, we commit ourselves to pursue You and Your Son, by the power of the Holy Spirit. Please Father, give us the grace to surrender, to be courageous, and to persevere through all that stands between us. Give us ears to hear and hearts to respond. In Christ's name; Amen.

Introduction

God lost three things when mankind rebelled in the Garden: His reign, His habitation and His intimate relationship with man. In this lesson, we will explore the restoration of His relationship with man; accomplished through intimate prayer. There has never been a more critical time for the followers of Christ to search out this matter.

> *Call my people to repentance. Yea, call them to their knees for prayer and fasting, for confession and vigilance. For this is a strategic hour. The enemy is rejoicing already over his anticipated victories. Ye can disappoint him and thwart his evil designs if ye lay hold upon the throne of God in steadfast, believing prayer.*   *Come Away My Beloved*, Francis Roberts

This is a strategic hour – perhaps the most strategic hour in the history of the church. Something must be done. But what? "Only God knows" may have jumped into your mind. So why don't we ask Him? That is exactly what He desires for us.

Map 8 - Intimacy With God

Every Christian knows that the effective fervent prayer of a righteous man avails much (James 5:16). Prayer is powerful (at least it's supposed to be), and nothing of heavenly value is possible without prayer. So why do we struggle to pray, both individually and corporately?

Why are we so unsure about the effectiveness of our prayers? Why does it seem that so many of our prayers go unanswered? Why is our prayer life so ineffective, difficult and dissatisfying?

The first strategic move in every war is to cut off communications between the forces on the ground and the central command center. Consequently, much energy and intelligence is focused on keeping the lines of communication open. The situation is no different in the war we are fighting against our greatest enemy, Satan. We must be fiercely diligent to defend what we have been given: The means for effective communication – and relationship – with God.

It is no coincidence that God has made prayer man's most powerful weapon in the battle for the kingdom. This is the place where God is most intimate in revealing His plans and encouraging His children. As we battle with Him through prayer, He establishes His relationship with us. There is no more important thing we can do in our search for joyful, Spirit-filled ministry.

Definition

Prayer (*deēsis*): Need, indigence, want, privation, extreme poverty; a seeking, asking, entreating, entreaty to God or to man. From *deomai*: to want, lack; to desire, long for; to ask, beg; the thing asked for; to pray, make supplications. *Outline of Biblical Usage, BlueLetterBible.org*

There are three things to notice about the definition of prayer. First, it is more about need than want. Second, that need is out of an extreme sense of poverty (i.e., it is humble). Third, prayer includes seeking and desiring – its relational aspects.

Searching Out the Matter
(All Scripture references, but those noted, are NKJV; Thomas Nelson, Inc.; footnotes and headings excluded)

Changing the Way We Pray

> Our common ideas regarding prayer are not found in the New Testament. We look upon prayer simply as a means of getting things for ourselves, but the biblical purpose of prayer is that we may get to know God Himself. It is the only way we can get in touch with the truth and the reality of God Himself. To say that "prayer changes things" is not as close to the truth as saying, "Prayer changes me and then I change things." God has established things so that prayer, on the basis of redemption, changes the way a person looks at things. Prayer is not a matter of changing things externally, but one of working miracles in a person's inner nature.
> *My Utmost for His Highest*, Oswald Chambers

Prayer is difficult because our enemies do not want us communicating with God. Satan is a powerful being. An opposing power is needed – God's power. Is it possible that our prayer life lacks God's power because we do not pray in the way God has designed? Have we chosen our own way in prayer?

In his book, *The PAPA Prayer*, Larry Crabb discusses how many in the church turn to God in prayer as if He were Santa Claus sitting behind a vending machine. If we just put in the right change (our time) and push the right buttons (our requests), He will give us what we want. As Crabb laments, this approach has drawn us far from God's intention in our prayer time with Him: To establish and nurture an intimate relationship with us.

That's right! Believe it or not, God desires our relationship more than He desires to give us things. Our motivation in prayer must begin with a desire to know God. Only then do we find ourselves in a position to hear what He wants to give us, so we can pray effectively.

Map 8 - Intimacy With God

Practicing the PAPA Prayer

As Larry Crabb says, "Once you get a feel for it, praying relationally comes as naturally as breathing. Relating to God is what we were destined and designed to do. The most important thing is to be honest with God in each of the following areas."

Present yourself to God: With authentic transparency, present whatever you discover in yourself – good or bad. Are you happy, sad, or mad? Disappointed or depressed? Be who you are, where you are.

> *Let us therefore come boldly to the throne of grace, that we may obtain mercy and find grace to help in time of need.* Hebrews 4:16

Have you ever considered that "in time of need" just might be in our prayer time? Humble children come as they are; and they trust their Father to receive them. Pretending can actually be a sign of pride.

Attend to how you are thinking of God: Focus on who God really is versus who you think God is, or who you want Him to be. Meditate on His name: El Elyon (Most High God), Adonai (Master), El Shaddai (God Almighty), Elohim (Eternal Creator).

> *Our Father in heaven, hallowed be Your name.* Matthew 6:9

Purge yourself of anything that blocks your relationship with God: Eliminate whatever is blocking your intimacy with God by acknowledging, without excuse or explanation, the self-obsession that the Spirit chooses to reveal. Begin by surrendering to His reign, followed by confession and repentance.

> *Your kingdom come. Your will be done on earth as it is in heaven.* Matthew 6:10

> *Search me, O God, and know my heart; try me, and know my anxieties; and see if there is any wicked way in me, and lead me in the way everlasting.* Psalm 139:23-24

> *If we confess our sins, He is faithful and just to forgive us our sins and to cleanse us from all unrighteousness.* 1John 1:9

Approach God as the "first thing" in your life: Lay aside everything but God. Focus on Him as the only provider of truly good things. As you put Him first, you can then approach Him with the confidence that what He loves to give you is what you need the most.

> *For after all these things the Gentiles seek. For your heavenly Father knows that you need all these things. But seek first the kingdom of God and His righteousness, and all these things shall be added to you.* Matthew 6:32-33

Each step in the PAPA Prayer may expose a need for confession and repentance: For trying to hide your true feelings, for presuming Him to be something less than He is, for allowing things or people to come between you and Him, or for making Him anything less than first. The conversation you have with Him in these areas will deepen and strengthen your relationship. As Larry Crabb effectively argues, once we have found this place of intimacy with God, we are perfectly positioned to offer pure worship and thanksgiving, and to hear His voice in our intercession for others and in petition for ourselves.

To receive the full blessing of the PAPA Prayer, use it to begin your prayer time, each morning, for at least 30 days. Initially, you should go through each step multiple times during your daily prayer time, and as many times as possible during the day. In this way, you will renew your mind to pray more relationally. You will also discover one of the most wonderful blessings of our walk with God...

Map 8 - Intimacy With God

The Continuous Presence of God

> *Rejoice always, pray without ceasing, in everything give thanks; for this is the will of God in Christ Jesus for you.* 1Thessalonians 5:16-18

To "pray without ceasing" has also been called "practicing the presence of God". It is the blessing of a continual, conversational relationship with the One that has all the answers. For most followers of Jesus, this seems like an unobtainable goal. Nothing could be further from the truth. The key to enjoying the continuous presence of God is relational prayer.

As we lay down our agenda – even our prayer list – and focus on Christ, a new dimension and opportunity for spiritual growth opens up to us.

> *But we all, with unveiled face, beholding as in a mirror the glory of the Lord, are being transformed into the same image from glory to glory, just as by the Spirit of the Lord.* 2Corinthians 3:18

As we behold the Lord's glory, the Holy Spirit works to renew our mind and open our mind's eye to see what we have been created and commanded to pursue.

> *But seek first the kingdom of God and His righteousness, and all these things shall be added to you.* Matthew 6:33

Jesus said that it was the Father's good pleasure to give us the kingdom of God (Luke 12:32). We are to seek the very thing He intends to give. He is eager to give it.

> *Come to Me, all you who labor and are heavy laden, and I will give you rest. Take My yoke upon you and learn from Me, for I am gentle and lowly in heart, and you will find rest for your souls. For My yoke is easy and My burden is light.* Matthew 11:28-30

The relational approach to prayer is not a burden. If it seems to be, then back up and ask God to expose why this is so with you. Most likely, you are still seeing Him as something He is not, or you are not praying out of a motivation to know Him.

Taking Every Thought Captive

It is quite common for potentially distracting thoughts to fight for our attention during prayer. Rather than immediately pushing these out of your mind, take them captive to the obedience of Christ.

> *For the weapons of our warfare are not carnal but mighty in God for pulling down strongholds, casting down arguments and every high thing that exalts itself against the knowledge of God, bringing every thought into captivity to the obedience of Christ, and being ready to punish all disobedience when your obedience is fulfilled.* 2Corinthians 10:4-6

Ask the Lord what He would have you do with each of the thoughts you capture. He may tell you to put it aside. He may just as well tell you something He would like for you to do with it. For example, if the distracting thought is about a meeting you have that day, He may want you to pray for the anticipated attendees. Or, the thought may be about an issue for which He wants to give you wisdom.

Whatever the case may be, our dedicated time of prayer is the perfect training ground for practicing His presence. As our conditioned response to distractions in prayer is transformed and we begin to turn to Him with them, it becomes easier to do the same when confronted with events and distractions during the day. Consequently, we are drawn further into the abiding life.

> *If you abide in Me, and My words abide in you, you will ask what you desire, and it shall be done for you.* John 15:7

This verse highlights the relationship of the abiding life and the life of relational prayer. The prayer that discovers and accomplishes the desires of our hearts must begin in this abiding relationship. Our abiding in

Map 8 - Intimacy With God

Him, and Him in us, is the relationship He desires. We will search further into the power of the abiding life in a future lesson. For now, it is enough that you begin to practice the relational prayer that cultivates the abiding life. In so doing, you participate in God's plan to restore intimate relationship with His people.

Conclusion

God does not waste anything – including His voice. He is not speaking to us continuously, as some have suggested. His words do not bounce off our eardrums. They will not return void. They are alive and powerful. God is waiting to speak. He is waiting for those that have a heart to hear – a heart that desires intimacy with Him more than getting something from Him.

Practicing the presence of God begins with the desire to know Him. Those that seek Him in this way will know His voice. They will be able to distinguish His voice from all others. His purposes will become clearer to them, including the purpose of restoring His relationship with His children.

Application

Intimacy takes time. Leaders are normally the busiest people in an organization. This conflict must be resolved. It all comes down to priority and value. The priority you give to developing intimacy with God is directly proportional to the value you place on your relationship with Him. It is time for a heart check: How much time would you spend with the leading consultant in your field? Are his words more valuable to you than the Father's?

People in your spheres of influence will notice, and be inspired, when they discover that you have made prayer a part of your business strategy. They will desire to know how to have that same intimacy with Him.

Reckoning

There is no more valuable time than time spent with our Father in heaven.

Assignment

1. Review your notes and the Scripture passages from this week's module. Share the ones that are most meaningful to someone in your spheres of influence.

2. Practice the PAPA Prayer as described in the lesson.

Devotion

From Os Hillman TGIF: Discovering Your Purpose

If you are going to discover how God wants to use your life and work, you must know why you were created. If you start trying to determine your purpose in life before understanding why you were created, you will inevitably get hung up on the things you do as the basis for fulfillment in your life, which will only lead to frustration and disappointment.

First and foremost, God created you to know Him and to have an intimate relationship with Him. In fact, God says that if a man is going to boast about anything in life, "boast about this: that he understands and knows me" (Jer. 9:24). Mankind's relationship with God was lost in the Garden when Adam and Eve sinned. Jesus' death on the cross, however, allows us to restore this relationship with God and to have an intimate fellowship with Him. The apostle Paul came to understand this when he said, "I gave up all that inferior stuff so I could know Christ personally, experience his resurrection power, be a partner in his suffering, and go all the way with him to death itself" (Phil. 3:10, THE MESSAGE).

Map 8 - Intimacy With God

Establishing this relationship with God is vital to understanding your purpose. If you don't have this relationship with God, you will seek to fulfill your purpose out of wrong motives; such as fear, insecurity, pride, money, relationships, guilt, or unresolved anger. God's desire is for you to be motivated out of love for Him and to desire to worship Him in all that you do. As you develop your relationship with God, He will begin to reveal His purpose for your life. "For I know the plans I have for you, declares the Lord" (Jer. 29:11).

Reprinted by permission from the author. Os Hillman is an international speaker and author of more than 10 books on workplace calling. To learn more, visit http://www.MarketplaceLeaders.org.

The Map Maker's Guide

Map 9 - The Gospel of the Kingdom

Spiritual Exercise

Assuredly, I say to you, whatever you bind on earth will be bound in heaven, and whatever you loose on earth will be loosed in heaven. Again I say to you that if two of you agree on earth concerning anything that they ask, it will be done for them by My Father in heaven. For where two or three are gathered together in My name, I am there in the midst of them. Matthew 18:18-20

Binding and loosing, and "it will be done for them", are awesome promises of God! They are a part of the life all serious Christians long for. So why are we not seeing more of it?

As with all of God's promises, there is a condition that must be met. The promises of binding, loosing and agreeing are conditioned on being "gathered together in My name". What does this mean?

Consider that Jesus, as your king, has sent you to a meeting of nations. You are His ambassador. As His ambassador, you are required to put aside your agenda for His. Though you may have, in your own mind, many wise and wonderful things to say, your focus is on what He wants and what He wants said. What has He instructed you to bind, loose and agree on? How will you know if He is not your king?

Prayer

Father in heaven, we recognize that You have appointed Jesus as our king. We surrender to His reign. We are blessed to be His ambassadors to this world. As we gather to discuss the matters of Your kingdom, we subject our ideas and agendas to those of our King. Thank You, Lord Jesus, for being in the midst of us. It is enough. This time belongs to You. Blessed be Your holy name. Amen.

Introduction

Many in the church have grown up with the philosophies of a "democratic republic". Democracy has been a great political experiment. However, it has created a cultural mindset that makes it difficult to live in a healthy relationship with God.

In God's kingdom, there is no "of the people, by the people, for the people". The King has the only and final vote. He is the one that determines and executes mercy and justice. Our rights are what He determines them to be.

For the rebellious, this is an unacceptable situation. And that is exactly what got us into this mess. The first sin was more than disobedience; it was outright rebellion. Before Adam and Eve disobeyed God, they decided that they should determine what was best for them. They decided that they would become the captains of their ship. They mutinied, and all was lost (for a time).

Thankfully, God has a plan to take back the throne of mankind's heart. Re-establishing His reign is one of God's greatest pursuits. The first step in the journey towards joyful, Spirit-filled ministry is our surrender to this, one of the three primary purposes of God.

Map 9 - The Gospel of the Kingdom

Our surrender must be complete; for the Creator will not share His reign with the created. From His position on the throne of our hearts, God reveals the desires He has placed there. In our surrendered state, we are positioned to receive all that God has purposed for our lives.

Definition

Kingdom (*basileia*): Royal power, kingship, dominion, rule (not to be confused with an actual kingdom but rather the right or authority to rule over a kingdom; of the royal power of Jesus as the triumphant Messiah; of the royal power and dignity conferred on Christians in the Messiah's kingdom); [secondarily] a kingdom, the territory subject to the rule of a king; used in the N.T. to refer to the reign of the Messiah. *Outline of Biblical Usage, BlueLetterBible.org*

Notice that the primary meaning of *basileia* is the power and right to rule over a kingdom. It is only secondarily the place or people of that rule. This will be a critical distinction as we explore the gospel of the kingdom that Jesus came to preach and establish.

Searching Out the Matter

(All Scripture references, but those noted, are NKJV; Thomas Nelson, Inc.; footnotes excluded)

The Gospel of the Kingdom

Surrender is easier when we understand the gospel of the kingdom, its place in God's story, and our place in it.

> *Now after John was put in prison, Jesus came to Galilee, preaching the gospel of the kingdom of God, and saying, "The time is fulfilled, and the kingdom of God is at hand. Repent, and believe in the gospel."* Mark 1:14-15

What gospel are we to believe? The gospel of the kingdom. This is the full gospel. It is more than the good news of Jesus Christ's death, burial and resurrection. Though it is of first importance, the good news that most have been taught is only a part of the good news; for the gospel of the kingdom is literally "the good news of God's reign in the hearts of mankind".

Consequently, when Jesus preached, "Repent", He meant that we were to turn from self-rule to His kingdom rule. We are commanded to move from rebellion to surrender. This was the major theme of His preaching in all of Galilee and throughout Israel.

> *And Jesus went about all Galilee, teaching in their synagogues, preaching the gospel of the kingdom, and healing all kinds of sickness and all kinds of disease among the people.* Matthew 4:23

> *Now when it was day, He departed and went into a deserted place. And the crowd sought Him and came to Him, and tried to keep Him from leaving them; but He said to them, "I must preach the kingdom of God to the other cities also, because for this purpose I have been sent."* Luke 4:42-43

Jesus was sent with a purpose: To preach the gospel of the kingdom everywhere He went. It was not just for private conversations with His disciples. It was good news for everyone. As you might expect, the gospel of the kingdom continued to be preached after Jesus ascended to sit at His Father's right hand.

> *But when they believed Philip as he preached the things concerning the kingdom of God and the name of Jesus Christ, both men and women were baptized.* Acts 8:12

Map 9 - The Gospel of the Kingdom

So when they had appointed him [Paul] a day, many came to him at his lodging, to whom he explained and solemnly testified of the kingdom of God, persuading them concerning Jesus from both the Law of Moses and the Prophets, from morning till evening. Acts 28:23

For more references to the gospel of the kingdom, see Matthew 9:35; 10:7; 24:14; Luke 8:1; 9:2, 6, 11; 10:9; and Acts 1:3; 8:12; 19:8; 20:25.

I have three points to make before we go on: First, Jesus began preaching the gospel – and had the disciples do the same – well before He discussed His death, burial and resurrection. Second, the gospel is more about Him than it is about us – it is His good news, His kingdom, and His reign. Therefore, and thirdly, the gospel is much bigger than most have been taught.

The One Who Reigns

Jesus Christ is the One Who reigns over His Father's kingdom:

Then comes the end, when He delivers the kingdom to God the Father, when He puts an end to all rule and all authority and power. For He must reign till He has put all enemies under His feet. 1Corinthians 15:24-25

And He put all things under His feet, and gave Him to be head over all things to the church, which is His body, the fullness of Him who fills all in all. Ephesians 1:22-23

Then the seventh angel sounded: And there were loud voices in heaven, saying, "The kingdoms of this world have become the kingdoms of our Lord and of His Christ, and He shall reign forever and ever!" Revelation 11:15

This Jesus – our Savior – is the Christ, the Anointed Lord of the kingdom of God.

A New Creation

Furthermore, Scripture tells us that this kingdom is an entirely new creation.

Therefore, if anyone is in Christ, he is a new creation; old things have passed away; behold, all things have become new. 2Corinthians 5:17

For in Christ Jesus neither circumcision nor uncircumcision avails anything, but a new creation. Galatians 6:15

Nevertheless we, according to His promise, look for new heavens and a new earth in which righteousness dwells. 2Peter 3:13

Now I saw a new heaven and a new earth, for the first heaven and the first earth had passed away. Also there was no more sea. Then I, John, saw the holy city, New Jerusalem, coming down out of heaven from God, prepared as a bride adorned for her husband. Then He who sat on the throne said, "Behold, I make all things new." And He said to me, "Write, for these words are true and faithful." Revelation 21: 1-2, 5

These verses beg the question, "Has the Kingdom come, or is it coming?" It is both. Christ came to establish the spiritual beginnings of the physical kingdom that He will eventually complete.

This is good news for us in that we get to participate in the restoration of His kingdom. We are children of the kingdom, for the kingdom resides in us. We are kingdom warriors, for it has been given to us to be instruments (aka, weapons) of righteousness.

Those of us that are alive and in Christ at this time in history are truly blessed. These are exciting strategic times. It is critical that we understand the general purposes of the Kingdom of God, and find the specific

Map 9 - The Gospel of the Kingdom

ones (aka, our assignments) that He has given to each of us. It is in these assignments that the violent (that's us!) take the kingdom by force (Matthew 11:12).

This Kingdom's Purposes

Now that we understand the gospel of God's reign, let's look at a few passages that speak to the purposes that flow out of it. As you read these, listen carefully to the Spirit. He may use one or two of them to identify the specific desire of your heart for this season of your life.

When you are ruled by a king, it is desirable to know what kind of king you have ruling over you. In something of an inaugural address, Jesus announced the purposes of His reign.

> *And He was handed the book of the prophet Isaiah. And when He had opened the book, He found the place where it was written:*
>
> > *" The Spirit of the LORD is upon Me,*
> > *Because He has anointed Me*
> > *To preach the gospel to the poor;*
> > *He has sent Me to heal the brokenhearted,*
> > *To proclaim liberty to the captives*
> > *And recovery of sight to the blind,*
> > *To set at liberty those who are oppressed;*
> > *To proclaim the acceptable year of the LORD."*
>
> *Then He closed the book, and gave it back to the attendant and sat down. And the eyes of all who were in the synagogue were fixed on Him. And He began to say to them, "Today this Scripture is fulfilled in your hearing."* Luke 4:17-21

Wow! What good news!! The kingdom is ruled by a good king!! He has come to heal, rescue, enlighten and protect His subjects. These purposes did not end with His ascension. He left specific instructions that we were to continue in them.

> *So Jesus said to them again, "Peace to you! As the Father has sent Me, I also send you."* John 20:21

Now, notice how God's description of "The True Fast" parallels Christ's inaugural address, and gives us more insight into our participation in His kingdom rule:

> *Is this not the fast that I have chosen:*
> *To loose the bonds of wickedness,*
> *To undo the heavy burdens,*
> *To let the oppressed go free,*
> *And that you break every yoke?*
> *Is it not to share your bread with the hungry,*
> *And that you bring to your house the poor who are cast out;*
> *When you see the naked, that you cover him,*
> *And not hide yourself from your own flesh?* Isaiah 58:6-7

God is calling us to continue the fulfillment of Jesus Christ's purposes here on Earth. As heirs of God and co-heirs with Christ we are called to the family business: The fulfillment of the gospel of the kingdom.

The Isaiah 58 passage goes on to describe the outcome of our participation in God's purposes for His kingdom people:

> *Then your light shall break forth like the morning,*
> *Your healing shall spring forth speedily,*
> *And your righteousness shall go before you;*

Map 9 - The Gospel of the Kingdom

The glory of the LORD shall be your rear guard.
Then you shall call, and the LORD will answer;
You shall cry, and He will say, 'Here I am.' Isaiah 58:8-9

As we join Jesus in fulfilling the purposes of God, His life ("your light") will break forth as He ("your righteousness") goes before us. Healing (i.e., in our spheres of influence) will spring forth, and His glory will protect us; for He will be ever with us. Who could refuse such an awesome adventure!?!

This is the same adventure found in the Sermon on the Mount:

> *You are the light of the world. A city that is set on a hill cannot be hidden. Nor do they light a lamp and put it under a basket, but on a lampstand, and it gives light to all who are in the house. Let your light so shine before men, that they may see your good works and glorify your Father in heaven.* Matthew 5:16

As one who delights in searching out the matters of God's Word, it excites me to discover the connections that exist between the Old and New Testaments. It encourages me in the eternality of God, and in His purposes and promises for His children.

Conclusion

God is establishing His kingdom as a new creation that is ruled by His Son, Jesus Christ. The good news is the power and character of our King. He is sovereign, He loves us, and He has a plan for us. To enjoy His reign, we must first surrender to Him as our king.

As King, Christ has shared His desires with His subjects. These connect our hearts with His. We can be sure that there is a desire in our hearts for every command of Christ. As we surrender to them, they become purposes in our lives. Not just our purposes, but the purposes of God; and this makes all the difference.

In our surrender to God's desire to reign in our heart, and Jesus Christ's desire that we love Him by continuing His work here, we will discover the personal and specific desires God has put in our hearts. Our surrender to these desires begins the transformation process that culminates in our strategic assignment for His kingdom. It is in these assignments that we find joyful, Spirit-filled ministry.

Application

The gospel of the kingdom – the good news of Christ's reign over the hearts of mankind – is the solution for most of the problems facing the church. When leaders give up their reign for His, many will follow – thus creating a mass movement from the enemies' camp, into the kingdom. You have been given influence for such a movement. It is time to get moving.

Reckoning

His reign is better than my own.

Assignment

1. Review the Bible passages for this week. Share at least one of the concepts with someone in your spheres of influence.

2. Each day this week, ask the Lord to show you the areas of your life where you are reigning. Repent of this rebellion and trust Him to forgive you and lead you into His reign (1John 1:9).

3. Consider Christ's announcement of the good news of His reign (Luke 4:16-21). As His bondservant and steward, ask Him how He wants you to represent Him. Be careful to record His answers.

Map 9 - The Gospel of the Kingdom

Devotion

Sin and Culture

John Eldredge

Guys are unanimously embarrassed by their emptiness and woundedness; it is for most of us a tremendous source of shame, as I've said. But it need not be. From the very beginning, back before the Fall and the assault, ours was meant to be a desperately dependent existence. It's like a tree and its branches, explains Christ. You are the branches, I am the trunk. From me you draw your life; that's how it was meant to be. In fact, he goes on to say, "Apart from me you can do nothing" (John 15:5). He's not berating us or mocking us or even saying it with a sigh, all the while thinking, I wish they'd pull it together and stop needing me so much. Not at all. We are made to depend on God; we are made for union with him, and nothing about us works right without it. As C. S. Lewis wrote, "A car is made to run on gasoline, and it would not run properly on anything else. Now God designed the human machine to run on himself. He himself is the fuel our spirits were designed to burn, or the food our spirits were designed to feed on. There is no other."

This is where our sin and our culture have come together to keep us in bondage and brokenness, to prevent the healing of our wound. Our sin is that stubborn part inside that wants, above all else, to be independent. There's a part of us fiercely committed to living in a way where we do not have to depend on anyone-especially God. Then culture comes along with figures like John Wayne and James Bond and all those other "real men," and the one thing they have in common is that they are loners; they don't need anyone. We come to believe deep in our hearts that needing anyone for anything is a sort of weakness, a handicap.

(*Wild at Heart*, 121-122)

The Map Maker's Guide

Map 10 - Desires and Assignments

Spiritual Exercise

The Holy Bible contains many models for prayer, including the following.

> *For this reason I bow my knees to the Father of our Lord Jesus Christ, from whom the whole family in heaven and earth is named, that He would grant you, according to the riches of His glory, to be strengthened with might through His Spirit in the inner man, that Christ may dwell in your hearts through faith; that you, being rooted and grounded in love, may be able to comprehend with all the saints what is the width and length and depth and height—to know the love of Christ which passes knowledge; that you may be filled with all the fullness of God. Now to Him who is able to do exceedingly abundantly above all that we ask or think, according to the power that works in us, to Him be glory in the church by Christ Jesus to all generations, forever and ever. Amen.* Ephesians 3:14-21

This prayer is one of four "Apostolic Prayers" recorded in Paul's epistles. The others are found in Ephesians 1:15-23, Philippians 1:3-11, and Colossians 1:9-14. Each one can be adapted as a prayer for oneself, or for someone in your spheres of influence, by replacing the appropriate pronouns. In this form, they become instruments of promise and truth that will transform both the person being prayed for and the person that prays. Let the following example encourage your turning to the Lord.

Prayer

Father of our Lord Jesus Christ, from whom the whole family in heaven and earth is named, we pray that You would grant us, according to the riches of Your glory, to be strengthened with might through Your Spirit in our inner man, that Christ may dwell in our hearts through faith; that we, being rooted and grounded in love, may be able to comprehend with all the saints what is the width and length and depth and height— to know Christ's love which passes knowledge; that we may be filled with all the fullness of God.

We pray to you Father, knowing that You are able to do exceedingly abundantly above all that we can ask or think, according to the power that works in us. We choose to believe it. To You be glory in the church by Christ Jesus to all generations, forever and ever. Amen.

Introduction

We previously discussed some of the more significant processes God uses to restore His creation. We learned that salvation is the process that brings us into an eternal relationship with Christ; beginning with our justification and ending with our glorification. Sanctification is the process whereby we are separated from profane things, purified and dedicated to God. Through the transformation process, we are changed into the very image of Christ's glory.

Transformation is unique in that it occurs iteratively in the lives of every Christian that has submitted to the Holy Spirit's work. Through our beholding Christ's glory, the Holy Spirit transforms us from one level of glory to the next, "out-raying" more of the light that is His life. The mature Christian can look back on their life and see where the Holy Spirit has transformed them step-by-step, and season-by-season. If they look

Map 10 - Desires and Assignments

carefully, most will see that each of these seasons of transformation were bookended by a desire and an assignment. This lesson explores the desires of our hearts and the assignments of God that bring Him glory. We will also discover the relationship these have to the purposes of God for each season of our lives.

Definition

Desire (*mish'alah*): Request, petition, desire. *Outline of Biblical Usage, www.BlueLetterBible.org*

Good (*kalos*): Beautiful, handsome, excellent, eminent, choice, surpassing, precious, useful, suitable, commendable, admirable; beautiful to look at, shapely, magnificent; good, excellent in its nature and characteristics, and therefore well adapted to its ends; beautiful by reason of purity of heart and life, and hence praiseworthy; honourable, conferring honour; affecting the mind agreeably, comforting and confirming. *Outline of Biblical Usage, www.BlueLetterBible.org*

Work (*ergon*): Business, employment, that which any one is occupied; that which one undertakes to do, enterprise, undertaking; any product whatever, anything accomplished by hand, art, industry, or mind; an act, deed, thing done: the idea of working is emphasized in opposition to that which is less than work. *Outline of Biblical Usage, www.BlueLetterBible.org*

"Searching out the Matter" has become a passion for me. In my searching, I have discovered that one of the easiest and most rewarding discovery methods is digging into the meaning of the Hebrew and Greek words that are used in Scripture. God purposefully created these two languages to express Himself and the doctrine of our Lord Jesus Christ. Both are far richer than the English language – particularly Americanized English. In His providence, God has hidden mysteries for us in the meaning of many Greek and Hebrew words.

For example, the Hebrew word that is translated as "desire" is more than a passive wishing or hoping for something. It includes the action of request and petition. Many Hebrew and Greek words are more active than the meaning we have given them. The people of the Bible – God's children – are to be active participants in His story and in their spheres of influence.

The concepts of beauty and comfort included in the Greek word for "good" add a relational character to its meaning. Furthermore, with meaning that includes "surpassing", "excellent" and "magnificent", it is not surprising that this word is used to describe the work that glorifies our heavenly Father (Matthew 5:16). Interestingly, a different Greek word – *agathos* – is used in Ephesians 2:10 to describe the work we are created to walk in (a matter I will leave for you to search out and consider).

Searching Out the Matter
(All Scripture references, but those noted, are NKJV; Thomas Nelson, Inc.; footnotes excluded)

Creatures of Purpose

Man (consisting of both male and female) was created in the image of God (Genesis 1:26-27). One trait of this image is our purposefulness. For us humans, "What is my purpose?" is one of the more revealing worldview questions; because it defines what we believe about ourselves and the world around us. As Creator and Father, God intends for us to know the purposes He has for us.

> *[God] who has saved us and called us with a holy calling, not according to our works, but according to His own purpose and grace which was given to us in Christ Jesus before time began...* 2Timothy 1:9

Our salvation and calling are in accordance with the purposes of God. They were given to us – along with His necessary grace – before the beginning of time. However, and this is critically important, they are not for us; "but according to His own purposes".

Map 10 - Desires and Assignments

But indeed for this purpose I have raised you (Pharaoh) up, that I may show My power in you, and that My name may be declared in all the earth. Exodus 9:16

God uses both good and evil people to accomplish His purposes. This is a great encouragement. If God would use someone as evil as Pharaoh to show Himself strong, then why not every one of His children?

To everything there is a season, a time for every purpose under heaven... Ecclesiastes 3:1

Every season in the life of every child of God has a purpose. Seasons come and seasons go (as they say); and with them, the purposes of God for that season. If we miss it, the purpose God has for us may be lost entirely, or passed on to someone that will respond. By His grace, God may decide to offer a purpose to someone multiple times. How God orchestrates the many purposes of the many seasons of His many children is a mystery. But one thing we know...

God Reveals His Purposes

Simply stated, God reveals His purposes through the desires of our hearts. As we mentioned earlier, the process of transformation begins with the discovery of these desires. The secret to this discovery is found in the following verses:

Trust in the LORD, and do good;
Dwell in the land, and feed on His faithfulness.
Delight yourself also in the LORD,
And He shall give you the desires of your heart. Psalm 37:3-6

"He shall give you" is an emphatic promise of God. Of course, these are not our carnal desires, but those He intended before He established the foundations of the earth (Ephesians 2:10). How exciting is that!?! And there's more.

God has been orchestrating events for thousands of years to help you discover the desires of your heart. Why? So He can give them to you!!

Some father's are blessed with the resources to plan ahead for a special gift they want to give their child (e.g., an education, a home, the family business), but no father has been planning as long as your Heavenly Father, for the desires He has put in your heart.

How do we discover this gift and put ourselves in position to receive it? By following the conditions of the promise:

1. Trust in the LORD – In the face of evildoers that are getting ahead through works of iniquity, will we trust God to give us our desires?

2. Do good – Will we resist the temptations to pursue our desires in unethical and evil ways?

3. Dwell in the land – The land to the Psalmist represented the promises of God – their inheritance. Psalm 37 contains many promises of God for the righteous man. Dwelling in them means to believe, reckon and cherish them. Are His promises enough of a dwelling place for His children?

4. Feed on His faithfulness – Will we look to His faithfulness as our sustenance – trusting nothing or no one else for our desires? Will we be satisfied in Him and what He wants to give us?

5. Delight yourself in the LORD – This last condition is my favorite; because it contains a hidden matter – one of God's mysteries. I found this treasure as I was searching out the meaning of "desire". Using BlueLetterBible.org, I discovered that the Hebrew word that is translated as "delight" is not used in any of the other 149 Psalms. Here it is the word `anag. `Anag has a very simple meaning: to be soft. Now, what does that make you think of? For me, it was the softness of clay in the Potter's hands.

Map 10 - Desires and Assignments

And so, by searching out this matter, we have discovered that the hidden key to receiving the desires of our heart is to be surrendered to the LORD. He will reveal the desires of our heart and give them. In essence, they will become the purposes of God for the one so surrendered. This is an incredible treasure; for the Scriptures have much to say regarding the promises of God's purpose.

> *And we know that all things work together for good to those who love God, to those who are the called according to His purpose.* Romans 8:28

Find His purpose for this season of your life and all things (past, present and future; good and bad) will work together for your good. What an amazing promise!! Furthermore, we can know that it will be accomplished.

> *I know that You can do everything, and that no purpose of Yours can be withheld from You.* Job 42:2

> *Commit your way to the LORD,*
> *Trust also in Him,*
> *And He shall bring it to pass.* Psalm 37:5

No matter how bad it looks, once we are walking in God's purpose, we can rest in the assurance that it will come to pass. It is an awesome encouragement to know that we share in the desires of our Father's heart. That powerful and intimate connection with the heart of God will carry us through the trials and tribulations of transformation; and into the assignment He has called us to walk in with Him.

Transformed for Our Assignment

The end of the transformation process comes when we are adequately prepared for the assignment that will glorify our Father in heaven. This assignment is the physical manifestation of the desire of our heart. There is a mystery here that we will cover briefly. Consider these verses:

> *For by grace you have been saved through faith, and that not of yourselves; it is the gift of God, not of works, lest anyone should boast. For we are His workmanship, created in Christ Jesus for good works, which God prepared beforehand that we should walk in them.* Ephesians 2:8-10

> *Let your light so shine before men that they will see your good works and glorify your Father in heaven.* Matthew 5:16

> *He shall bring forth your righteousness as the light,*
> *And your justice as the noonday.* Psalm 37:6

We have been created in Christ Jesus to walk in good works. These works are the assignments that are birthed from the desires of our hearts. As we walk in these assignments, men will see them and glorify our Father in heaven. But how will someone see a work of man and say something like, "Isn't God awesome!" Will God take the glory of His children's work? Of course not! That is the mystery.

We can begin to understand this mystery by recognizing that the command of Matthew 5:16 is not to do good works. The command is to "let your light shine". What is this light? And what is "your righteousness" that He (the Father) has promised to bring forth (Psalm 37:6)?

> *In Him [the Word, Christ] was life, and the life was the light of men.* John 1:4

> *But of Him you are in Christ Jesus, who became for us wisdom from God—and righteousness and sanctification and redemption—that, as it is written, "He who glories, let him glory in the Lord."* 1Corinthians 1:30-31

Christ Jesus is our righteousness and His life is our light! In Him, we will shine forth… IF we are not getting in the way! This is one of the primary purposes of transformation – to get us out of the way.

Let me explain. If we are children of God, we have the Holy Spirit. If we have the Holy Spirit, we have His fruit.

Map 10 - Desires and Assignments

But the fruit of the Spirit is love, joy, peace, longsuffering, kindness, goodness, faithfulness, gentleness, self-control. Against such there is no law. Galatians 5:22-23

Consequently, and as one example, we don't need to pray for patience. Every Christian has within them the supernatural patience of God. Hard to believe, I know. But it's true! God's way for our finding patience is in our beholding Christ's glory and submitting to the Holy Spirit's work of removing the impatience that is in us (putting to death the deeds of the flesh).

Similarly, we don't need more love. We need to be delivered from the judgmental spirit that has built a barrier between us and those we should love unconditionally. It is a process of subtraction.

Each portion of the Spirit's fruit has an opposing carnal poison, found in our flesh, which inhibits the life of Christ in our relationships. If we will allow Him, the Spirit will transform these things out of us. As God determines, the Holy Spirit's transformational work will be completed, giving way to the assignment that God will use to glorify His name, expand His kingdom and give us the desires of our hearts.

Conversely, through transformation, the Holy Spirit will work into us the things we need to live the normal Christian life: Faith, courage, virtue, etc. As we have previously pointed out, this includes a renewal of our minds; a change in the way we understand and consider this world and the kingdom of God.

Conclusion

We will more fully search out the matter of good works and God's glory in future lessons. For now, it is important to recognize that we are "created in Christ Jesus for good works", "that we should walk in them". The purpose of transformation is to prepare us for the assignment that God reveals in the desires of our hearts. A heart surrendered will reveal its desires. Desires surrendered will become the purposes of God – purposes filled with promise and certain fulfillment. His assignments for us are our part in His larger eternal work. Large or small, they are critical to His kingdom and a blessing to each person that is involved in them.

Application

Many Christians go through life longing for ministry that is joyful and Spirit-filled. Regrettably, they most often find disappointment, discouragement and disillusionment. Why? Because they do not know where to find the purposes of God for this season of their lives. God has raised up Leaders in the Workplace to show all His children that His purposes can be found in the desires He has placed in their hearts. One of the greatest blessings a Leader in the Workplace can give to someone in his sphere of influence is to help them discover those desires.

Reckoning

God has created me with His desires carefully placed in my heart.

Assignment

1. Review the Bible passages for this week. Study and meditate on those that may have challenged your understanding. Ask the Lord to give meaning to them for you. Share this with another.

2. The Hebrew word for delight in Psalm 37:4 means "to be soft" – like clay in the Potter's hands. How does this affect your understanding of the verse?

3. Create a four column table with the following headings: God's Promises, What It Is Worth, The Condition, What It Will Cost Me. Read through Psalms 34, recording each promise in column one (e.g., in verse 7: The Lord hears my cry). In column two put a value, from 1 to 10, for the promise's worth to you. In column three, record the condition for the promise (e.g. being righteous). In column four, put a value

Map 10 - Desires and Assignments

(again from 1 to 10) that indicates the cost of the condition to you. Weigh the value versus the cost and see just how profitable it would be to "go all in" for the Life that has been offered.

Devotion

Dreaming Big

From Rob Streetman, The inLight Adventure Blog

God has not left us to our own devices to understand the desires that He has for us. He has been orchestrating events for a very long time so that we would discover what He wants to give us in this very season! Why would we consider for even a moment that He would not do all in His power to manifest these very desires?

It is so very important that we receive the faith that He has given us. It is a faith proportional to the sum of every desire. It is the faith of Christ!!

Of course, these desires are not necessarily for us. They are primarily for His Name sake, His glory and His kingdom. Beyond that, they may be for our children's future, our neighbor's salvation, our spouse's spiritual strength or for a thousand other people.

Having said that, let me tell you what gets me up in the morning (literally). Every desire is also very much about us. What can I say? It is a wonderful, amazing mystery. Now don't miss this:

> **The desires that He gives us are absolutely and directly out of the desires of His own heart!!**

Read that at least one more time. Read it in light of your strongest desire. He not only put it there, but He shares it with you. I ask again: Why would we consider for even a moment that He would not do all in His power to manifest these very desires?

You might be wondering if this could possibly be true. Why me? Why now? The answer can be found in the hidden meaning of the condition for the promise:

> "Delight yourself also in the LORD..."

You see, the Hebrew word translated as "delight" has a special meaning in the 37th Psalm. It is not the *chaphets* (to take pleasure in) that is found in the other Psalms. It is *anag* (to be soft, delicate or dainty). It is an effeminate word in the Hebrew language.

Do you see it? It is the definition of the Bride's heart toward the Bridegroom – soft, delicate and surrendered. It is the Bride trusting her Husband King with all Her heart, mind, soul and strength. This sharing of His desire is the way in which He woos us and melds our heart into His. Yes, it is the melding of two hearts in the most intimate love we will ever know.

And so I encourage you: Find the time to be softly surrendered before your Bridegroom. Let Him show you the desires of your heart, and His, for this season of your life. Recognize that these are the desires that were put in you before the foundations of the earth. Surrender and He will give you the desires of your heart. He will include all the faith and courage you need to take the adventure with Him. And in the process, you will find a love for Him that you could never have imagined.

Dream with Him! Dream big!! He is the Dream Giver!!!

The Map Maker's Guide

Map 11 - Surrendering to His Purpose

Spiritual Exercise

For My thoughts are not your thoughts,
Nor are your ways My ways," says the Lord.
For as the heavens are higher than the earth,
So are My ways higher than your ways,
And My thoughts than your thoughts. Isaiah 55:8-9

Delight yourself also in the Lord,
And He shall give you the desires of your heart.

But the meek shall inherit the earth,
And shall delight themselves in the abundance of peace. Psalm 37:4, 11

If you turn away your foot from the Sabbath,
From doing your pleasure on My holy day,
And call the Sabbath a delight,
The holy day of the Lord honorable,
And shall honor Him, not doing your own ways,
Nor finding your own pleasure,
Nor speaking your own words,
Then you shall delight [surrender] yourself in the Lord;
And I will cause you to ride on the high hills of the earth,
And feed you with the heritage of Jacob your father.
The mouth of the Lord has spoken. Isaiah 58:13-14

And whoever exalts himself will be humbled, and he who humbles himself will be exalted.
Matthew 23:12

Prayer

Father God, have mercy on us. We have exalted ourselves, thinking we knew best and assuming we could accomplish something important independent of your ways, thoughts and purpose. We come again to say that we surrender. Protect us from our enemies: Satan, the world and our flesh. As your children, we desire to know Your heart that we might love You more. In Christ's name. Amen.

Introduction

This module marks the formal end of our exploration into Surrendering to His Purpose. We have learned that God is bringing His created order back into alignment with His original purposes. In His mercy toward mankind, He has determined to include us (rather than start over). As we surrender to His purposes, he will show us His plans for accomplishing them.

Before moving on to Sacrificing for His Plan, we must establish a point of reckoning, a memorial to God's revelation and the work He has done to this point in our adventure. Our memorial will be a reminder of the

Map 11 - Surrendering to His Purpose

love and power He has towards those that are loyal to Him. We will establish our memorial as a group, in facilitated discussion and prayer.

Definition

Memorial (*mnemosunon*): That which keeps alive the memory of someone or something. *Vines Expository Dictionary*

When the children of Israel crossed the Jordan, into the Promised Land, God instructed them to build a memorial "that all the peoples of the earth may know the hand of the Lord, that it is mighty, that you may fear the LORD your God forever" (Joshua 4:24). It was a memorial of God's purpose and promise to give them the land. After their crossing, He began to reveal His plan for their adventure. In much the same way, this time of reflection and reckoning marks our crossing over into God's promise – to give us the desires of our hearts.

Searching Out the Matter
(All Scripture references, but those noted, are NKJV; Thomas Nelson, Inc.; footnotes and headings excluded)

Preparation

Remember the PAPA Prayer when answering the following questions. Invite the Lord to reveal Himself to you as you consider them. Then share with the group what the Lord has been revealing.

If you are trying to take on this adventure by yourself, I suggest you stop now and find at least two others that will join you. You will be richly blessed to do this in the fellowship of other believers. You will not make it much farther on your own. There are no lone rangers in God's great adventures.

> *Again I say to you that if two of you agree on earth concerning anything that they ask, it will be done for them by My Father in heaven. For where two or three are gathered together in My name, I am there in the midst of them.* Matthew 18:19-20

While it is true that God dwells with us in times of solitude, I am convinced that He has more to say in regard to His purposes and plans when we are meeting with His Son and two or three others.

Building a Memorial

God instituted the practice of memorial building so that His people would have something to go back to when they needed to remember His purposes and promises. Use these questions – and any others He has for you – to build your memorial.

> What are the three eternal, or foundational, purposes of God?
>
> How do we surrender to them?
>
> Which one inspires you the most?
>
> What are some of the other purposes we find in Scripture?
>
> To which of these are you most drawn?
>
> What are the desires/burdens that God has placed in your heart for this season?
>
> Has He given you vision for the associated assignment?
>
> Have you surrendered to His preparation?
>
> What are the one or two things that will inhibit you from this pursuit?
>
> What are you going to do to overcome them? Who will help you?

Map 11 - Surrendering to His Purpose

Conclusion

At this point, it is important to recognize that the journey toward joyful, Spirit-filled ministry is a process; and that God is a very creative and dynamic orchestrator. He does not transform any one of us in the same manner as another. Do not be discouraged if you do not have a clear understanding of God's specific purpose for this season of your life. That has not surprised Him. He has an adequate measure of grace for your journey. Continue to ask, seek and knock.

Application

God has raised up Leaders in the Workplace to be disciple makers and transformation agents. As leaders, we must draw upon God for the grace to persevere through the tough times. As disciple makers, we are called to encourage, edify and equip others as they follow our lead. As transformation agents, we must continually remind ourselves, and those with us, of the purposes and promises of God.

The next section – Sacrificing for His Plan – will be the most challenging. It will distinguish you as a leader. Press on toward the goal for the prize of the upward call of God in Christ Jesus (Philippians 3:14). Run the race to win it (1Corinthians 9:24). The Lord, our God, will use you to transform lives and communities. Continue to prepare yourself.

Reckoning

Surrender is the key to security.

Assignment

1. Discuss the questions from this module with someone close to you; and with someone in your spheres of influence.

2. Find three people that will pray for your spiritual protection and growth during the remainder of this adventure.

3. Write your own devotion: What is the most significant thing God has revealed to you in the beginnings of this journey?

Devotion

Your testimony of God's revelation for this season of your life goes here.

The Map Maker's Guide

Section Three - Sacrificing for His Plan

With that, the Map Maker, Somebody, and Somebody's friends came to what Somebody assumed must be the room reserved for the next leg of their journey. Strangely, this door did not have a powerful looking, beautifully engraved word on it. There was no word at all.

The Map Maker stopped at the door and waited for Somebody and His friends search out the matter of the door with no title. One of Somebody's hobbies was woodworking, so he was the first to noticed that the door was masterfully crafted. He could tell that a master carpenter has used various woods, grains and stains to fashion an intricate mosaic. Somebody had to step back to make out the beautifully-crafted image.

"Why, it's a cross!" exclaimed Somebody.

"That's right", the Map Maker proudly affirmed. "This is My Son's room. He calls it 'The Plan Room'".

After discovering and surrendering to the Lord's purpose for this season in our lives, He begins to show us His plan for accomplishing it. We soon learn, in counting the cost, that we cannot be His disciple if we do not take up our cross daily and follow Him. This will create THE decisive moment – what Henry Blackaby called, "The crisis of belief."

In this section, we will discover how Leaders in the Workplace are to navigate the chaos of transformation, and help others to do the same. We will also explore the lifestyle of making disciples the way God intended.

The Mapmaker's Guide

Map 12 - Counting the Cost - Our Investment

Spiritual Exercise

And when you offer a sacrifice of thanksgiving to the LORD, offer it of your own free will. Leviticus 22:29

Offer the sacrifices of righteousness, and put your trust in the LORD. Psalm 4:5

I beseech you therefore, brethren, by the mercies of God, that you present your bodies a living sacrifice, holy, acceptable to God, which is your reasonable service. And do not be conformed to this world, but be transformed by the renewing of your mind, that you may prove what is that good and acceptable and perfect will of God. Romans 12:1-2

Prayer

LORD God, we come of our own free will to offer You thanksgiving and praise for Your patient work in our lives. We desire to bring our entire being as a sacrifice of righteousness to You. We trust Your completed and continuing work that makes this possible. By Your mercies, we present ourselves to You. We surrender to the transforming work of the Holy Spirit, and to Your good, acceptable and perfect will. In Jesus Christ's name we pray. Amen.

Introduction

After we discover and surrender to God's purpose, He begins to show us His plan for accomplishing it. Some He trusts with the whole plan; but for most, He reveals just enough of the plan to allow a counting of the cost. This is in accordance with Luke 14:25-33, where Jesus Christ instructs us in the wisdom of weighing the cost of discipleship.

The cost of discipleship can be understood as our investment in God's kingdom. In a sense, it is the toll we pay on the way toward joyful, Spirit-filled ministry. As disciple makers, the demonstration of our faith in counting and paying the cost encourages others when they face the tests and requirements of a sacrificial walk.

Definition

Disciple (*mathētēs*): Literally, "a learner" (from *manthano*, "to learn," from a root *math--*, indicating thought accompanied by endeavor), hence it denotes "one who follows one's teaching"; it is used of the "disciples" of Jesus: of Jews who became His adherents, some being secretly so; especially of the twelve Apostles; of all who manifest that they are His "disciples" by abiding in His Word; in the Acts, of those who believed upon Him and confessed Him. A "disciple" was not only a pupil, but an adherent; hence they are spoken of as imitators of their teacher. *Vine's Expository Dictionary*

"Disciple" is not the title for a higher rank of Christian – something that we can opt out of. We are either His disciple or we are not His. Additionally, the teacher/student relationship that has been adopted by modern Western culture is fundamentally different than the teacher/disciple relationship of the Bible. Generally speaking, a student listens to a teacher to pass a test or complete a task. A disciple follows a teacher, or

Map 12 - Counting the Cost - Our Investment

Master, to become like him. A more accurate understanding of "disciple" is apprentice – someone who joins with, to become exactly like, a master craftsman.

Lastly, disciples are made; and they are made by the master. Only those trained by Jesus Christ will be like Him. Disciple makers are instruments of righteousness (Romans 6:13) used by the Lord to make His disciples. They must be disciples to Him, not to any human.

Searching Out the Matter
(All Scripture references, but those noted, are NKJV; Thomas Nelson, Inc.; footnotes and headings excluded)

Why Count the Cost?

Counting the cost comes natural to most Leaders in the Workplace. They have been trained to weigh the risks and rewards of investments and major operational decisions. Wise business men and women will make sure they have the funds to complete a new facility before beginning the project. They will not move into a new territory without an in-depth understanding of the competition and demographics of the area.

Similarly, if we are to be disciples of Christ, we would be wise to know what "being His disciple" means; and what is required. In the kingdom of God, there are many sound reasons for counting the cost:

1. It reminds and encourages us that He is in charge and in control.

2. It protects us from presumption and a false discipleship.

3. It reaffirms our commitment to the Lord.

4. It protects us from the embarrassment of not finishing what we have started.

5. It reveals our dependence on Him.

6. It protects us from paying a cost that is not required.

Many have been invited "to accept Jesus as their savior", "to join the church", "to ask Jesus into their hearts", etc. without being instructed to count the cost. I must admit, as a leader sincerely trying to "bring in the harvest", I have attempted to make the "decision" as easy as possible. My business background, and our culture, has taught me not to lead with the cost.

But hiding the cost of discipleship does not a good disciple make. Many do not discover there is a cost for many years. Most are not investing what's required. Where does that leave them? Still others, when faced with the cost, assume it is optional, since it was not explained to them when they signed up.

Is it any wonder the church is in the shape it is in? How many are true disciples of Jesus Christ? And, if not disciples, can they be called Followers?

These are difficult questions. Questions that no one likes to ask. But the days are getting short. Time is running out. We must start asking ourselves, and each other, "Have you counted the cost?"

The Proper Mindset

Jesus did not soft pedal the investment required to be His disciple. It is impossible to ease into the subject. So, let me go ahead and say it now: The cost of discipleship is high.

In consideration of what lies ahead, it would be helpful to pause for a moment and reckon these truths for ourselves:

1. Whatever the cost, whatever investment is required, the return is far greater than anyone can imagine.

Map 12 - Counting the Cost - Our Investment

2. More importantly, we must keep in mind that, though we benefit, we are not doing this for ourselves but for the One who loved us and gave His life for us.

3. Therefore, our investment is an opportunity to participate in His love for His Bride; and, as His wife, in the return of that love to Him.

The Cost for Every Disciple

With our minds set on the wonder of His love, we can now safely and soberly explore the cost of discipleship. There are more than a dozen passages where Jesus communicated what was expected of those that desired to be His disciples. I offer here some of the more challenging ones.

Love Him More Than

> He who loves father or mother more than Me is not worthy of Me. And he who loves son or daughter more than Me is not worthy of Me. Matthew 10:37

> If anyone comes to Me and does not hate his father and mother, wife and children, brothers and sisters, yes, and his own life also, he cannot be My disciple. Luke 14:26

Our love for Jesus must make every other love a distant second – even the love of our own life. To make the point, He used a very strong word to describe (in hyperbole) just how distant the second loves must be. Jesus is jealous for His Bride.

Our investment as His disciples is putting every love in subordination to our love for Him. His return is a love that is worthy of the love He offers. In a beautifully mysterious way, our elevated love for Him makes it possible for us to love one another as He requires.

Love One Another

> By this all will know that you are My disciples, if you have love for one another. John 13:35

> This is My commandment, that you love one another as I have loved you. Greater love has no one than this, than to lay down one's life for his friends. You are My friends if you do whatever I command you. John 15:12-14

The love Jesus requires is *agapē* – sacrificial love. Jesus expresses His love for us in His Passion of suffering, shame and death. He has commanded each of us to do the same for one another. As we obey His command to love one another, we live out of the "greater love" – *agapē*.

Our investment is our life laid down for others. His return is "all will know that you are My disciples". Being like Him, we will reveal and remind the world of His love for them.

Abide and Bear Much Fruit

> Then Jesus said to those Jews who believed Him, "If you abide in My word, you are My disciples indeed. John 8:31

> If you abide in Me, and My words abide in you, you will ask what you desire, and it shall be done for you. By this My Father is glorified, that you bear much fruit; so you will be My disciples. John 15:7-8

Abide means "to continually remain" and "not to depart". There is no going in and out of abiding. A branch that is abiding in the vine one day and trying to live out of its own life the next will not bear much fruit. In fact, it will die away from the vine.

Our investment is the continual commitment to draw our life from Him and His word. His return is the bearing of much fruit – fruit that will glorify His Father.

Map 12 - Counting the Cost - Our Investment

Denial of Self

> Then He said to them all, "If anyone desires to come after Me, let him deny himself, and take up his cross daily, and follow Me. For whoever desires to save his life will lose it, but whoever loses his life for My sake will save it. Luke 9:23-24

For each of us, to become a disciple of Christ requires the complete denial of self. By the grace He supplies, we must refuse – even refuse to desire – our inalienable rights as humans. We must make ourselves "of no reputation, taking the form of a bondservant" (Philippians 2:5-7).

Our investment is our independence. His return on that investment is a fellowship that is dependent on Him, and dependable to Him for others.

The Cost of Being the *Ekklesia*

The call to be a counter-culture *ekklesia* has not changed in 2000+ years; and the call remains the same in every community, culture and country. The church is the church, and the world is the world. They are at enmity with each other. The world will hate us when we stand against it – a good measure of our devotion to the Lord's purpose; a good sign that we are His disciples.

> Jesus answered, "My kingdom is not of this world. If My kingdom were of this world, My servants would fight, so that I should not be delivered to the Jews; but now My kingdom is not from here.
> John 18:36-37

> Adulterers and adulteresses! Do you not know that friendship with the world is enmity with God? Whoever therefore wants to be a friend of the world makes himself an enemy of God. James 4:4

> If you were of the world, the world would love its own. Yet because you are not of the world, but I chose you out of the world, therefore the world hates you. John 15:19

> Yes, and all who desire to live godly in Christ Jesus will suffer persecution. 2Timothy 3:12

Rubbing the prevailing society the wrong way is expected of Christ's disciples. So is the world's resistance, aggravation and (dare we say) offense. The question for us: How will we respond?

> For we do not wrestle against flesh and blood, but against principalities, against powers, against the rulers of the darkness of this age, against spiritual hosts of wickedness in the heavenly places.
> Ephesians 6:12

> For though we walk in the flesh, we do not war according to the flesh. For the weapons of our warfare are not carnal but mighty in God… 2Corinthians 10:3-4

We must resist the temptation to respond from our carnal nature (like the world). Our response must be supernatural.

> But I tell you not to resist an evil person. But whoever slaps you on your right cheek, turn the other to him also. If anyone wants to sue you and take away your tunic, let him have your cloak also. And whoever compels you to go one mile, go with him two. Give to him who asks you, and from him who wants to borrow from you do not turn away. Matthew 5:39-42

I am sure you will agree that it takes more than human will power to turn the other cheek, give up more than is asked, and go farther for someone than required. Only the supernatural life of Christ can do these things. His command demands our obedience. It must be possible; and we must discover how (more on this later).

It is also important to recognize that the world has found its way into the church; and, as in Jesus' day, may be the source of the most severe cost.

> Then the Pharisees went out and immediately plotted with the Herodians against Him, how they might destroy Him. Mark 3:6

Map 12 - Counting the Cost - Our Investment

But they cried out, "Away with Him, away with Him! Crucify Him!" Pilate said to them, "Shall I crucify your King?" The chief priests answered, "We have no king but Caesar!" John 19:15

Now Saul was consenting to his death. At that time a great persecution arose against the church which was at Jerusalem; and they were all scattered throughout the regions of Judea and Samaria, except the apostles. And devout men carried Stephen to his burial, and made great lamentation over him. As for Saul, he made havoc of the church, entering every house, and dragging off men and women, committing them to prison. Acts 8:1-3

Like Christ, we will feel abandoned and betrayed. Perhaps our own family and friends will turn on us. But we will implore them just the same, because that is what disciples of Christ do.

Now then, we are ambassadors for Christ, as though God were pleading through us: we implore you on Christ's behalf, be reconciled to God. 2Corinthians 5:20

To be a transforming agent, the Church must consciously and continuously stand apart from the world; and from those in the church who are worldly. This is the risk we take when we invest ourselves as disciples of Jesus Christ.

Conclusion

Becoming a disciple is not an elective course in Jesus' school of ministry. A disciple is something He makes of everyone that desires to follow Him. Furthermore, counting the cost of discipleship is something best done at the beginning.

How many have raised their hand, walked the aisle, and said a prayer – only to become frustrated and confused when they later found out there was a cost? How many years were wasted in easy believism? What could have been invested for kingdom return – in this life and the one to come?

It saddens and sobers me to ask these questions. It saddens, because I am one of those who wasted too many years of my life (and God's investment in me). It sobers, because I know it is true for others; and, as a Leader in the Workplace, I am responsible for rescuing others from their condition.

There must come a time in every Christian's life when they solemnly count the cost of being a disciple of Christ. As they say, "Better late than never, and better early than late." It seems to me that God requires a general cost counting when we first receive Him as Lord and Savior. He then reveals the cost more specifically over time as He iteratively transforms us from glory to glory.

As the Leader surrenders to God's desire for this season of His life, that desire becomes a purpose of God (that will not be denied Him). God then reveals the beginning portion of His plan for accomplishing His purpose – enough to allow the Workplace Leader to count the cost. This is the decisive moment in the journey!

Application

For Leaders in the Workplace, there may not be a more important activity than counting the cost. God has invested authority and influence into us. These investments are for the sake of His kingdom. Our resistance reveals our self-reign and/or our lack of faith. Counting the cost empowers us to face ourselves and overcome the enemies that seek to distract us from joyful, Spirit-filled ministry. It will also qualify and prepare us to help others do the same.

As Leaders in the Workplace, it is important to recognize that we are responsible to help those we are discipling through this decisive step. It is much easier to teach something that we have experienced ourselves. Sit down with God, and count the cost of discipleship with Him.

Map 12 - Counting the Cost - Our Investment

Reckoning

Whatever the cost, the return will always be greater – for me and for God.

Assignment

1. Review your notes and the Scripture passages from this week's module. Share the ones that are most meaningful to someone in your spheres of influence. Ask them if they have counted the cost of discipleship.

2. Using the passages provided, count the cost. Decide if you are willing to pay it.

3. Consider the following devotion, and the hymn *All to Jesus I Surrender*. The Vineyard version on YouTube is a good one (http://www.youtube.com/watch?v=7x2IpLSfqp8).

Devotion

Fortitude (from Come Away My Beloved, Francis J. Roberts, pg. 170)

Through a multitude of tests, you will learn courage. It does not matter the price you pay, but at any cost you must obtain strength of character and the fortitude to endure. I would build your resources until you are able to carry unusually heavy loads and withstand intense pressures.

You will become an ambassador of the Kingdom of Heaven to whom I can assign critical missions, confident that you are equipped to fulfill them.

It will be in vain if you anticipate resting in a comfortable place. Zion is already filled with those who are at ease. No, you will find yourself put in a place of training and discipline, so that when the moments of crisis come you will not become fainthearted, and you will not be the victim of unwonted fear.

Trust My instruction in all of this, as you have in various past experiences. I am faithful and loving, and I am doing this so that you may meet the future days and not be found wanting.

The Mapmaker's Guide

Map 13 - Suffering for the Kingdom

Spiritual Exercise

James, a bondservant of God and of the Lord Jesus Christ, to the twelve tribes which are scattered abroad: Greetings. My brethren, count it all joy when you fall into various trials, knowing that the testing of your faith produces patience. But let patience have its perfect work, that you may be perfect and complete, lacking nothing. James 1:1-4

Prayer

Father God, finding joy in trials and tests is counter-intuitive in our culture. We confess our fear and avoidance of all things difficult and uncomfortable. Give us grace to welcome the trials and tests You bring our way. Give us wisdom and understanding to count the whole of each trial as a joyful exercise. Give us the grace and courage to walk through each trial with patience – that we may be found perfect and complete, lacking nothing. Do this Father for Your Name's sake and for Your kingdom. In Jesus Christ's name, Amen.

Introduction

Many Christians are prevented from finding joyful, Spirit-filled ministry by their misunderstanding of the suffering that accompanies the normal Christian life. To think that our loving Father would allow tribulation, trial and persecution is difficult for many. Even those that have heard the truth hope that it will not come to them.

Many of us have a tendency to exaggerate our "suffering". Some of us do it very well. Many times our "suffering" is only discomfort, or our not getting what we want. True suffering involves the loss of something that is needed for survival, or the introduction of something that threatens our safety or health. Going without dessert is not suffering. Living without proper nutrition is suffering. Cutting a finger is not suffering (even when it bleeds). Having a finger chopped off for one's faith is suffering.

True suffering comes in many forms: Physical, emotional, mental and spiritual. Suffering in one area readily affects the others. Regardless of the area that is most greatly affected, the most productive way to overcome suffering is to begin in the spiritual realm. From this perspective, we can better understand God's purpose in creating or allowing the suffering – giving us a better chance of taking full advantage of the pain we have been called to endure.

As we search out this matter of suffering, we will discover that it is promised for all that would lead a righteous life, and a blessing that is worthy of our pursuit. It is another of the Kingdom mysteries – something that is foolishness to the world, but grace and liberation to the children of God. Yes, even the truth about suffering will make us free.

For many, this lesson will shift their paradigm about the normal Christian life. This is a good thing. They will be made free in the renewing of their minds. Others will reject the truth and remain captive to the deception. As disciple makers, our responsibility is to present the truth and trust God for the rest.

Map 13 - Suffering for the Kingdom

Definition

Tribulation (*thlipsis*): Primarily means a pressing or pressure, anything which burdens the spirit. It is used of: The calamities of war; want; the distress a of woman in child-birth; persecution; the "afflictions" of Christ, from which his followers must not shrink, whether sufferings of body or mind; sufferings in general. *Vine's Expository Dictionary*

Searching Out the Matter
(All Scripture references, but those noted, are NKJV; Thomas Nelson, Inc.; footnotes and headings excluded)

If It Doesn't Kill You…

What doesn't kill you will make you stronger. If you have done anything difficult in your life – and particularly, if you have whined about it – you've probably heard this from someone. It's a favorite of strength and conditioning coaches, parents and Tour de France cyclists. You may not have appreciated the encouragement at the time, but, deep down, you knew it was true.

Still no one wants to suffer. In fact, most people avoid it as much as possible. Most of us prefer to maneuver around the sufferings that come our way – a major reason why we strive to stay in control of our lives. This does us more harm than good. Counter-intuitive? Of course, but we are talking about His ways and thoughts – not our own, nor those of this world.

Few want to talk about suffering. It makes us uncomfortable. When was the last time your pastor or teacher spoke on the benefits of suffering? Why has suffering gotten such a bad reputation in the church? It's strange, really, given all the Bible has to say to encourage us in suffering, trial, tribulation, etc.

As you read the following passages, open your heart to God's encouragement. By His grace, you will discover the promise, reason, requirement, blessing and joy of suffering for His Kingdom. Reckon these truths to be true for yourself. Invite the Holy Spirit to transform you by the renewing of your mind.

> *These things I have spoken to you, that in Me you may have peace. In the world you will have tribulation; but be of good cheer, I have overcome the world.* John 16:33

Christ promised that we "will have tribulation". Tribulation reminds us that we are in a place that is not our home. It comes with a promise: That in Christ, we can overcome the worst that the world has to throw at us.

> *Yes, and all who desire to live godly in Christ Jesus will suffer persecution.* 2Timothy 3:12

> *Blessed are those who are persecuted for righteousness' sake, for theirs is the kingdom of heaven.* Matthew 5:10

Persecutions are a part of the normal Christian life ("to live godly in Christ Jesus"); and they are a blessing. Having personally experienced persecution in the Workplace, I can testify that God used it to bless me both spiritually (by removing pride and teaching me a deeper forgiveness and love for others), and practically (by saving me from the persecutor and moving me into a better position in the company).

> *And when they had preached the gospel to that city and made many disciples, they returned to Lystra, Iconium, and Antioch, strengthening the souls of the disciples, exhorting them to continue in the faith, and saying, "We must through many tribulations enter the kingdom of God."* Acts 14:21-22

> *And you will be hated by all for My name's sake. But he who endures to the end will be saved.* Matthew 10:22

Map 13 - Suffering for the Kingdom

In these passages, we see the connection between tribulation and our salvation. God allows persecution and tribulation in our lives as a vehicle for our entry into His kingdom. It begs the question: What are we doing to ourselves when we resist, or work around, the trials and tribulations that come our way?

> *And not only that, but we also glory in tribulations, knowing that tribulation produces perseverance; and perseverance, character; and character, hope. Now hope does not disappoint, because the love of God has been poured out in our hearts by the Holy Spirit who was given to us.* Romans 5:3-5

The Greek word translated here as "glory" means "to boast in a thing". Paul boasted in tribulations because it marked him as belonging the Jesus Christ. He boasted because he was being prepared and strengthened him for another "glory" – the one that was to come. He spoke of it this way:

> *Therefore we do not lose heart. Even though our outward man is perishing, yet the inward man is being renewed day by day. For our light affliction, which is but for a moment, is working for us a far more exceeding and eternal weight of glory…* 2Corinthians 4:16-17

> *The Spirit Himself bears witness with our spirit that we are children of God, and if children, then heirs—heirs of God and joint heirs with Christ, if indeed we suffer with Him, that we may also be glorified together. For I consider that the sufferings of this present time are not worthy to be compared with the glory which shall be revealed in us.* Romans 8:16-18

There is a direct correlation between our suffering, God's glory, and our participation with Him in it. Afflictions, trials, tribulations and persecutions are all opportunities for us to invest in God's purposes and plans. Additionally (and this is something we need to lay hold of), God has also established that we would benefit from the investment. In fact, the return is far greater than we can imagine.

> *And we know that all things work together for good to those who love God, to those who are the called according to His purpose.* Romans 8:28

You can be sure that God is careful with His words. He does not waste them, nor does He misuse them. Whenever I see "all" in the Scriptures, I know that my Father in heaven is challenging me to believe for more. One of those challenges is believing that God works our suffering "together for good". Paul helps us understand how:

> *For as the sufferings of Christ abound in us, so our consolation also abounds through Christ. Now if we are afflicted, it is for your consolation and salvation, which is effective for enduring the same sufferings which we also suffer. Or if we are comforted, it is for your consolation and salvation. And our hope for you is steadfast, because we know that as you are partakers of the sufferings, so also you will partake of the consolation.* 2Corinthians 1:5-7

Our suffering produces consolation and salvation for others, supernaturally empowering them to endure the same suffering. Their suffering does the same for us. This is one of the great mysteries of fellowship and disciple-making.

For example, it is no coincidence when a woman loses her husband within six months of the same tragedy happening to a couple of her friends. There is more supernatural going on here than we recognize – or leverage for God's kingdom and the benefit of His children. God intends for us to share with each other in the blessings that come with suffering for His kingdom.

> *I now rejoice in my sufferings for you, and fill up in my flesh what is lacking in the afflictions of Christ, for the sake of His body, which is the church…* Colossians 1:24

In suffering, we are joined with Christ in His afflictions for His body. Only those that have experienced such suffering can appreciate the level of intimacy this brings to the believer.

Map 13 - Suffering for the Kingdom

Therefore, since Christ suffered for us in the flesh, arm yourselves also with the same mind, for he who has suffered in the flesh has ceased from sin, that he no longer should live the rest of his time in the flesh for the lusts of men, but for the will of God. 1Peter 4:1-2

Amazing!! Our suffering in the flesh works to eradicate sin in our lives, and encourage our living for the will of God. Suffering plays a significant role in our transformation.

Beloved, do not think it strange concerning the fiery trial which is to try you, as though some strange thing happened to you; but rejoice to the extent that you partake of Christ's sufferings, that when His glory is revealed, you may also be glad with exceeding joy. If you are reproached for the name of Christ, blessed are you, for the Spirit of glory and of God rests upon you. On their part He is blasphemed, but on your part He is glorified. 1Peter 4:12-14

The word "partake" is important to our understanding of suffering. It means "partner with", signifying that we are joined with Jesus Christ in our suffering. Could this be one of God's ways for our abiding in His Son?

Additionally, our suffering well with Him brings Him glory. In the process, we are blessed by the joy that comes from that glory resting upon us. In this way, we are obeying Christ's command to "let your light so shine before men that they see your good works and glorify your Father in heaven." (Matthew 5:16)

Sources of Suffering

The more mature we become, the more we can be trusted to suffer for God's kingdom. And as we mature, the source of our suffering changes – becoming more impactful for the purposes of God. There are at least four sources of suffering, and each one is possible in the life of every disciple of Jesus Christ.

1. Many have suffered from the consequences of their foolishness. For example:

    a. Being fined for filing an inaccurate tax return;
    b. Having something stolen from an unlocked car.

2. It is certainly true that a loving Father chastens, rebukes and even scourges His children. This is in response to our childish immaturity or waywardness. It is an exercise in discipline and training (Hebrews 12:5-7).

3. Then there is the tribulation and trial that comes from living in a fallen world. Job is a good example. Other Scripture references include John 16:33; Acts 14:22; Romans 5:3-4; 1Thessalonians 3:4; and 2Thesselonians 1:3-8; 1Peter 4:12-13; and Revelation 3:10.

4. Lastly, there is the "suffering with Christ", or "fellowshipping in His sufferings". References here include Matthew 5:10; Philippians 1:29-30, 2:5-8, and 3:8-11; Romans 8:16-17; and other in the lists above.

This "suffering with Christ" is a mysterious and awesome truth. Paul, Peter and John considered sharing in His suffering a great privilege. There is a depth of fellowship with the Savior, in His suffering, that few in the church have experienced. How do we find it? How did He suffer? How should we share is His suffering now?

Let this mind be in you which was also in Christ Jesus, who, being in the form of God, did not consider it robbery to be equal with God, but made Himself of no reputation, taking the form of a bondservant, and coming in the likeness of men. And being found in appearance as a man, He humbled Himself and became obedient to the point of death, even the death of the cross. Philippians 2:5-8

Christ laid down his reputation, became a slave and died a humiliating and painful death. We have been given the mind of Christ. This passage encourages us to "let this mind be in you". Said another way, "Let the Holy Spirit transform you by the renewing of your mind. Think like Christ."

Map 13 - Suffering for the Kingdom

So what might this look like for His disciples? Isaiah 53 gives us a good deal of understanding:

> *He is despised and rejected by men,*
> *A Man of sorrows and acquainted with grief.*
> *And we hid, as it were, our faces from Him;*
> *He was despised, and we did not esteem Him.*
>
> *Surely He has borne our griefs*
> *And carried our sorrows;*
> *Yet we esteemed Him stricken,*
> *Smitten by God, and afflicted.*
>
> *But He was wounded for our transgressions,*
> *He was bruised for our iniquities;*
> *The chastisement for our peace was upon Him,*
> *And by His stripes we are healed.* Isaiah 53:3-5

He is despised and rejected by men, bearing our griefs and carrying our sorrows, wounded for our transgressions, bruised for our iniquities, and oppressed and afflicted. Certainly, there are sufferings that were for Christ alone; however, we must be careful not to assume that all these are only for Him.

> *So Jesus said to them again, "Peace to you! As the Father has sent Me, I also send you."* John 20:21

The Pursuit of Suffering

There is much for us to unlearn about suffering. For example, I've heard some say, "It would be foolish to invite, accept or acknowledge suffering in my life." This contradicts most of the scriptures we have reviewed thus far. Acts 14:21-22, Romans 5:3-5 and Romans 8:16-17 are good places to start in helping someone see the truth and importance of suffering.

Others have said, "It is one thing to accept suffering, but another to go seeking after it. God does not command us to do that." I remember agreeing to this – more than once. Searching out the matter of suffering has changed my mind. Here is what Jesus had to say about it.

> *A new commandment I give to you, that you love one another; as I have loved you, that you also*
> *love one another. By this all will know that you are My disciples, if you have love for one another.*
> John 13:34-35

How are we to love one another? As He loved us! And how was that? To make it clear, He later added:

> *Greater love has no one than this, than to lay down one's life for his friends.* John 15:13

Taking up this theme of sacrificial love, Paul encourages the Galatians to "Bear one another's burdens, and so fulfill the law of Christ." (v. 6:2) We cannot bear the burdens of another if we are not actively seeking to know what they are.

Additionally, if it is God's intention for us to bear them, then we must hear Him say so. To best hear His intention, we must have a heart that is willing to respond to whatever He commands – including what may be our suffering for that person. Our preceding "amen" will only come out of our desire to suffer for them. This is a radical shift in the leaning of our hearts toward one another. It is something the world will not understand. But, by God's grace and power, our suffering will draw them to the glory that suffering produces.

Conclusion

The truth of Scripture regarding the various forms of suffering requires a counter-intuitive and counter-cultural perspective on life and ministry. It requires a great deal of trust and humility. It requires sacrificial love.

Map 13 - Suffering for the Kingdom

As with most mysteries, a little bit of understanding raises more questions. Here are a few for your continuing consideration:

1. If the various forms of suffering are a blessing, promise and condition, then how much time and energy should we invest in delivering others from them?

2. What about our children? Are we delivering them from a blessing when we bail them out of trial or discomfort? What does this teach them about the normal Christian life?

3. How do we disciple others before, during and after their suffering? How do we know whether to rescue or walk with someone that is suffering?

Once again, we are faced with kingdom challenges that are beyond our understanding. Only the Lord has the answers to these (and so many other questions) about suffering for His Kingdom. In our weakness, we find ourselves wholly incapable of living the normal Christian life.

Be encouraged that there is a way; for our hope lies in the life of the One that can live this life. This will be the subject of future lessons. For now, let us rest in the truth that "with God all things are possible." (Mark 10:27)

Application

As disciple makers, Leaders in the Workplace have been given a solemn responsibility to help others walk through the tribulation that God allows for their transformation. Understanding and believing the truth of suffering positions the Workplace Leader to speak life and liberty into the body of Christ. Only those that have been made free are used as instruments of this freedom for others.

Reckoning

The sufferings of this present time are not worthy to be compared with the glory which shall be revealed in us.

Assignment

1. Review your notes and the Scripture passages from this week's module. Share the ones that are most meaningful to someone in your spheres of influence.

2. What are your convictions and fears about suffering? Share these with someone you can trust to pray for you. For any fears you have, remember: Behind every fear is a lie. Deal with the lie, and the fear will fly.

3. Consider the following devotion. Ask God to work out of you what doesn't belong, and replace it with His thoughts and ways regarding suffering.

Devotion

From Os Hillman TGIF: Responses to Adversity

Though the fig tree does not bud and there are no grapes on the vines, though the olive crop fails and the fields produce no food, though there are no sheep in the pen and no cattle in the stalls, yet I will rejoice in the LORD, I will be joyful in God my Savior. Habakkuk 3:17-18

When we experience adversity, we generally respond in one of three ways: (1) we become angry; (2) we try to gut it out; or (3) we accept it with joy.

Anger

When adversity comes our way, we say, "Why me, Lord?" We become bitter and resentful and blame God and others for our problems. We view ourselves as victims and demand that God answer our accusing questions: "Why don't You love me, Lord? We feel entitled to life, health, wealth, and happiness.

Map 13 - Suffering for the Kingdom

Gutting It Out

Another way we respond to adversity is by adopting a stoic attitude, repressing our emotions. We lie to ourselves and say, "I'm gutting it out. I'm demonstrating endurance." In reality, we are merely isolating ourselves with a shell of false bravado. We don't meditate on God's love, we don't pray, we don't believe God really has anything good planned for us. We simply tell ourselves, "This will soon be over. I'm a survivor." We never receive what God has planned for us if we stay here.

Acceptance with Joy

This is the response God seeks from us. When adversity comes, we rest in His love and trust that He knows best. We realize that nothing can happen to us without His permission. If there is pain in our lives, we know it's because God deems it necessary for our growth or wishes to use our pain to minister to others.

God revealed to the prophet Habakkuk that Israel was soon to be invaded by the Babylonians. Habakkuk knew that Israel was about to suffer intense adversity as part of God's loving discipline of His people. Habakkuk faced the looming national tragedy with an attitude of acceptance with joy.

If Habakkuk could be joyful in the face of a national calamity, then we can rejoice in the Lord no matter what comes our way.

Reprinted by permission from the author. Os Hillman is an international speaker and author of more than 10 books on workplace calling. To learn more, visit http://www.MarketplaceLeaders.org.

The Map Maker's Guide

Map 14 - Chaos Navigation

Spiritual Exercise

Therefore, my beloved, as you have always obeyed, not as in my presence only, but now much more in my absence, work out your own salvation with fear and trembling; for it is God who works in you both to will and to do for His good pleasure. Philippians 2:12-13

Do not fear, little flock, for it is your Father's good pleasure to give you the kingdom. Luke 12:32

Not that I have already attained, or am already perfected; but I press on, that I may lay hold of that for which Christ Jesus has also laid hold of me. Philippians 3:12

He cannot do a work through me until He has done a work in me. Unknown

Prayer

Father God, how wonderful it is to know that You are working in us, for Your good pleasure. This is where we will focus our attention – on Your pleasure. We surrender to your work in and through us. We trust You to reveal Your perfect will for our lives. We know that we shall be satisfied as we seek Your satisfaction. Give us grace to work out our salvation with fear and trembling – to lay hold of that for which Christ Jesus laid hold of us; nothing more and nothing less. In Jesus' name. Amen.

Introduction

As we learned in the first two lessons of this section, the normal Christian life requires our investment and risk; and it includes tribulation, trial, persecution and affliction. These play a supernatural part in God's work, as He transforms us into the image of the glory of His Son. It is encouraging to know that our investment and suffering for the kingdom has eternal value.

But what is it that persuades us to go where so many fear to tread? And how do we persuade others to go with us? Here are some good reasons to get us started:

1. The desire in our heart tells us that there must be more to life than the old status quo.

2. He has called us; and we desire to obey His call.

3. We are eager to see what's on the other side.

4. He has promised to go with us.

We also know that the Holy Spirit uses our sacrifice and suffering to transform us into the image of the glory of Christ. The Greek word for transformed is *metamorphoo*. Like the inside of a cocoon, *metamorphoo* can be quite a messy process. In fact, it can be chaotic. In this lesson, we will explore the ways God would have us navigate the chaos – to His and our advantage.

Definition

Navigate (verb): To plan, record, and control the course and position of (a ship or aircraft); to follow a planned course on, across, or through (e.g., navigate a stream); to make one's way. *www.thefreedictionary.com*

Follow (*akoloutheō*): To follow one who precedes, join him as his attendant, accompany him; to join one as a disciple, become or be his disciple (i.e., side with his party). *Blue Letter Bible Outline of Biblical Usage*

Map 14 - Chaos Navigation

Jesus Christ is our Captain; the Holy Spirit, our Navigator. The children of God make their way through chaos by following Jesus, in step with the Spirit. This is easier said than done, but a great place to start.

Searching Out the Matter
(All Scripture references, but those noted, are NKJV; Thomas Nelson, Inc.; footnotes excluded)

Expect and Embrace Chaos

To prepare us for our future assignment, God allows – even creates – chaos in our lives. Entering into it willingly is a critical step in our Sacrificing for His Plan. Chaos tests us, helping us see what we truly believe. Chaos can be a great teacher, exposing our flesh and revealing the hard places of unbelief in our hearts. God uses chaos to search our hearts and to shake loose the things that don't belong (Psalm 139:23-24).

There are several ways to respond to chaos: Satan's way, the world's way, our way, and God's way. Satan's way is to lash out at those we think are causing the chaos; to manipulate others to get us out of it; even throwing innocent bystanders under the bus to feel better about our own discomfort. The world's way is to negotiate or ignore the chaos, so as to minimize its impact on our lives. Responding to chaos "our way" usually includes our taking control of the situation, using whatever soulish skills we have to maneuver around it.

I have attempted many of the wrong ways for navigating through the chaos in my life. None have ended well. The times I have chosen to follow God's way have been incredibly blessed. God's deliverance from persecution in a previous job was one of those times.

A more recent example has been my family's navigation through the trauma of a house fire and the chaos of finding another permanent residence. By God's grace, we followed Christ in an incredible adventure that taught us much about chaos navigation. This lesson is based on that experience. You can find our testimony to God's amazing sovereignty, love and plan at http://www.inlightconsulting.com/MMtraining/House%20Fire%20Chaos%20and%20Blessing.pdf.

The Ways of God

God intends to do something in us: Our transformation. He intends to give something to us: His kingdom. And He intends to do something through us: Glorify Himself. It is safe to assume that the God of this universe, the One who is King, will insist on doing what He wants, in the way He wants to do it.

We can also safely assume that God's ways are the best ways for everyone involved. It is important to regularly remind ourselves that His ways are higher – more intelligent and more virtuous – than we can think or imagine.

> *For as the heavens are higher than the earth, so are My ways higher than your ways, and My thoughts than your thoughts.* Isaiah 55:9

How high are the heavens? It's hard to say, but scientists tell us that, in the heavens that we can see, there is a star over 13 billion light years from Earth. Yes, the heavens are very high above the earth.

Our God spoke that vast expanse, and everything in it, into existence. He measures it with a span (Isaiah 40:12). By His word it is held together in its placement and movement.

It is this power – inherent in His ways – that God uses to guide us through the chaos of our lives. Why would we settle for anything less? Sadly, we are a knuckleheaded, rebellious people – even the children of God.

> *For thus says the Lord GOD, the Holy One of Israel:*
> *"In returning and rest you shall be saved;*
> *In quietness and confidence shall be your strength."*
> *But you would not,*

Map 14 - Chaos Navigation

And you said, "No, for we will flee on horses"—
Therefore you shall flee!
And, "We will ride on swift horses"—
Therefore those who pursue you shall be swift!
One thousand shall flee at the threat of one,
At the threat of five you shall flee,
Till you are left as a pole on top of a mountain
And as a banner on a hill. Isaiah 30:15-17

Israel could have turned to the One that promised to protect them, but they would not. And it wasn't going to turn out well for them. But God is patient.

Therefore the LORD will wait, that He may be gracious to you;
And therefore He will be exalted, that He may have mercy on you.
For the LORD is a God of justice;
Blessed are all those who wait for Him.
For the people shall dwell in Zion at Jerusalem;
You shall weep no more.
He will be very gracious to you at the sound of your cry;
When He hears it, He will answer you.
And though the Lord gives you
The bread of adversity and the water of affliction,
Yet your teachers will not be moved into a corner anymore,
But your eyes shall see your teachers.
Your ears shall hear a word behind you, saying,
"This is the way, walk in it,"
Whenever you turn to the right hand
Or whenever you turn to the left. Isaiah 30:18-21

As He did with the nation of Israel, God waits for us to come to the end of our ways and return to Him. He is then gracious, exalted and merciful. Moreover, though He may give us adversity and affliction, He uses them to return us to His direction and protection.

For since the beginning of the world
Men have not heard nor perceived by the ear,
Nor has the eye seen any God besides You,
Who acts for the one who waits for Him. Isaiah 64:4

God is not waiting on us to act. Now, that is a paradigm shift! Let this sink in. God is waiting on us to wait for Him, so He can act on our behalf. Amazing! He is like no other god, including those of the world that we turn to for solutions. He is not at all like the god we subconsciously make of our self-sufficient ingenuity.

A man's heart plans his way,
But the LORD directs his steps. Proverbs 16:9

I once thought that planning my way was okay, because God would then direct my steps. I wanted to own the plan. Then I discovered that even my way is not the best way.

O LORD, I know the way of man is not in himself;
It is not in man who walks to direct his own steps. Jeremiah 10:23

How awesome and liberating it is to know that the LORD has taken responsibility for both the way and the steps!! It's a good thing, too, because the work is way above my pay grade. Why would I think differently? Am I that arrogant? Consider the way of transformation:

Map 14 - Chaos Navigation

But we all, with unveiled face, beholding as in a mirror the glory of the Lord, are being transformed into the same image from glory to glory, just as by the Spirit of the Lord. 2Corinthians 3:18

Do we really think that we can transform ourselves into the glory of Christ? Of course not… when we really think about it. The trouble is: We don't. We just go off trying to do it the best way we know how. Many times, we behold our self for the solution. Or, we choose to behold the "well known" author and his latest improvement program. In our desperation to find a quick and easy fix, we fail to behold the One that has the way and power we need.

Graciously, as with Israel, God waits patiently for us to run ourselves up a pole and turn to Him for help. Then, with grace and mercy, the Holy Spirit begins the work that only He can do – in His way – for His glory.

Keys to Patiently Persevering Through the Chaos

As Beth and I watched our house go up in flames, the Lord said two things. First there was, "I am sovereign. Nothing happens outside of my will. I am a good God, I love you, and I have a plan for you. Reckon it in your hearts." The second was, "You will have to grieve." That was enough to get us started in the way of God for our season of chaos.

Our obedience to these commands enabled us to walk confidently with the Lord in the adventure that would follow. Along the way, we learned a few other things about navigating chaos. I trust God will use them to help you (and help you to help others) navigate through the chaos that can transform you and them into the image of the glory of the Lord. Meditate on the referenced verses. Allow them to renew your mind.

1. Intentionally recognize the sovereignty of God – that all He allows works to our good.

    And we know that all things work together for good to those who love God, to those who are the called according to His purpose. Romans 8:28

2. Praise Him for His faithfulness; for He inhabits the praises of His people.

    Therefore let those who suffer according to the will of God commit their souls to Him in doing good, as to a faithful Creator. 1 Peter 4:19

3. Come to terms with the ending of the old status quo – grieve as necessary. This will free you to look forward and see how powerfully God is going on before you.

    Do not remember the former things,
    Nor consider the things of old. Isaiah 43:18

4. Stay focused on Him – distractions are your enemies.

    But Jesus said to him, "No one, having put his hand to the plow, and looking back, is fit for the kingdom of God." Luke 9:62

5. Stay in the now - recognize this is as much about your transformation as it is about your future.

    But we all, with unveiled face, beholding as in a mirror the glory of the Lord, are being transformed into the same image from glory to glory, just as by the Spirit of the Lord. 2Corinthians 3:18

6. Daily choose to surrender, sacrifice and submit.

    Then He said to them all, "If anyone desires to come after Me, let him deny himself, and take up his cross daily, and follow Me." Luke 9:23

7. Exercise your faith by challenging yourself with His promises. Psalms 34 and 37 are good places to start. If you believe these promises, then speak them to yourself – out loud. If you do not, ask God to

Map 14 - Chaos Navigation

give you the faith you need. He uses chaos to increase our faith. Here's a sampling of His promises for those in chaos:

> *The angel of the LORD encamps all around those who fear Him,*
> *And delivers them.*
> *Oh, taste and see that the LORD is good;*
> *Blessed is the man who trusts in Him!*
> *Oh, fear the LORD, you His saints!*
> *There is no want to those who fear Him.* Psalm 34:7-9

> *The steps of a good man are ordered by the Lord,*
> *And He delights in his way.*
> *Though he fall, he shall not be utterly cast down;*
> *For the Lord upholds him with His hand.* Psalm 37:23-24

8. Pursue a deeper relationship with the Lord by practicing *The PAPA Prayer* (by Larry Crabb). There is no more important time to protect your intimacy with the Lord than when you are in chaos.

> *Therefore let us draw near with confidence to the throne of grace, so that we may receive mercy and find grace to help in time of need.* Hebrews 4:16

9. Go with others, leaning on your kingdom community. Add to these at least three others that you can trust to pray for your protection and transformation.

> *And the glory which You gave Me I have given them, that they may be one just as We are one: I in them, and You in Me; that they may be made perfect in one, and that the world may know that You have sent Me, and have loved them as You have loved Me.* John 17:22-23

10. Draw your strength and encouragement from the Lord. Aggressively resist all sources of assistance that are not clearly from Him.

> *Finally, my brethren, be strong in the Lord and in the power of His might.* Ephesians 6:10

Following these ten steps will not only help you survive the chaos, it will ensure that you maximize God's purpose and plan in it. It will turn what would otherwise be an utterly miserable experience to one of exciting adventure. It will encourage, edify and equip you for joyful, Spirit-filled ministry; making you a better disciple maker and transformation agent in your spheres of influence.

Conclusion

For those bound for more glory, there is no getting around the chaos. It is part of the normal Christian life. So, let's not waste the pain. Take full advantage by knowing, and accepting, the ways of God in the chaos that accompanies the transformation process.

No one should face trials and tribulations alone. Chaos is best met within communities where we can trust others to watch our back and encourage us to keep moving forward. The Leader in the Workplace is the rallying point for that community. God has encouraged and equipped you to be His agent of encouragement and guidance. Without a shepherd, the sheep will be scattered. Many will become discouraged, and will be destroyed, without God's Leader in the Workplace.

Application

Teaching others reinforces what we ourselves have learned. So share what God has revealed. Here are some additional thoughts I have heard from others – for you to consider and share.

- The journey of transformation is a formation process to prepare us for a divine assignment.

Map 14 - Chaos Navigation

- God uses the chaos of transformation to work His way, truth and life into us; and to work out hooks, habits and hang-ups that will interfere with our glorifying Him and enjoying His presence.

- The measure of success in a divine journey is a divine measure – namely, obedience (it may look like failure to the world).

- Transformation will take as long as it takes for the preparation to be completed. There is a reason it takes nine months to birth a baby.

- God talks more to us in the depths of the transformation than on the mountaintops of peace and pleasure.

- Rapid, repetitive transformation will be the norm in the last days – like the birth pangs of a woman in labor.

Reckoning

I can do all things – and face all things – through Christ, Who gives me strength.

Assignment

1. Review your notes and the Scripture passages from this week's module. Share the ones that are most meaningful to someone in your spheres of influence.

2. What are your convictions and fears about transformation and the chaos that may come? Share these with someone you can trust to pray for you. Remember: Behind every fear is a lie. Deal with the lie, and the fear will fly.

3. Consider your past seasons of transformation and chaos. Was God with you? What did He do to prepare you for this season? Let faith arise.

4. As we continue this section on "Sacrificing for His Plan", consider your propensity to take control when things start going wrong. What motivates this response? Invite the Lord to deal with this and give you grace to surrender it to Him.

Devotion

You Were Made to Fly
by Os Hillman

"Naked I came from my mother's womb, and naked I will depart. The LORD gave and the LORD has taken away; may the name of the LORD be praised" (Job 1:21).

Can a caterpillar fly? If you said, "No," you would be partially correct. Actually, a caterpillar can fly, but it must have a transformation first.

The butterfly begins life as a caterpillar, a wormlike larva that spins a cocoon for itself. For weeks, the larva remains hidden within the cocoon as it undergoes metamorphosis. When it's time for the butterfly to emerge, it must struggle and fight its way out of the cocoon. We might be tempted to help this process by tearing open the cocoon - but that's the worst thing we could do. The struggle makes it strong and enables it to fly. Butterflies need adversity to become what God intended them to be. So do we.

The Book of Job is the story of a wealthy and successful community leader named Job. He was a successful and righteous businessman with huge holdings of livestock and real estate. One day Satan came before God and asked him, "Where have you come from?" Satan replied, "From roaming through the earth and going back and forth in it."

Map 14 - Chaos Navigation

God said to Satan, "Have you considered my servant Job? He is blameless and upright, a man who fears God and shuns evil." Notice that God pointed Job out to Satan! God gave Satan permission to put Job through a trial of adversity. Job's herds were stolen, his servants were murdered, and all of Job's children were killed by a sudden tornado.

Through his trial of adversity, he grows in strength, wisdom and faith. His entire perspective on God is transformed by his suffering. He was even accused of sin by his closest friends.

We must get beyond the immature notion that God is interested only in making us healthy, wealthy and happy. More than anything, He wants us to be like Christ. And the road to becoming like Christ often leads through the wilderness of adversity.

In order for the butterfly to fly, there must be a transformation process that is often developed through adversity.

Reprinted by permission from the author. Os Hillman is an international speaker and author of more than 10 books on workplace calling. To learn more, visit http://www.MarketplaceLeaders.org

The Map Maker's Guide

Map 15 - The One Another Fellowship

Spiritual Exercise

We have learned that, to be faithful stewards of the mysteries of God, we must explore those mysteries and put them to use for His kingdom. God has hidden mysteries in the Scriptures. God has hidden truth in the stories and prophecies of the Old Testament. Jesus spoke in parables to hide the mysteries of the kingdom. The Holy Bible is the most obvious place to search out the mysteries of God.

We are wise to also recognize that the mysteries of God can be found all around us. God's creation reveals the nature and character of its Creator; from the substance of the cosmos to the birth of a child. Who but God can understand the complex workings of our brains? God has hidden great mysteries in His creation.

Furthermore, all of God's creation operates in mysterious relationships: Mankind's responsibility to the earth and its responsibility to us; generational relationships (e.g., passing down curses and blessings); and the incredible relationship of a husband and wife – helping to reveal Jesus Christ's relationship with the church. These and many more mysteries are going on all around us. How we consider them can greatly affect our knowledge of God.

For the faithful steward, all of creation is a mystery to be explored – including our relationship with one another. As we pray, consider the One that creates: He hides and encourages our searching, that we might know and love Him more.

Prayer

Father God, You are the greatest of all mysteries. Your ways and thoughts are so far above our own that we are tempted to shrink back – discouraged that we will never understand Your mysteries. Help us, Heavenly Father. Thank You for making us curious people. Thank You for encouraging us to keep on searching. Thank You, that in our searching, we are promised to find You. Strengthen us in the adventure. Use us as faithful stewards and instruments of righteousness to deliver Your liberating truth. In Jesus' name. Amen.

Introduction

God never intends for us to do things in isolation. Sacrificing for His Plan is to be experienced in community. It is another of God's ways that are directly opposed to the ways of man. In every worldly system (e.g., sports, business, government), the individual is recognized above the team. The man that is the captain of his own ship is praised and emulated. The "star" gets the big bucks.

This is not the way of God! From the Old Testament (where God pleaded with the people not to desire a king) to the New Testament (where the Body of Christ becomes the Bride), the people of God are those that live in community, for the sake of building the community of Jesus Christ. How are we to be made into the fellowship of His habitation? Where do we start?

We start by searching it out: Beholding the Lord as we seek the revelation and transformation that the Holy Spirit will provide. We will begin with the meaning of fellowship.

Map 15 - The One Another Fellowship

Definition

Fellowship (*koinōnia*): Fellowship, association, community, communion, joint participation; intimacy; a gift jointly contributed, a collection, a contribution, as exhibiting an embodiment and proof of fellowship. *BlueLetterBible.org Outline of Biblical Usage*

It is important to recognize that fellowship is a noun that assumes action. It describes a group of people that are doing something. That something is living together in the way of God for fellowship.

Not sitting or standing around together, though this is a part. Not talking, playing or working together, though this is more a part. The whole of *koinōnia* is found in living... together. ALL living; and ALL together. It is no coincidence that more than eighty-five percent of the you/your pronoun usages in Scripture are plural. Independence is one of the greatest deceptions and sins of our day.

Searching Out the Matter
(All Scripture references, but those noted, are NKJV; Thomas Nelson, Inc.; footnotes excluded)

The Mystery of Fellowship

> *I do not pray for these alone, but also for those who will believe in Me through their word; that they all may be one, as You, Father, are in Me, and I in You; that they also may be one in Us, that the world may believe that You sent Me. And the glory which You gave Me I have given them, that they may be one just as We are one: I in them, and You in Me; that they may be made perfect in one, and that the world may know that You have sent Me, and have loved them as You have loved Me.* John 17:20-23

Jesus Christ's desire is that we would be "made perfect in one". He has been praying for more than 2000 years that we would be perfectly unified. He gave us the glory that the Father gave Him for this very purpose!!

The Father intends to answer His Son's prayer. Every purpose that God has given us includes this underlying objective. Therefore, every purpose of God involves more than one person, and will by its nature draw more people to it.

Notice that Jesus asked His Father to make us one (versus helping us do it). It is a work that only the Father can accomplish. Our response must be agreement with Jesus' prayer, and surrender to the Father's work.

> *To me, who am less than the least of all the saints, this grace was given, that I should preach among the Gentiles the unsearchable riches of Christ, and to make all see what is the fellowship of the mystery, which from the beginning of the ages has been hidden in God who created all things through Jesus Christ; to the intent that now the manifold wisdom of God might be made known by the church to the principalities and powers in the heavenly places, according to the eternal purpose which He accomplished in Christ Jesus our Lord, in whom we have boldness and access with confidence through faith in Him.* Ephesians 3:8-12

It is almost too amazing to believe that "the manifold wisdom of God" and the "eternal purpose which He accomplished in Christ Jesus our Lord" is "the fellowship of the mystery". The church is the "mystery fellowship"; for by this fellowship His wisdom and purpose will be made known to principalities and powers beyond this place and time.

Let that sink in for a moment. How amazing that we share in the mystery of God's manifold wisdom to this age!! What a privilege!! We are to proclaim and live in the fellowship of His mystery.

Map 15 - The One Another Fellowship

Recognize, if you can, how important our fellowship is to God. It is a precious thing to the Father, Son and Holy Spirit. I dare say we do not treat her so well. It would do us good to mourn with Jesus Christ over the dismemberment of the Body of Christ – His Bride to be.

Make no mistake about it: She will be spotless and without wrinkle. The question we must ask ourselves is this: Are we participating with God in His unifying work, or are we allowing ourselves to be pulled apart by our enemies – Satan, our flesh and the world?

If you are pierced to the heart as I am, you will be asking the question, "Lord, what must we do?" If I may be so bold to suggest, I believe He would say:

> *God is faithful, by whom you were called into the fellowship of His Son, Jesus Christ our Lord.*
> 1Corinthians 1:9

Trust your Father in Heaven to complete the work He has begun. Join Him, as the early followers did, by continuing steadfastly in the apostles' doctrine and fellowship, in the breaking of bread, and in prayers (Acts 2:42). Become part of the "one another" fellowship.

The "One Another" Fellowship

Now that we have the Holy Spirit's conviction and the Lord's perspective, we can move on to a deeper understanding of the fellowship He desires. We will do so by searching out the "one another" verses. As we review these, let the truth convict and encourage you in the potential of fellowship.

> *But if we walk in the light as He is in the light, we have fellowship with one another, and the blood of Jesus Christ His Son cleanses us from all sin.* 1John 1:7

Fellowship with one another is evidence of our walk with Christ; and important enough to include with the promise of our being cleansed from all sin.

> *Salt is good, but if the salt loses its flavor, how will you season it? Have salt in yourselves, and have peace with one another.* Mark 9:50

"Have peace with one another" is not an option; it is a command of our King. Note His use of the word "with". Our peace is to be found with one another, not in avoiding one another.

> *A new commandment I give to you, that you love one another; as I have loved you, that you also love one another. By this all will know that you are My disciples, if you have love for one another.* John 13:34-35

> *This is My commandment, that you love one another as I have loved you.* John 15:12

Another command: To love one another… as He loved us. Lest we forget, that love was sacrificial, even unto death on a cross. It is a condition of our being His disciples.

> *For as we have many members in one body, but all the members do not have the same function, so we, being many, are one body in Christ, and individually members of one another.* Romans 12:4-5

Not only are we members of Christ's body, we are members of one another. There is to be a closeness that exceeds the powers of observation – something beyond the natural.

> *Be kindly affectionate to one another with brotherly love, in honor giving preference to one another…* Romans 12:10

Giving preference means letting the other choose, not choosing for them. This type of love requires humility and trust in our Father. One another fellowship encourages our spiritual maturity.

Map 15 - The One Another Fellowship

Now may the God of patience and comfort grant you to be like-minded toward one another, according to Christ Jesus, that you may with one mind and one mouth glorify the God and Father of our Lord Jesus Christ. Therefore receive one another, just as Christ also received us, to the glory of God. Romans 15:5-7

One another fellowship empowers the renewal of our minds (i.e., transformation) through the appropriation of the mind of Christ. We become unified in thought and worship. Christ received us with sacrificial love. As the Father sent Him, so He sends us. It is for God's glory that we receive one another (i.e., to grant another access to one's heart).

Now therefore, it is already an utter failure for you that you go to law against one another. Why do you not rather accept wrong? Why do you not rather let yourselves be cheated? No, you yourselves do wrong and cheat, and you do these things to your brethren! 1Corinthians 6:7-8

Our ill-treatment of one another in the public square brings shame to Jesus Christ, and the rest of His Body. Our acceptance of being wronged protects Him and His Body.

And if one member suffers, all the members suffer with it; or if one member is honored, all the members rejoice with it. 1Corinthians 12:23-26

Our suffering and honor with one another is not an option, it is a reality of life in God's kingdom. The only way to avoid this reality is to disconnect from the Body. That is what we are doing when we live with indifference to our brothers and sisters in Christ.

For you, brethren, have been called to liberty; only do not use liberty as an opportunity for the flesh, but through love serve one another. Let us not become conceited, provoking one another, envying one another. Galatians 5:13, 26

Do not grumble against one another, brethren, lest you be condemned. Behold, the Judge is standing at the door! James 5:9

One of the saddest things to see are fellowships in close geographic proximity living apart from one another. Rather than serve each other, they glory in themselves. Satan uses this to set in motion a cycle of vain glory pursuit, envy, and one-upmanship.

We are called to a much higher witness of God's love for one another; as we see in the following verses.

I, therefore, the prisoner of the Lord, beseech you to walk worthy of the calling with which you were called, with all lowliness and gentleness, with longsuffering, bearing with one another in love, endeavoring to keep the unity of the Spirit in the bond of peace. Therefore, putting away lying, " Let each one of you speak truth with his neighbor," for we are members of one another. And be kind to one another, tenderhearted, forgiving one another, even as God in Christ forgave you. Ephesians 4:1-3,25,32

Once again, we see that we are not just members of Christ, but members of one another. What we do to each other, we do to ourselves. Furthermore, our worth as followers of Jesus Christ is measured by our bearing with one another in love.

And let us consider one another in order to stir up love and good works, not forsaking the assembling of ourselves together, as is the manner of some, but exhorting one another, and so much the more as you see the Day approaching. Hebrews 10:24-25

The issue is not how we assemble – from small groups to large denominations – but the heart we have for each other as we assemble. Is our desire for ourselves and our group, or for something greater? To fight the temptations of sectarianism, we must be intentional about our assembling together in love for the whole Body of Christ.

Map 15 - The One Another Fellowship

Finally, all of you be of one mind, having compassion for one another; love as brothers, be tenderhearted, be courteous; not returning evil for evil or reviling for reviling, but on the contrary blessing, knowing that you were called to this, that you may inherit a blessing. 1Peter 3:8-9

Our love for one another is no less than our calling, and the source of our inheritance in Christ. This alone should be enough motivation; but God, knowing how difficult such fellowship would be for us, promised even more.

No one has seen God at any time. If we love one another, God abides in us, and His love has been perfected in us. 1John 4:12

God has established the conditions and the promises of His kingdom. His abiding in us, and the perfection of His love in us, are conditional on our love for one another.

Dear God, have mercy on us! Transform us into the people (plural) that will follow your plan, and follow it your way. We know there is no other. We lay down our lives, that we would find the life of love - whatever the cost. In Jesus' name. Amen.

Conclusion

I confess that this is the most challenging facet of my walk with the Lord. My heart is so far from the revelation of these verses. The church in America is so divided. How far have we drifted from God's plab? How did we get here? More importantly, how do we find God's perfect will in our love for one another?

Application

Leaders in the Workplace are in a unique position to experience God's blessing through the "one another" fellowship. By bringing together employees, customers, and others within their spheres of influence, Leaders in the Workplace will be used by God to break down the walls that separate us. The church in the Workplace will once again experience the power of love in community, and the world will see God in our love for one another. Answer God's call and receive your kingdom inheritance in Christ.

Reckoning

All Christians are members of one another. No part of the Body can survive in isolation.

Assignment

1. Review your notes and the Scripture passages from this week's module. Share the ones that are most meaningful with someone in your spheres of influence.

2. Ask God to search your heart (Psalm 139:23-24) for the anxiety, prejudice and motivation that is weakening the Body of Christ. Confess your sin and receive His forgiveness and deliverance (1John 1:9).

3. Exercise at least one act of "one another" service for someone within your spheres of influence that is outside your denomination. Commit to making this a regular occurrence.

Devotion

From Chuck Colson : How Now Shall We Live? (pp. 303-304)

The new millennium is a time for Christians to celebrate, to raise our confidence, to blow trumpets, and to fly the flag high. This is the time to make a compelling case that Christianity offers the most rational and realistic hope for both personal redemption and social renewal.

Map 15 - The One Another Fellowship

But if we are to have an impact on our culture, the beginning point must be to take our stand united in Christ, making a conscious effort among all true believers to come together across racial, ethnic, and confessional lines. In His high-priestly prayer, Jesus prayed fervently that we would be one with one another, as He is one with the Father. Why? *So that the world will know* that He is the Christ (see John 17:20-23). The unavoidable implication of Jesus' words is that Christian unity is the key to evangelism and cultural renewal. Much of the church's weakness can be traced to its inability or unwillingness to obey the command to strive for unity in Christ.

The Map Maker's Guide

Map 16 - Who Is Serving Who?

Spiritual Exercise

The plans we pursue are either from God or they are distractions. There really are no gray areas in His kingdom. There is a center of God's will for every one of His children. The key to finding that center is surrendering to God's purpose, and sacrificing for His plan.

> *Prayer does not mean that I am to bring God down to my thoughts and my purposes, and bend his government according to my foolish, silly, and sometimes sinful notions. Prayer means that I am to be raised up into feeling, into union and design with him; that I am to enter into his counsel and carry out his purpose fully.* D. L. Moody
>
> *God does not exist to answer our prayers, but by our prayers we come to discern the mind of God.* Oswald Chambers
>
> *If anyone is willing to do His will, he will know of the teaching, whether it is of God or whether I speak from Myself.* John 7:17 (NASB)

Knowing the will of God is a challenge for most Christians. God has given us the keys to hearing: Trust, humility, fear, surrender, and a heart turned toward obedience. It is not His intention that we "work up" any of these. They have been given as expressions of His grace. Our part is choosing to take hold of them – like a child receiving a gift.

Prayer

Father God, may Your kingdom come and Your will be done, on earth as it is in heaven. We surrender to Your ways and thoughts for the fullness of our lives, but particularly in the area of relationship with You. Teach us to pray. It is by grace that we have been saved. Thank You. It is by grace that we will lay hold of the intimacy You have given each of us. We receive it; in Jesus' name. Amen.

Introduction

In their appointed positions, it is critical that Leaders in the Workplace understand "who is serving who" to accomplish God's ultimate purposes. Who is serving who? The answer to this question will challenge your thinking, renew your mind, and change the way you "serve God".

Perhaps you have been where I once found myself: Having returned from a long period of wandering from the Lord, I desperately desired to make up for lost time. And so began many years of serving Him. Sounds good, doesn't it.

The problem is I had it all wrong. I wasn't serving God the way He wanted me to serve; and I didn't have someone to disciple me in the way I should go about it. Consequently, much of my serving was wasted effort. My hope and prayer is that the Holy Spirit will give you a renewed understanding about serving God; that you will experience the fullness of His grace in your kingdom adventure.

Map 16 - Who is Serving Who?

Definition

Paradigm (noun): A typical example or pattern of something; a worldview underlying the theories and methodology of a particular scientific subject. www.google.com

Worldview (noun): The overall perspective from which one sees and interprets the world; a collection of beliefs about life and the universe held by an individual or a group. www.thefreedictionary.com

Everyone has a worldview; and everyone has a paradigm regarding the nature of God and His church (i.e., how it works). Some hold onto their worldviews and paradigms quite firmly, resisting anything new or uncomfortable. As we've discovered, this limits our revelation of the mysteries of God. To fully experience the adventure of searching out the kingdom of God – and to be made free by the truths found there – we must not resist the truth's work in our lives.

There are times when the mysteries of God fly in the face of our paradigms about God and our relationship with Him. This is one of those times. It may be helpful to remember that the Holy Spirit is leading us. He is a capable and loving teacher.

Searching Out the Matter
(All Scripture references, but those noted, are NKJV; Thomas Nelson, Inc.; footnotes excluded)

Who is Serving Who?

Let's start with the assumption that God needs something from us; that there is some service we can do for Him.

> *Indeed heaven and the highest heavens belong to the LORD your God, also the earth with all that is in it.* Deuteronomy 10:14

> *The earth is the LORD's, and all its fullness,*
> *The world and those who dwell therein.* Psalm 24:1

> *If I were hungry, I would not tell you;*
> *For the world is Mine, and all its fullness.* Psalm 50:12

The LORD owns all He needs and, as much as we might think differently, He is not in the habit of telling us when He needs it. Seems like one of those "duh!" things once you think about it. However, most of us would have to admit we really want Him to need us. We want to give back to the One who has done so much for us.

But what would we do? Wash His car? Buy Him dinner? Shine His shoes? There is a humbling aspect to this whole matter of serving God. Once we accept the fact that He really doesn't need us, we can begin to experience just how much He wants us – and how much He is willing to do for His children.

> *For since the beginning of the world*
> *Men have not heard nor perceived by the ear,*
> *Nor has the eye seen any God besides You,*
> *Who acts for the one who waits for Him.* Isaiah 64:4

Our God is different from all other gods because He intends to act for us – after we wait for Him. Let that sink in. Instead of waiting on us to act, God is waiting on us to wait – so He can act for us. Why would He do such a thing?

> *For the eyes of the LORD run to and fro throughout the whole earth, to show Himself strong on behalf of those whose heart is loyal to Him.* 2Chronicles 16:9

Map 16 - Who is Serving Who?

The LORD is looking to show Himself strong; and He knows that we are the ones that need His help – not the other way around. It is exactly the reason He sent His son.

> *Even to your old age, I am He,*
> *And even to gray hairs I will carry you!*
> *I have made, and I will bear;*
> *Even I will carry, and will deliver you.* Isaiah 46:4

In God's economy, it is the strong that serve the weak. This is the heart of a God that is *agapē* – God's sacrificial love. It was also the heart of His Son; for He is a good King.

> *For even the Son of Man did not come to be served, but to serve, and to give His life a ransom for many.* Mark 10:45

> *And He was handed the book of the prophet Isaiah. And when He had opened the book, He found the place where it was written:*

> > *"The Spirit of the Lord is upon Me,*
> > *Because He has anointed Me*
> > *To preach the gospel to the poor;*
> > *He has sent Me to heal the brokenhearted,*
> > *To proclaim liberty to the captives*
> > *And recovery of sight to the blind,*
> > *To set at liberty those who are oppressed;*
> > *To proclaim the acceptable year of the Lord."* Luke 4:17-19

The Father sent His Son to serve His subjects. I hope this has overwhelmed you as it does me. If there's a lump in your throat right now, don't resist the urge to praise our Father and our Savior King. Go ahead: Give Him praise!

Then Who Do I Serve?

Now that we are beginning to understand who is serving who in our relationship to God, let's turn to the question that is niggling at the back of your mind; something like, "We are suppose to be serving, right? Doesn't the Bible say something about that?"

Of course we are; and, of course, it does.

> *So Jesus said to them again, "Peace to you! As the Father has sent Me, I also send you."* John 20:21

We have been sent by our King exactly as He was sent… to serve others.

> *As each one has received a gift, minister it to one another, as good stewards of the manifold grace of God.* 1Peter 4:10

> *And the King will answer and say to them, "Assuredly, I say to you, inasmuch as you did it to one of the least of these My brethren, you did it to Me."* Matthew 25:40

God's way in serving is for His children to serve each other (i.e., love one another). In doing so, we minister to Him – completing the circle and satisfying our desire to love Him as He first loved us.

It is important to recognize that serving others is harder than serving God. As someone has said, sheep are ornery, smelly animals. They bite and they wander off. And they don't regularly return favors. Therefore, we must regularly and intentionally commit ourselves to the sacrificial service of others. It is a battle against Satan, the world and our flesh that we must aggressively fight.

Map 16 - Who is Serving Who?

The Return on His Investment

God has been very clear and direct about our working relationship with Him. He serves us as we serve each other. But why would He serve us? Is it just for our benefit – because He loves us? Or, does He get something out of it, too?

While it is certainly true that God serves us out of His love, there is more to the story. In this case, there is something that God receives in His service to us – something like a return on His investment.

> *Call upon Me in the day of trouble;*
> *I will deliver you, and you shall glorify Me.* Psalm 50:15

> *And whatever you ask in My name, that I will do, that the Father may be glorified in the Son.* John 14:13

By showing Himself strong on our behalf; by responding to our need for His deliverance; by doing whatever we ask in His will, God is glorified.

Furthermore, God expects His investment in us to have an impact for His kingdom. Most everyone is familiar with the parable of the talents, but God's expectation and His provision go far beyond finances. God has also entrusted authority to His Son. His Son has entrusted it to us.

> *And when He had said this, He breathed on them, and said to them, "Receive the Holy Spirit. If you forgive the sins of any, they are forgiven them; if you retain the sins of any, they are retained.* John 20:22-23

> *Now all things are of God, who has reconciled us to Himself through Jesus Christ, and has given us the ministry of reconciliation... and has committed to us the word of reconciliation. Now then, we are ambassadors for Christ...* 2Corinthians 5:18-20

The very ministry that Jesus came to institute – the ministry of reconciliation – has been invested in us as His ambassadors. As His ambassadors, we have been given influence and authority to serve those within our spheres of influence.

How does this influence, authority and ministry manifest itself? Much more dramatically than many of us have been taught to expect.

> *Let your light so shine before men, that they may see your good works and glorify your Father in heaven.* Matthew 5:16

When you follow God's way, what men see in "your good works" will not be something that will have them saying, "Isn't he a wonderful builder?", or "I think she is the best teacher in the church." Instead, they will be left awed at the presence and power of God. It is Him, and not our work, that people will notice. But, how is this possible?

> *For we are to God the fragrance of Christ among those who are being saved and among those who are perishing. To the one we are the aroma of death leading to death, and to the other the aroma of life leading to life. And who is sufficient for these things?* 2Corinthians 2:15-16

> *Not that we are sufficient of ourselves to think of anything as being from ourselves, but our sufficiency is from God, who also made us sufficient as ministers of the new covenant, not of the letter but of the Spirit; for the letter kills, but the Spirit gives life.* 2Corinthians 3:5-6

These verses remind us that it is not our sufficiency that accomplishes these things, but God. This is not about our measuring up, but about our surrender and sacrifice – so the light that is His life can shine out from us; that His sufficiency would be to His glory.

Map 16 - Who is Serving Who?

Now, going back to Matthew 5:16, we recognize that there will be "good works". These are works that we were created to walk in (Ephesians 2:10). The good works that are done according to God's plan will be the greater than works Jesus spoke of in John 14:12. They will be works that glorify the Father.

The Nature of Our Influence

The way God constructs our spheres of influence may not always be what we expect, but He is the King; the Grand Orchestrator whom we can trust. There are no coincidences for His children. That includes the types of people He has given for the Workplace Leader to serve.

Influence in the kingdom of God most often occurs in parent-child relationships: Boss to employees, elected official to constituents, teacher to students, etc. However, this is not always the case; and we must be careful to avoid being confined in our thinking by the world's hierarchies.

God also gives Leaders in the Workplace spiritual influence with customers, peers, and partners. Additionally, the most spiritually mature Christians may be the lowest in the corporate hierarchy, and still have the most spiritual influence. The most mature Christian in the Boardroom carries the authority of God for everyone in attendance.

Leaders in the Workplace must seek God's wisdom and revelation regarding the influence they have been given – be it obvious or hidden – to make disciples and transform communities. They must go to Him humbly – without presumption or pretense – seeking to know who He has drawn into their spheres of influence for inclusion in His plan.

Conclusion

Let's face it: The expectations are high. Very high! There is lot riding on our participation in God's plan. We don't want to fail Him; and other people are counting on us (whether they know it or not).

A wise pastor once told me, "Whom God appoints, God anoints." Much depends on our "taking hold of that for which Christ Jesus took hold of us." (Philippians 3:12) We must, by grace, through faith, walk into our anointing. We must pray that God will give us the grace to feel the weight of the mantle of influence and authority He has given each of His Leaders in the Workplace.

Application

God desires to show Himself strong on your behalf – if you are one whose heart is loyal to Him. Those that are loyal are the ones that share His desire to serve others. Now is a good time to renew your search for the ones that He has orchestrated into your sphere of influence; and look for opportunities to sacrificially serve them.

Reckoning

God will be strong on my behalf.

Assignment

It is important to know who we are in God's plan and who He wants us to be.

1. What are your leadership roles in the Body of Christ and your community (e.g., employer, deacon, chair of _____)? Describe your relationship with the fellowships, ministries and groups with whom you are involved. Ask God to clarify His intention for your involvement in each of them.

2. Each day this week, pray the prayer of Psalm 139:23-24. Ask God to reveal any role you may have dismissed out of fear, misunderstanding, false-humility or disobedience.

Map 16 - Who is Serving Who?

3. Consider carefully any opportunities you have been offered to lead a group, ministry or fellowship. Let God, through the Holy Spirit, reveal the ones that are His intention (versus the ones that are distractions).

Devotion

Who Must I Serve? (A Confession)
From Rob Streetman, The inLight Adventure Blog

I must confess that, in my flesh, I would rather serve God than serve other people. God is holy and deserves my service. People are difficult, lazy and, well, undeserving of my service. They don't always have the means to reward me for my service. So, I have been easily deceived into thinking that the highest service is service to God; and service to others is secondary, even unnecessary.

This deception has had a tragic impact on my relationship with others, and my relationship with God. It has inhibited my spiritual growth, and the growth of those I am responsible to disciple. It has separated me from the Body of Christ, and the love in them that God has for me. It has had me serving God for His acceptance, and reflecting that lie onto others. Like I said... it's tragic.

But - praise God! – I have been made free by this truth: God doesn't need me to serve Him. He wants me to serve others. And not just for them, but for me. Loving one another has broken me out of the isolation chamber that imprisoned my life in Him. I am free to love, and be loved, as God intends. I have learned that *agapē* is sacrificial love – a love that requires action. I have experienced that love flowing through me, from God to others. I am excited that there is infinitely more of that life in me... for others. I pray the same is true for you.

Loving Him and you more,

Rob

The Map Maker's Guide

Map 17 - Our Identity in Christ

Spiritual Exercise

One of the mistakes I made in my early Christian life was to assume that the verse I heard someone quote was the whole thought of the passage. As I began to search for deeper meaning, I discovered that the rest of the truth helped me understand more of what had been a mystery to me. Here is one example.

> *Therefore, my beloved, as you have always obeyed, not as in my presence only, but now much more in my absence, work out your own salvation with fear and trembling; for it is God who works in you both to will and to do for His good pleasure.* Philippians 2:12-13

When all I knew of this passage was "work out your own salvation with fear and trembling", it left me confused. Why should I do anything regarding salvation with fear (*phobos*) and trembling? God didn't give us a "spirit of fear". What should I be trembling with fear about?

Then someone showed me verse 13, and understanding came. My fear should be that I might miss or get in the way of God's work in me. This discovery led to another.

> *Do not fear, little flock, for it is your Father's good pleasure to give you the kingdom.* Luke 12:32

How awesome to discover that God's good pleasure is to give us His kingdom!! As we prepare to turn our hearts to God in prayer, let's praise Him for the full revelation of His word. Let's commit ourselves to His good pleasure; and ask Him for a personal understanding about His will and work in us.

Prayer

Father God, You are a mystery to us, but only because we have not sought You with our whole hearts. Forgive us. Help us. Thank you for making surrender all the more easy, as we come to understand You in our searching. Thank you for encouraging us in such a loving way. We love because You first loved us. The revelation of Your love is our heart's desire – that we may love You and others more. In Jesus' name. Amen.

Introduction

In the one another fellowship, every member has a role to play – an identity, in Christ, for service to the fellowship. One of the Workplace Leader's primary responsibilities is helping each one in their spheres of influence discover that identity. Doing so will free them from one of the enemy's most effective deceptions; that of our identity in Christ.

Perhaps more dramatically than at any other time in her history, the church has lost her identity. Don't believe me? When was the last time you saw the royal priesthood in action? How about a temple of God being, well, a temple of God? Smelled the aroma of Christ lately? Where are the "greater than" works that Christ promised for those who believe?

We have been deceived about our identity in God's story. Like the man in James epistle, we have forgotten who we are (vv. 1:22-25). This is particularly important for Leaders in the Workplace; for without a true sense of identity, we are additionally deceived about our authority and influence. Consequently, the people God has called to lead the implementation of His plans are inadequately prepared.

Map 17 - Our Identity in Christ

Sadly, most Christians have allowed the world to define their identity. From well-intentioned parents, teachers and pastors, to mean-spirited oppressors, controllers and bullies, we have heard and accepted an identity that is much lower than our Creator intends. Of course, Satan is behind much of this. He is conspiring with our carnal nature, suggesting that we settle for less.

Finding and keeping our identity is one of most challenging and critical battles we will face. Peter, Susan, Edmund and Lucy had no idea of their importance in the battle for Narnia until they discovered that they were the Kings and Queens. Like them, it is time we discovered who we are – not for ourselves, but for God's glory and for His kingdom. Experiencing joy and power in His plan is dependent on our participation in the full identity and influence we have been assigned.

Definition

Authority (*exousia*): power of choice, liberty of doing as one pleases; physical and mental power (the ability or strength with which one is endued, which he either possesses or exercises); the power of authority (influence) and of right (privilege). *Blue Letter Bible Outline of Biblical Usage*

Influence (noun): The capacity to have an effect on the character, development, or behavior of someone or something, or the effect itself. *www.google.com*

The Greek word for authority, *exousia*, is more often translated "power" (in no less than sixty-nine verses). *Exousia* is the delegated authoritative power of God. With it comes privilege and influence. While the world holds authority to mean something like "the power to tell others what to do", the authority delegated by God is the privilege to influence the world as instruments of God's power.

Consider for a moment what this means about God's love for mankind. He has delegated His power to His children that they might overcome the Evil One; that many might be saved. He has made them a vessel for that power; that they would learn to be instruments and weapons of righteousness; for He is preparing the Bride to co-reign with His Son.

Searching Out the Matter
(All Scripture references, but those noted, are NKJV; Thomas Nelson, Inc.; footnotes excluded)

This lesson will carry us deeper into the mysteries of God. However, it is important to note that you will not find your identity and influence defined here. Your identity is something you must discover by the Holy Spirit. The questions you will find are provided as a help in your search. They are not rhetorical. I challenge you to consider each one carefully – to use them with the intention of hearing from God. Faith comes by hearing; and hearing by the (*rhema*, spoken) word of God.

A Different Perspective

In the Old Testament, the people of God were led by kings, priests and prophets. Under the New Covenant, the leadership identities have changed. Jesus is now the King over many kings; and everyone in His kingdom is a royal priest. Prophet is now part of a five-fold gift given by the King; along with pastor, teacher, evangelist and apostle. Quite a few new identities have been added (e.g., disciple, bondservant, ambassador, elder and deacon).

As we explore our identity in Christ, lay aside how you see your identity, and consider what it means to Christ. Put yourself in His shoes. Why has He identified you the way He has – both generally (as a member of the church) and in your specific roles? What are His expectations of you?

It will also be helpful to consider your identity in Christ's kingdom from the perspective of His followers within your spheres of influence. Who you are to the Body of Christ says something profound about your identity. What are their expectations of you? And what does Christ desire you to be to them, and for them?

Map 17 - Our Identity in Christ

Lastly, even the lost are drawn to you by the Holy Spirit. Why are they coming to you? What do they hope to see or find?

Each of these identities comes with the King's delegated authority, influence and power to serve the church and impact a lost and fallen world. There are no coincidences for God's children. Every Leader in the Workplace has been placed in spheres of influence that God intends to transform. God has appointed each leader to an assignment that will require the assistance and fellowship of other individuals within their spheres of influence. We must get to know, and leverage, each other's identities.

It can be a challenge to consider your identity and influence from another's perspective. We have become such self-focused people. You will have to be other-focused and self-controlled. I assure you it will be worth the effort; for you will discover that there is more to you than you have believed.

Our Foundational Identity

God has established three identities that all Christians are called to fulfill in the New Covenant: Disciple, bondservant, and ambassador.

> Then He said to them, "Follow Me, and I will make you fishers of men. Matthew 4:19
>
> Now when He got into a boat, His disciples followed Him. Matthew 8:23
>
> A disciple is not above his teacher, but everyone who is perfectly trained will be like his teacher. Luke 6:40

Disciples follow their teacher and are made to be like him. As we have learned, this is much different than "student". Students seek to learn only what they need to know, while disciples surrender to a relationship with the One that will make them – to know Him and His life fully.

> For this is the will of God, that by doing good you may put to silence the ignorance of foolish men — as free, yet not using liberty as a cloak for vice, but as bondservants of God. 1Peter 2:15-16

A bondservant of God is one who has volunteered to serve; believing that life under the Master's reign is better than a life of independence. A bondservant is eager to know his Master's heart and to do his bidding.

> Now then, we are ambassadors for Christ, as though God were pleading through us: we implore you on Christ's behalf, be reconciled to God. 2Corinthians 5:20

It is important to recognize that we are ambassadors for Christ, responsible to His kingdom, and not to the kingdoms where we have been sent. We are the *ekklesia*, called out to transform cultures, not become subordinate to them. Ambassadors carry with them the rights of the kingdom of origin. As we shall see, the responsibilities and rights of our Master are far greater than those of this world.

The lifestyle of a bondservant-disciple-ambassador looks very different from what we see in the lifestyle of the average Christian – different mindset, different activity, etc. What do you think our King expects to see when He looks out over His kingdom people? What should He see in your life? What influence do you carry?

Greater Than...

Now that we have an understanding of our foundational identity, let's look as Christ's description of us as His followers.

> For I say to you, among those born of women there is not a greater prophet than John the Baptist; but he who is least in the kingdom of God is greater than he. Luke 7:28
>
> Most assuredly, I say to you, he who believes in Me, the works that I do he will do also; and greater works than these he will do, because I go to My Father. John 14:12

Map 17 - Our Identity in Christ

Have you considered what Christ must have imagined for those that would follow Him? Don't let your opinion of yourself limit your consideration of this. What exploits filled His anticipations for us? Greater than the prophets! Doing greater things than He! What does He expect His designated leaders to accomplish with those within their spheres of influence?

Kings and Priests

> To Him who loved us and washed us from our sins in His own blood, and has made us kings and priests to His God and Father, to Him be glory and dominion forever and ever. Amen. Revelation 1:5b-6

> But you are a chosen generation, a royal priesthood, a holy nation, His own special people, that you may proclaim the praises [virtues] of Him who called you out of darkness into His marvelous light; who once were not a people but are now the people of God, who had not obtained mercy but now have obtained mercy. 1Peter2:9-10

God and His children, in heaven and on earth, know that you have been made a king and a priest – together a royal priesthood. What does this mean to Him, and to them? Are we carrying the demeanor of a king – or that of a pauper?

> Coming to Him as to a living stone, rejected indeed by men, but chosen by God and precious, [5] you also, as living stones, are being built up a spiritual house, a holy priesthood, to offer up spiritual sacrifices acceptable to God through Jesus Christ. 1Peter 2:4-6

The holy priesthood were the only ones that could enter the Holy of Holies, where God dwelt between the cherubim and seraphim. What did the people think of those that walked worthy of such an anointing and privilege? What influence did they have with the people?

Christ's Gifts to the Church

Expectations are a normal part of life. We are surrounded by them. Our employer expects us to perform at an acceptable level. Our tennis or bridge partner expects us to keep our head in the game. And our children... well, our children expect more than we ever imagined someone could expect of another human being.

Drowned in the expectations of those we know and love are the expectations of the One we love most of all. What do we do with the expectations of the Gift Giver?

> But to each one of us grace was given according to the measure of Christ's gift. And He Himself gave some to be apostles, some prophets, some evangelists, and some pastors and teachers, for the equipping of the saints for the work of ministry, for the edifying of the body of Christ, till we all come to the unity of the faith and of the knowledge of the Son of God, to a perfect man, to the measure of the stature of the fullness of Christ; Ephesians 4:7,11-13

Did you know that Christ gave these gifts to the church? Have you ever considered that you might be one of them? Have you asked Him which gift He intends for you to be for Him and His church? What do these gifts and identities mean to Him and them? What should the church anticipate from you as His gift? What influence have you been given to accomplish Christ's intention? What is the consequence if these gifts are not in operation?

Furthermore, what about the "positions" of elder and deacon?

> Is anyone among you sick? Let him call for the elders of the church, and let them pray over him, anointing him with oil in the name of the Lord. And the prayer of faith will save the sick, and the Lord will raise him up. And if he has committed sins, he will be forgiven. James 5:14-15

> For those who have served well as deacons obtain for themselves a good standing and great boldness in the faith which is in Christ Jesus. 1Timothy 3:13

Map 17 - Our Identity in Christ

What is Christ and His Body looking for out of these individuals? Are we taking full advantage of their anointing for the spiritual and physical needs of the fellowship? Why not? Are you one of them?

The Temple of God

Lastly, let us considered our identity in the world – with those lost and wandering outside the Kingdom of God. Have you ever considered what it means to be the temple of God on the earth?

> *And what agreement has the temple of God with idols? For you are the temple of the living God. As God has said:*
>
> > *"I will dwell in them*
> > *And walk among them.*
> > *I will be their God,*
> > *And they shall be My people."* 2Corinthians 6:16
>
> *So Jesus said to them again, "Peace to you! As the Father has sent Me, I also send you." And when He had said this, He breathed on them, and said to them, "Receive the Holy Spirit. If you forgive the sins of any, they are forgiven them; if you retain the sins of any, they are retained."* John 20:21-23

We are the temple of the New Covenant; dedicated for the habitation of God. Like temples past, the presence and glory of God should fill us, and we should become the place where God can be seen and experienced. Most important to Jesus here, we are to be the place where the rest of humanity will know that God works on their behalf; to repair all that has been broken; to know our God forgives and restores. God established the temple as a holy place of sacrifice, forgiveness, atonement, meeting, and restoration. Those in the world that are drawn by the Holy Spirit, though they may not know it, are looking for this in us.

Conclusion

Now that we know God has planted a desire in our hearts, and surrounded us with fellowship for the adventure, we must continue to search out the center of God's will in the identity He has given us. This may be an identity we have already been given – explicitly or implicitly. It may be one that He is waiting for us to step into. We may be resisting it – out of fear, disobedience, misunderstanding or false-humility. It is time we stepped into the identity and influence given to each of us individually, and as a fellowship, by God Almighty.

Application

The things of God are foolishness to the world. This includes the way we think of ourselves. We must resist the deception of the enemies of God to dumb down our identity. On the other hand, we must be careful to avoid presumption. The only way to know our personal identity and spheres of influence is to ask and receive the Lord's revelation.

Reckoning

My identity and influence in this life is beyond the world's assessment – it is of an eternal kingdom.

Assignment

1. Review your answers to the questions asked throughout this lesson. Discuss the ones that most impacted you with someone in your spheres of influence.

2. In a two column chart record what God has had to say about your identity (column 1) and your influence potential (column 2). Periodically review this as a reminder of your identity and influence for the kingdom and glory of God.

Map 17 - Our Identity in Christ

3. Revisit the Sphere of Influence tool with consideration of your identity and influence for those God has placed there. What are you to each one of them?

Devotion

The Conflict of Dreams
From Rob Streetman, The inLight Adventure Blog

Dear Dreamers,

There is something wrong with the church in America. If that comes as a surprise to you, then I strongly (but tenderly) suggest you get your head out of the sand. The statistics are irrefutable: Divorce and abortion rates the same in the church as in the world; 65 – 87% of college freshman, who were raised in Christian families, are leaving the church; the total dollars spent by the church in America divided by the number of baptisms - $1.55 million. The question is no longer "Do we have a problem?", but "What can be done about it?"

Personally, I have not given up hope in God's grace and mercy for the church in American. I believe that His eyes are still roaming, to and fro across this Earth (and our nation), looking for those in whom He can show Himself strong. I just wonder how much more He will tolerate. It is time for decisive action; action that will not come from the corporate church, but from each individual and family.

The answer is radical, but simple.

I am convinced that every Christian must intentionally, and solemnly, return the American Dream – trade it back in – for the dream God has had for you since before time began. As I've said before, the American Dream has cast a spell on the church in America. We have drunk deeply of its potion, and have become drunk with its intoxication. It is impossible to overestimate the damage our worldly drunkenness and stupor has brought down on our children, grandchildren... Oh, Lord, when will it stop?

Let me be clear – the American Dream and God's dream are not the same. It is an insult to Him to even suggest such a thing. The abundant life is not measured in square footage, retirement savings and legacies. America is no longer a Christian nation. America is more like the world than many nations on this Earth. And friendship with the world is enmity toward God. When will we stop investing in, and depending on, the kingdoms of this world? Are we not called to be fully committed to the kingdom of God?

Dear brethren, we are so far from God's dream for us that it's just too difficult to describe it in terms that are understandable in our current situation. In fact, it would be better to challenge you with seeking that perspective from Him and His word. Here are a few good starting points:

> But you are a chosen generation, a royal priesthood, a holy nation, His own special people, that you may proclaim the praises of Him who called you out of darkness into His marvelous light; who once were not a people but are now the people of God, who had not obtained mercy but now have obtained mercy. 1Peter 2:9-10

> ...that you may know what is the hope of His calling, what are the riches of the glory of His inheritance in the saints, and what is the exceeding greatness of His power toward us who believe, according to the working of His mighty power... Ephesians 1:18-19

Please, please, please, don't stop with a mental assent to these verses. Take this to the Lord and ask Him to show you how much greater His dream is for you and your family – not in the sweet-by-and-by, but in the abundance of His life right now.

And ask for the grace to repent of such a tragic, foolish transaction. Our children's eternal lives depend on it.

Your fellow ambassador,

Rob

The Map Maker's Guide

Map 18 - Disciple Making God's Way

Spiritual Exercise

So I say to you, ask, and it will be given to you; seek, and you will find; knock, and it will be opened to you. For everyone who asks receives, and he who seeks finds, and to him who knocks it will be opened. If a son asks for bread from any father among you, will he give him a stone? Or if he asks for a fish, will he give him a serpent instead of a fish? Or if he asks for an egg, will he offer him a scorpion? If you then, being evil, know how to give good gifts to your children, how much more will your heavenly Father give the Holy Spirit to those who ask Him! Luke 11:9-10

Prayer

Father God, we believe that you are the Giver of great gifts. You are Jehovah Jireh, our Provider. Yet most of us have experiences where You did not give us what we had asked for. We have sought, only to find dead ends. We have knock on doors that have not opened. We take this time to acknowledge that You are a perfect loving Father. We acknowledge that the only explanation is our selfish asking, our misguided seeking, and our knocking on the wrong doors. We desperately need the Holy Spirit to transform, guide and direct us. We believe You have given Him to those of Your children that have asked You. We submit to His counsel and work in our lives. In Jesus' name. Amen.

Introduction

A search for "disciple-making" on ChristianBook.com returns 311 resources. Just imagine, if you read one "disciple-making" book a week, it would take you six years to complete your research. At the end of those six years, you would likely discover that ten or twelve more had been written... and you might decide to write one yourself.

We do not lack for resources when it comes to the Great Commission. So what's gone wrong? Why is it taking so long for us to complete the primary task that Jesus Christ gave to us – over 2000 years ago?

First, it bears repeating that we have lost our focus toward God's primary purposes. As we discovered in the section on Surrendering to His Purpose, God lost three things when man rebelled against Him in the Garden of Eden – and He plans to get them back. What He has done for us – in the midst of His story – is so wonderful we find it hard not to assume that the story is about us.

That is what Satan would have us believe. Such deception keeps our eyes on ourselves and what God can do for us. It distracts us from the prize and the One Who offers it. The story of the Bible is about the Father, Son and Holy Spirit getting back what They lost. The story is about Them!

Secondly, we are failing in Christ's Commission because we are going about our assignment in a most unproductive way. It is by grace that we are given a part in God's story. To play a part, we must see His plan from His perspective; and realize that He has His own way for getting things done. His ways, though sometimes uncomfortable, are the best ways.

Map 18 - Disciple Making God's Way

Dietrich Bonhoeffer said, "Christianity without discipleship is always Christianity without Christ." Notice that he did not say "Christianity without evangelism…" Becoming disciple makers is the way we enter into the work God is doing to redeem the world to Himself.

Similarly, discipleship without Christ will not produce a Christian. Our problem is not so much our neglect of making disciples, but of trying to make them in the ways of our own invention. Christ will only involve Himself in the ways of His Father.

In this lesson, we will discover just how involved Christ is when we surrender and sacrifice ourselves to disciple making God's way.

Definition

Edify (*oikodomē*): (the act of) building, building up; the act of one who promotes another's growth in Christian wisdom, piety, happiness, holiness; a building (i.e. the thing built, edifice). *Blue Letter Bible Outline of Biblical Usage*

There is a mystery here. Edifying the Body of Christ is a part of disciple making (along with equipping and encouraging). It is a "building up" of the Body of Christ. We are commissioned to make disciples (to build them up, together), yet Christ said that He would build His church (Matthew 16:18). So who is doing the work?

Searching Out the Matter
(All Scripture references, but those noted, are NKJV; Thomas Nelson, Inc.; footnotes excluded)

How Did Jesus Do It?

Have you ever considered that Jesus could have died, been buried and rose again in less than a week? That is all the time it would have taken for Him to accomplish what many believe to be His only mission. So why was He about the Father's business for more than three years? It is simple: Because death, burial and resurrection was not His only mission.

Jesus Christ also came to show His disciples how we should live in the kingdom of God. Having completed that work, He commissioned them to do the same:

> *So Jesus said to them again, "Peace to you! As the Father has sent Me, I also send you."* John 20:21

Notice that Jesus was sent by the Father. This may be news to some. It may also be surprising that we are sent as the Father sent Him. Recognizing the deeper meaning of this, A. W. Tozer said, "Only a disciple can make a disciple." Tozer understood – as we must – that Jesus was not only the first disciple maker…

Jesus was also the first real disciple!

Let that sink in for a minute. As the first real disciple, Jesus is the One we can and should look to as our example. He was a disciple – and He made disciples – God's way. Therefore, as our example for both, it is important to fully understand that Jesus was a man. That's right: The Son of God was a son of man.

> *Let this mind be in you which was also in Christ Jesus, who, being in the form of God, did not consider it robbery to be equal with God, but made Himself of no reputation, taking the form of a bondservant, and coming in the likeness of men. And being found in appearance as a man, He humbled Himself and became obedient to the point of death, even the death of the cross.*
> Philippians 2:5-8

In making Himself "of no reputation" (meaning, "empty, void, deprived of force"), the Son of God became the Son of Man to show us what was possible for a son of man that becomes a son of God. To make the point,

Map 18 - Disciple Making God's Way

Jesus called Himself "Son of Man" approximately 10 times more than "Son of God". It was His favorite title for Himself.

He Could Do Nothing...

> *Then Jesus answered and said to them, "Most assuredly, I say to you, the Son can do nothing of Himself, but what He sees the Father do; for whatever He does, the Son also does in like manner.* John 5:19

Very early in His ministry, Jesus said that He could do nothing of Himself. The Son watches what the Father is doing, so the Son can do them. As we will soon discover, this is more than doing <u>as imitation</u>. It is doing <u>in participation</u> – where the Father does the work. Lastly, it is important to note that "the Son gives life to whom He – the Father – will". All that Jesus did was the will and work of the Father.

> *For as the Father has life in Himself, so He has granted the Son to have life in Himself, and has given Him authority to execute judgment also, because He is the Son of Man.* John 5:26-27

Why did the Father grant life to the Son? Because He, the Father, has life to give. Why did He give him authority? Because He is the Son of Man.

> *I can of Myself do nothing. As I hear, I judge; and My judgment is righteous, because I do not seek My own will but the will of the Father who sent Me.* John 5:30

Again Christ says, of Himself, that He can do nothing apart from the Father. He also said that His judgment was righteous; not because of anything He had done and not because of who He was; but because He sought the will of the Father. His mission was about the Father's will and work, not His own.

> *If I do not do the works of My Father, do not believe Me; but if I do, though you do not believe Me, believe the works, that you may know and believe that the Father is in Me, and I in Him.* John 10:37-38

Jesus is saying that our belief in Him should be based on Him doing the works of His Father. Whose works were they? They were the Father's works. And it was the works that proved the Father was in Him. In other words, the Father was doing His works through Christ.

> *Then Jesus cried out and said, "He who believes in Me, believes not in Me but in Him who sent Me. And he who sees Me sees Him who sent Me. I have come as a light into the world, that whoever believes in Me should not abide in darkness.* John 12:44-46

Belief in Christ is not just belief in Him, but in the Father, also. And the One we see is not just Him, but the Father. To appreciate the mystery of Christ's identification with the Father we must keep in mind that He has become a Son of Man. The mystery of this is almost too deep for our understanding, but Christ is trying to show us the normal life of a son of man that is a son of God.

> *For I have not spoken on My own authority; but the Father who sent Me gave Me a command, what I should say and what I should speak. And I know that His command is everlasting life. Therefore, whatever I speak, just as the Father has told Me, so I speak.* John 12:49-50

Next, Jesus points out that the Father has given Him a command that "is everlasting life". What is this command? I believe the Father has commanded Jesus to only say what He (the Father) is saying. It's not that the Father told Jesus what to say and He later said it. It's more like He is an instrument of God's voice, saying what the Father says, as the Father says it. We see this again later in Chapter 14.

> *He who does not love Me does not keep My words; and the word which you hear is not Mine but the Father's who sent Me.* John 14:24

139

Map 18 - Disciple Making God's Way

Jesus is saying that the very word that is coming out of His mouth is not His word. How could Jesus say that the works that He did and the words that He spoke were not His; they were the Father's? Let's back up a few verses to better understand their relationship.

> "If you had known Me, you would have known My Father also; and from now on you know Him and have seen Him." Philip said to Him, "Lord, show us the Father, and it is sufficient for us." Jesus said to him, "Have I been with you so long, and yet you have not known Me, Philip? He who has seen Me has seen the Father; so how can you say, 'Show us the Father'? Do you not believe that I am in the Father, and the Father in Me? The words that I speak to you I do not speak on My own authority; but the Father who dwells in Me does the works. Believe Me that I am in the Father and the Father in Me, or else believe Me for the sake of the works themselves. John 14:7-11

Again, Jesus is doing everything He can to reveal the Father – Who is in Him. It is the Father who does the work. The works were enough to prove that the Father was in Christ. It's like Jesus was saying, "Look at the works that you have seen. Don't you know that I cannot do them? I'm just a man. Someone more powerful than me had to do the works. That was my Father."

The works prove that the Father and He are one, because only the Father in Him could be doing the work that they are seeing. And that is why He could immediately say...

> Most assuredly, I say to you, he who believes in Me, the works that I do he will do also; and greater works than these he will do, because I go to My Father. And whatever you ask in My name, that I will do, that the Father may be glorified in the Son. If you ask anything in My name, I will do it. John 14:12-14

The Father's works that Jesus did are to be the same works that we do. More so, now that He has gone to the Father, the works will be greater. How can this be? The secret is found in what Jesus had to say about His disciples.

The Master's Disciples

One of Jesus' primary missions was to show us how to be disciples that make disciples. He did exactly what He expects of us. If we are to be productive disciples in the kingdom of God, we must become like Him. He made this clear in a number of ways. First, He told them directly:

> It is enough for a disciple that he be like his teacher, and a servant like his master. Matthew 10:25a

> So Jesus said to them again, "Peace to you! As the Father has sent Me, I also send you." John 20:21

We must not confuse "disciple" for "student". "Disciple" is much closer in meaning to our understanding of "apprentice". For example, a disciple spends considerable time with his teacher (versus visiting a classroom once a week). A disciple's intention was to become like his teacher – to take on the teacher's lifestyle and character.

An apprentice also expected to be made into a man that would, so to speak, carry on his Master's "trade". And that is what Jesus does with His disciples; with one significant distinction. Jesus did not commission the disciples to make disciples of themselves, but disciples like them – those that would "observe all things that I have commanded you". Today's disciple-makers are called to the very same commission.

We Can Do Nothing

You will recall that Jesus said, "I can of Myself do nothing." He said the same for us in the Parable of the True Vine:

> I am the vine, you are the branches. He who abides in Me, and I in him, bears much fruit; for without Me you can do nothing. If you abide in Me, and My words abide in you, you will ask what

Map 18 - Disciple Making God's Way

you desire, and it shall be done for you. By this My Father is glorified, that you bear much fruit; so you will be My disciples. John 15:5, 7-8

It is in this abiding – "without Me you can do nothing" – relationship that our desires are met, the Father is glorified, we are productive fruit bearers, and we become His disciples.

In our abiding, we must walk as Jesus walk:

He who says he abides in Him ought himself also to walk just as He walked. 1John 2:6

How did He walk? His most famous walk was the Via Delarosa.

And being found in appearance as a man, He humbled Himself and became obedient to the point of death, even the death of the cross. Philippians 2:8

This section is called Sacrificing for His Plan for this very reason. Jesus sacrificed His life by first deny Himself for the three-plus years He spent making disciples, and then by dying on the cross at Calvary. He requires nothing less of us:

Then He said to them all, "If anyone desires to come after Me, let him deny himself, and take up his cross daily, and follow Me. For whoever desires to save his life will lose it, but whoever loses his life for My sake will save it." Luke 9:23-24

Denying oneself is putting aside all self-interest, self-centeredness and self-awareness. It is laying down all desire to protect our life in this world. It is a fundamental step in our receiving His life; the life that shall save us (Romans 5:10) and enable us to walk as He walked.

Taking up our cross does not mean becoming a martyr; and it does not mean suffering through some form of affliction. The Romans forced the one being crucified to carry a portion of their cross as a sign of their surrender to the nation they had been rebelling against. Our cross is a sign of our surrender… daily.

The following are a number of other ways Jesus demonstrated and instructed His followers in making disciples God's way.

Not Our Will

Looking back at John 5:30, we hear Jesus saying, "…I do not seek My own will but the will of the Father who sent Me." In the same way, through Matthew, He warns us:

Not everyone who says to Me, "Lord, Lord," shall enter the kingdom of heaven, but he who does the will of My Father in heaven. Matthew 7:21

Paul picks up on this in His letter to the Philippians:

Therefore, my beloved, as you have always obeyed, not as in my presence only, but now much more in my absence, work out your own salvation with fear and trembling; for it is God who works in you both to will and to do for His good pleasure. Philippians 2:12-13

As the Father was in Jesus, He is now in us – working that His will and work would be done. Discovering and doing the Father's will is as important in our disciple making as it was with Jesus.

The Works We Will Do

In John 5:20, Jesus states that the Father "will show Him [Jesus] greater works than these". To His disciples, He promises that:

… he who believes in Me, the works that I do he will do also; and greater works than these he will do, because I go to My Father. John 14:12-14

As with His Son Jesus, God desires to do greater works with is adopted sons and daughters.

Map 18 - Disciple Making God's Way

The Light of the World

The very thing that Jesus proclaimed of Himself, He affirmed in His followers:

> *I have come as a light into the world, that whoever believes in Me should not abide in darkness.*
> John 12:46

> *You are the light of the world. A city that is set on a hill cannot be hidden.* Matthew 5:14

These are but a few of the ways that Jesus identified Himself with those that would be His disciples. Some we have covered (e.g., "love one another as I have loved you"); others are yet to be searched out. It may be that you are still asking yourself, "How can this be possible?" I encourage you to be patient. We will search this out in the section on Submitting to His Power.

For now, it is enough that we focus on God's plan for making disciples.

Conclusion

The key to disciple making God's way is walking as the Lord Jesus walked. Not "trying" to walk as He walked; nor walking something like He walked. It is not about imitating His life, but allowing His life to do what It naturally does, in the work we were created to walk in (Ephesians 2:10).

How He walked is carefully recorded in the Gospels. It was a walk of surrender, sacrifice and submission to the will and work of His Father. We can do no less and still call ourselves His disciples.

Making disciples has been called the Great Commission for a reason. It is filled with the greatness of the Lord's purpose, plan and power for ministry. Through it, God's children involve themselves in the greatness of God's story. Out of it, His way, truth and life greatly impact the world – for His great glory, name and kingdom.

But this is only possible if we make disciples God's way.

Application

If you are a Leader in the Workplace, then you are called to make disciples. To whom much is given, much is expected. You are expected to understand your commission and carry it out to the best of your ability. Most of the work will be His, for He will get the glory. Our responsibility is to choose and passionately pursue His way, His truth, and His life; and to share what we have with others.

Reckoning

He can do exceedingly abundantly above all that we ask or think, according to the power that works in us (Ephesians 3:20).

Assignment

1. Review your notes and the Scripture passages from this week's module. Share the ones that are most meaningful to someone in your spheres of influence.

2. How does this understanding of "disciple" change your perspective of the relationship you have with Jesus Christ? How does this impact the disciple making God is doing in you? How does this impact the disciple making God is doing through you?

3. Identify the three to twelve people that God has placed in your spheres of influence for you to be more intentional about making into disciples of Jesus Christ.

Map 18 - Disciple Making God's Way

Devotion

Enable Others to Succeed

From Rob Streetman, Marketplace Ministry Tip, Chapel Hill News and Views Magazine

I recently heard a successful business owner share his heart for his employees, and what he was doing to better understand who they were as people. One thing stood out to me: This owner's heart for their success; and not just success in their vocation. He wanted to know how they defined success in the whole of their life – vocation, family, and personal/spiritual – and what he could do to help them.

His comments got me thinking about what our businesses might look like if they were truly mission fields. Think about that for a minute. Don't be frightened by the prospect until you have considered it before God. Is He not your CEO? Does He not have access to cattle on a thousand hills? Is He not looking to and fro to show Himself strong on behalf of those that will be loyal to Him?

It will help to understand, and consider, that He is infinitely wise with His resources. If He truly owns "your" company, will He not see to its success? How does He measure success in employee relations if not by the way we love those He has brought under our leadership?

In his book, *The 21 Indispensable Qualities of a Leader*, John C. Maxwell says, "… the best leaders desire to serve others, not themselves." Servant Leaders lead in service toward others. Every godly leader has the desire in their heart to serve others in their spheres of influence. Surrender to that desire and the Lord will give it to you (Psalm 37:4). In the process you will become the best leader you can possibly be.

Marketplace Ministry Tip: Ask God to reveal the desire He has placed in your heart for your employees. Remember, He is a process-oriented problem solver, who will direct your steps in this adventure. Start with those that report directly to you. Once you show them you care about their success, in their whole life, bring them into the adventure by encouraging and enabling them to serve those under their leadership. Contact me (rob@inlightconsulting.com) if I can help you become one of the best leaders.

The Map Maker's Guide

Map 19 - Workplace Ministry Formation

Spiritual Exercise

Now this is the confidence that we have in Him, that if we ask anything according to His will, He hears us. And if we know that He hears us, whatever we ask, we know that we have the petitions that we have asked of Him. 1John 5:14-15

For since the beginning of the world
Men have not heard nor perceived by the ear,
Nor has the eye seen any God besides You,
Who acts for the one who waits for Him. Isaiah 64:4

Show me Your ways, O LORD;
Teach me Your paths.
Lead me in Your truth and teach me,
For You are the God of my salvation;
On You I wait all the day. Psalm 25:4-5

Prayer

Father God, we are waiting on You. We are waiting on you to show us Your ways and teach us Your paths; to lead us in Your truth. Father, we are waiting on You to act. And Father, we are waiting on You to reveal Your will. Even now, there are specific situations and relationships in our lives in which we are waiting to know Your will. We are waiting, ready to respond from a heart that You have made willing. We trust You, for You are steadfastly faithful. In Jesus Christ's name. Amen.

Introduction

As God reveals His plan for accomplishing the purposes He has for each of us, we discover that He has His own way for getting things done. His ways are the best ways. In *Making Disciples God's Way*, we discovered that Jesus has shown us how to be a disciple maker – by being a disciple Himself. We now know that a true disciple lives for His Master's will, only doing and saying what His Master is doing and saying.

To close out this section, we will explore Jesus' expectations for us as His disciple-making disciples. Most Christians are familiar with the Great Commission. Some also know that portions of Jesus Christ's commission are recorded in Mark, Luke and John; and in the beginning of Acts. It is time all Leaders in the Workplace became faithful stewards of the mysterious depths of possibility and responsibility found there.

What we will discover is adventure beyond our imagination. We must be careful to avoid becoming overwhelmed or discouraged. We must remember that the Father is working in us for His good pleasure; that we need only do what our Master is doing and say what He is saying. The Holy Spirit has been sent to guide us. Our first responsibility is to surrender and take the first step of sacrificial obedience. To help with that, we will close this lesson with some suggestions for ministry in your spheres of influence.

Map 19 - Workplace Ministry Formation

Definition

Equip (*katartizō*): To render fit, sound, complete; to mend (what has been broken or rent), to repair; to complete; to fit out, equip, put in order, arrange, adjust; to fit or frame for one's self, prepare; ethically: to strengthen, perfect, complete, make one what he ought to be. *Blue Letter Bible Outline of Biblical Usage*

Disciple-makers are called to equip the body of Christ, into the fullness of Christ, in the love of Christ. The Greek word translated equip was also used as a medical term for setting a bone during surgery. It is the same word used when the disciples were "mending" their nets. Therefore, equip is best understood as "making fully qualified for service".

Searching Out the Matter
(All Scripture references, but those noted, are NKJV; Thomas Nelson, Inc.; footnotes excluded)

How It Will Look – Jesus Christ's Expectations

Jesus was sent by God to make a way for our salvation and to show us what it means to be a disciple and a disciple maker. He only did what the Father was doing; and He did it God's way. His final instructions to the first disciples reveal the immediate blessings and the Father's expectations in our being made a disciple; and in making disciples His way.

As you read each account of Jesus Christ's commission, consider the highlights recorded here. Before you begin, let me remind you that these were His final words before His ascension; the last things He wanted them to remember.

Each word, phrase and concept likely contains meaning beyond your current understanding. Search out the matter. Reckon each one to be true; to be truth that will make you a disciple, and a disciple making transformation agent; to make you free to walk fully into this great adventure.

Matthew 28:16-20

1. Christ first established that He had been given the authority to commission them.
2. He expected them to go to all the nations.
3. Baptizing was an important expectation.
4. They were to do more than "teach" Christ's commands. They were to teach others to observe the commands. From Vines Dictionary, this means to "to watch over, preserve" – a word close to "steward".

Mark 16:14-20

1. Signs will follow those who believe.
2. These signs are supernatural and involve the spiritual realm.
3. Though it was His followers that went out and preached, it was the "Lord working" to confirm their preaching.

Luke 24:44-53

1. An understanding of the Old Testament was important – particularly as it relates to Christ.
2. Repentance and remission of sins are to be an important part of the message.
3. It was important to note that He blessed them with the "Promise of My Father" – the Holy Spirit.
4. The result was great joy, and them praising and blessing God.

Map 19 - Workplace Ministry Formation

John 20:19-23

1. Disciple making produces peace – the peace of God that transcends all understanding.
2. Evidence of Christ's suffering and sacrifice are a part of the disciple maker's character.
3. Jesus sends His disciple makers as the Father sent Him – to do only what He is doing. A properly made disciple has exchanged their life for Christ's.
4. The Holy Spirit is given by Christ, and must be received.
5. Incredibly, disciples are given the authority to forgive and retain sins. This speaks both to our identity as disciples of Jesus Christ and to our Heavenly Father's trust in His children.

Acts 1:4-8

1. There is not only a baptism in water, but one in the Holy Spirit. This baptism requires a "waiting".
2. This baptism "when the Holy Spirit comes upon you" precludes the disciple bearing witness to Jesus Christ, wherever they are sent.

And what was the result?

> *And with great power the apostles gave witness to the resurrection of the Lord Jesus. And great grace was upon them all.* Acts 4:33

These passages should give great hope to every Leader in the Workplace. If we will only make disciples God's way, the glory and power of God will be manifest in our families, fellowships and communities. The Great Commission will be great in the greatest sense. Didn't Christ say we would do greater things than even He did? Perhaps a return to the way God did it, through Christ, is what we need. Perhaps it is time to lay down the lesser ways for the great way that He left to us.

Where Do We Start?

Be Doers of the Word

> *But be doers of the word, and not hearers only, deceiving yourselves. For if anyone is a hearer of the word and not a doer, he is like a man observing his natural face in a mirror; for he observes himself, goes away, and immediately forgets what kind of man he was. But he who looks into the perfect law of liberty and continues in it, and is not a forgetful hearer but a doer of the work, this one will be blessed in what he does.* James 1:22-25

> *Assuredly, I say to you, among those born of women there has not risen one greater than John the Baptist; but he who is least in the kingdom of heaven is greater than he. And from the days of John the Baptist until now the kingdom of heaven suffers violence, and the violent take it by force. For all the prophets and the law prophesied until John.* Matthew 11:11-13

The challenges Leaders in the Workplace face are very real. Most Christians spend most of their waking hours in the Workplace. It should not be surprising that God has begun a movement there – strategically placing His people in positions of authority and influence. But, as Jesus warned, "the kingdom of heaven suffers violence, and the violent take it by force." Satan has ruled the Workplace for far too long.

The Lord has been given the necessary authority and He has promised to be with His disciples. No challenge is too great for Him; but, He will not do it without those He is training for the battle. As Leaders in the Workplace, we must become "doers of the word".

Being "doers of the word" requires commitment and reckoning; and it assumes a beginning – taking that first obedient step. Begin here and you will avoid deceiving yourself; you will not forget what kind of man (or woman) you are; and you will be blessed in the work you do. In the process, you will become a violent one that takes the Kingdom by force.

Map 19 - Workplace Ministry Formation

Find Your Platoon

God's ways are above our ways, as the heavens are above the earth (Isaiah 55:9). In other words, they are infinitely better. They are also less threatening and stressful than those created by mankind. So why not begin to be the church in the Workplace in the same way God led the early church:

> And they continued steadfastly in the apostles' doctrine and fellowship, in the breaking of bread, and in prayers. Then fear came upon every soul, and many wonders and signs were done through the apostles. Acts 2:42-43

As you can see, it was only after they continued steadfastly in the disciplines of Bible study, fellowship, communion and prayer that God showed up – and showed up BIG! The fear of the Lord came upon every soul (not just those in the church). Work only God could do was done through His Leaders in the Workplace.

So, begin with the basics; but do them all. Follow the prescription. Do them in the way God intends that they be done. Let me say that again: Do them in the way God has prescribed!!! This will take some study on the Leader's part:

- What does God want us to study?

- What does God's kind of "fellowship" look like? (Let me help you here: Be careful not to assume that it is accountability, sharing everything, etc.)

- What is the reality of communion? Is it symbol, or sacrament? What does it have to do with abiding?

- And how are we to pray?

I cannot express here how important this small beginning will be for the church in the Workplace. It may seem too simple, too easy. But this is God's grace for His children. So, find a few brothers and sisters in Christ and meet with them weekly. Commit this time to the four disciplines and to determining what the King wants you to do for the church in your spheres of influence.

Conclusion

To conclude this lesson, as well as this section on sacrificing for His plan, I would like to offer a few other "starting points" that are close to my heart. I hope and pray they will encourage you to continue sacrificing for His plan as we move on to explore Submitting for His Power.

Become an explorer for yourself and those in your spheres of influence. We have discussed a number of foundational elements of the joyful, Spirit-filled life; including finding God's desire for this season, relational prayer, abiding in Christ, surrender, and sacrifice. It is beyond this study to include them all. For example, some important elementary principles that have been left out include repentance, the pursuit of holiness, and the doctrine of baptisms. Hopefully, you have been encouraged by the Holy Spirit to continue exploring these and the other mysteries of God.

> Jesus answered and said to him, "If anyone loves Me, he will keep My word; and My Father will love him, and We will come to him and make Our home with him. John 14:23

Love Jesus and keep His word. I once heard someone pray, "Father, give me the love for Your Son that You have for Him." What a great prayer!! Our love for Jesus is never as intimate as He deserves. Each new season of our lives – each new desire and assignment – is an opportunity to grow deeper in love with Him.

> Trust in the LORD, and do good;
> Dwell in the land, and feed on His faithfulness.
> Delight yourself also in the LORD,
> And He shall give you the desires of your heart.
> Commit your way to the LORD,

Map 19 - Workplace Ministry Formation

Trust also in Him,
And He shall bring it to pass.
⁶ He shall bring forth your righteousness as the light,
And your justice as the noonday. Psalm 37:3-6

Trust the Lord and do good; and dwell in His promises. I encourage you to reckon the truths of Psalm 34 and 37 as your own. Allow faith to rise up as you meditate on them. Be soft – like clay in the Potter's hand. Recognize that Christ is our righteousness (1Corinthians 1:30).

> *Therefore we do not lose heart. Even though our outward man is perishing, yet the inward man is being renewed day by day. For our light affliction, which is but for a moment, is working for us a far more exceeding and eternal weight of glory, while we do not look at the things which are seen, but at the things which are not seen. For the things which are seen are temporary, but the things which are not seen are eternal.* 2Corinthians 4:16-18

Do not lose heart. Paul's "light affliction" – stoning, drowning, scourging, etc. – would seem quite heavy to most of us today. Nevertheless, by experience, Paul realized that it was working for him the glory Jesus had passed on from the Father (John 17:22). This too is a mystery, but one to which many of us will testify.

The days ahead will include this "light" affliction. The trials and tribulations will prove what we believe, remove what doesn't belong, and grow in us the faith and character of Christ. We will learn to love one another as Christ loves the church. The world will be drawn to us, for we are the temple of the Living God. Most importantly, they will see and glorify our Father in heaven.

Application

Becoming a disciple maker begins with two choices – choosing to be made, and choosing to be used to make others. If you are a Leader in the Workplace, I can guarantee you that the Lord has put a desire in your heart to be a disciple that makes disciples. Surrender to His work in and through you, and you will be made as He gives you the desires of your heart.

Reckoning

God has placed people in my spheres of influence for a kingdom purpose.

Assignment

1. Review your notes and the Scripture passages from this week's module. Share the ones that are most meaningful to someone you are discipling.

2. Consider Jesus Christ's expectations in our disciple making. Which are most intriguing to you? Commit to explore these further. They may lead to God's purpose for you.

3. Do any of Jesus' expectations expose a fear? Remember, behind every fear there is a lie. Deal with the lie and the fear will fly. Commit to deal with the lie.

Devotion

Prepare Early to Finish Well

From Rob Streetman, Marketplace Ministry Tip, Chapel Hill News and Views Magazine

> *My legacy doesn't matter. It isn't important that I be remembered. It's important that when I stand before the Lord, he says, 'Well done, good and faithful servant.' I want to finish strong.* James Dobson

Map 19 - Workplace Ministry Formation

I think it is interesting that most do not think about finishing well until they are near the finish line. How would things have gone if you had thought about the finish when you started your business or career? Would you have done something different to prepare yourself and your company to insure you finished well?

Of course, the finishing well that I am talking about is not measured by the things of this world. It would be wise to consider how we are measuring our success. There are many that will hear, "Well done, good and faithful servant." Regrettably, others will be surprised:

> Not everyone who says to Me, "Lord, Lord," shall enter the kingdom of heaven, but he who does the will of My Father in heaven. Many will say to Me in that day, "Lord, Lord, have we not prophesied in Your name, cast out demons in Your name, and done many wonders in Your name?" And then I will declare to them, "I never knew you; depart from Me, you who practice lawlessness!" Matthew 7:21-23

To finish well, we have to prepare for it. This is common business sense. A sales executive doesn't wait until October to load up his pipeline if he hopes to finish the year well. The production manager hires and trains well before the delivery schedule on that new big order.

So, have you prepared to finish well? As they say, "Better late than never."

Marketplace Ministry Tip: The first step in finishing well is to think about it – in the right way. Who are you finishing well for? What does He want to accomplish through you and your business or vocation? Turn your heart and mind to Him, and start asking the hard questions. Contact me, at rob@inlightconsulting.com, if I can help you in this regard.

Humbly yours and His forever,

Rob

The Map Maker's Guide

Section Four - Submitting to His Power

As they continued down the hallway, Somebody began to feel something drawing him toward a particular room - like a tractor beam he had seen in science fiction movies. The name of the room was displayed in large, glowing and pulsating letters. It read, "THE POWER ROOM".

As you might expect, there was a low, rumbling sound coming from behind the door to The Power Room. Something powerful was definitely going on in there.

Somebody opened the door. Forgetting he had been drawn to the room and expecting to be shoved back by the Power inside, Somebody had braced himself forward. So, when the Power did exactly the opposite of what Somebody expected – forcefully drawing him and his adventure partners into the room – in they went. If they hadn't been huddled so close together, they surely would have pitched headlong across the room. As it was, they were barely able to remain on their feet.

Gathering his composure and his bearings, Somebody turned to the Map Maker. "Wow, that was weird", was all Somebody could think to say. The Map Maker couldn't help but laugh.

"You would be surprised how often that happens. I must admit, I enjoy watching it every time. Welcome to The Power Room."

As the darkness grows darker, God's light will shine ever brighter through the good works of His leaders and those within their spheres of influence. Individuals, families, fellowships, and communities will be transformed under the supernatural power of God as God's people walk together into their assignments. Most importantly, He will be glorified and His kingdom will be established for all to see.

This final section of the Map Maker's Guide explores God's power for joyful, Spirit-filled ministry. That power is available from one, and only one, source: The life of Jesus Christ. Finding that life requires submission to God's will and His Son's lordship. Without Him, we can do nothing. Abiding in Him, those that believe will do the greater than things that bring glory to the Father, and take the kingdom by force.

The Map Maker's Guide

Map 20 - The Life that Glorifies Our Father in Heaven

Spiritual Exercise

For My thoughts are not your thoughts,
Nor are your ways My ways," says the Lord.
For as the heavens are higher than the earth,
So are My ways higher than your ways,
And My thoughts than your thoughts. Isaiah 55:8-9

It is the glory of God to conceal a matter,
But the glory of kings is to search out a matter. Proverbs 25:2

To put this in a perspective we can understand, the heavens are at least 13 billion light years above the Earth – and our God measures this vast expanse we call the Universe in the span of His hand! Our God is a very big god! By comparison, we are so very small. Still, in His awesome sovereignty, God Almighty has condescended to conceal matters of His kingdom for His children to search out (anyone thinking scavenger hunt?). Furthermore, The Excellent Glory has established that searching out these matters is for our glory. How amazing is that!?!

Prayer

Gracious and merciful Father in Heaven, we are awed by your thoughts and ways. They are higher, more beautiful, more powerful and more magnificent than we can think or imagine. We praise You for Your thoughts and ways. We praise You for concealing these matters. We thank You for inviting us, in Christ, to search them out. We submit to our Lord and to our Teacher in the searching. We commit to do what we hear. In Jesus Christ's Name. Amen.

Introduction

As we move into this last leg of our adventure, let us consider once again the grand purposes of God. His story is about Him getting back that which was lost in the Garden: His reign, His habitation and His intimate relationship with His children. He has invited us to join Him in the work. A life of joyful, Spirit-filled ministry awaits those that will surrender to Him and sacrifice for His plan.

We now turn our attention to the exceeding greatness of His power toward us who believe, according to the working of His mighty power which He worked in Christ when He raised Him from the dead and seated Him at His right hand in the heavenly places, far above all principality and power and might and dominion, and every name that is named, not only in this age but also in that which is to come. Let us consider the One Who put all things under His Son's feet, and gave Him to be head over all things to the church, which is His body, the fullness of Him who fills all in all. (Ephesians 1:19-23)

There is a power that has exceeding greatness toward those who believe. It is – simultaneously – power (*dunamis*), energy (*energeia*), delegated authority (*exousia*), strength (*ischus*), and might (*kratos*). Jesus exercised this power and commissioned His followers to do the same (John 14:12; 20:21). As we submit to His

Map 20 - The Life that Glorifies Our Father in Heaven

power, God, through Jesus Christ and the Holy Spirit, transforms us into instruments and weapons of righteousness for the transformation of others in our spheres of influence. In so doing, He is glorified.

I want you to know right up front that there are verses in this lesson that I believe with all my heart, but cannot explain with my limited vocabulary. This mystery of glory is one that exposes the limitations of our minds. I encourage you: Do not settle for that which only your mind can comprehend. Trust Him to lead you into all understanding. May we desire to know the Lord fully, so that we may better love Him with our whole heart, mind, soul and strength.

Definition

Glory (*doxa*): Splendor, brightness, magnificence, excellence, preeminence, dignity, grace, majesty; a thing belonging to God; the kingly majesty which belongs to him as supreme ruler, majesty in the sense of the absolute perfection of the deity; a thing belonging to Christ; the kingly majesty of the Messiah; the absolutely perfect inward or personal excellency of Christ; the state of blessedness into which believers are to enter hereafter through being brought into the likeness of Christ. *Outline of Biblical Usage, BlueLetterBible.org*

The word glory appears in the NKJV 404 times. Needless to say, it is an important word in Scripture; important enough that we take time to understand it's full meaning. For starters, recognize that it belongs to God the Father and Christ His Son, and is a condition "which believers are to enter". There is a glory that has been reserved for the Father's many children – those that follow His Son.

Searching Out the Matter
(All Scripture references, but those noted, are NKJV; Thomas Nelson, Inc.; footnotes and headings excluded)

The Mysteries of Glory and Our Work

Let's start with the foundational verse for this leg of our adventure. It is here that we begin our exploration of the mystery of glory. It is a mystery that will radically change our work, ministry and family life.

> *Let your light so shine before men, that they may see your good works and glorify your Father in heaven.* Matthew 5:16

First, it is important to note that this is a command of our King. Second, His command is not, "Go do good works that will glorify God". God will glorify Himself. The command for us is to "let your light so shine before men..." This raises a few compelling questions:

1. Would God take credit for work done by His children?
2. If our Father in heaven is to be glorified in the "good work", who do you think will be doing the work?
3. Why does Jesus call it "your good work"?
4. If it's God's work – and somehow our work – what part of the work is His; and what part is ours?
5. Just what is our responsibility in a work that glorifies our Father in Heaven?

The answers to these questions, and the mystery they represent, will be found in searching out the matter of the glory of God, the glory given to Jesus Christ, and the glory subsequently passed on to those that would believe in Him. Yes, that's right: The Father has not only given glory to His Son, but He has determined to share it with His other children as well. But, I'm getting ahead of myself. Let's start at the beginning.

A Vision of Glory

> *Then God said, "Let Us make man in Our image, according to Our likeness; let them have dominion over the fish of the sea, over the birds of the air, and over the cattle, over all the earth and over*

Map 20 - The Life that Glorifies Our Father in Heaven

every creeping thing that creeps on the earth." So God created man in His own image; in the image of God He created him; male and female He created them. Genesis 1:26-27

Being created in His likeness and image is more than we can think or imagine. What was mankind capable of? Apparently, quite a lot! God created and positioned us strategically – to have dominion over all creation. But, then we fell.

So He drove out the man; and He placed cherubim at the east of the garden of Eden, and a flaming sword which turned every way, to guard the way to the tree of life. Genesis 3:24

… for all have sinned and fall short of the glory of God… Romans 3:23

Without His redemption and restoration, we will not see, nor will we partake of, His glory. But there is hope.

The Hope of Our Return

Adam, the one who would be king of the earth, was cast out; to become a common laborer. He gave up his crown for independence. What a foolish exchange! But, as we know, God has a restoration plan. He has not given up on mankind.

When I consider Your heavens, the work of Your fingers,
The moon and the stars, which You have ordained,
What is man that You are mindful of him,
And the son of man that You visit him?
For You have made him a little lower than the angels,
And You have crowned him with glory and honor. Psalm 8:3-5

Even in their fallen state, God acknowledged the position of those created in His image. When does a king crown someone? When he is crowning his heir – giving him the resources, responsibility and authority to reign. Think about that for a moment. What does it say about your identity in Jesus Christ?

It is the glory of God to conceal a matter,
But the glory of kings is to search out a matter. Proverbs 25:2

There is glory reserved for the kings that will search out a matter. God has been encouraging us to find His glory – and ours – since the beginning. He has great plans for His children: Inauguration, dominion, and glory. He has gone to great lengths to make sure His plans are accomplished.

For it was fitting for Him, for whom are all things and by whom are all things, in bringing many sons to glory, to make the captain of their salvation perfect through sufferings. Hebrews 2:10

It is important to note that glory and heaven are not the same things. This is not about being brought into our "heavenly rest". It is the hope of our return to glory on this side of eternity. That very hope is secured in Jesus Christ's mission and suffering.

Glory Returns to Man

And the glory which You gave Me I have given them, that they may be one just as We are one: I in them, and You in Me; that they may be made perfect in one, and that the world may know that You have sent Me, and have loved them as You have loved Me. John 17:22-23

Over 2000 years ago, Christ gave us the glory He had received from His Father. So, when did God give glory to the Son?

For He received from God the Father honor and glory when such a voice came to Him from the Excellent Glory: "This is My beloved Son, in whom I am well pleased." And we heard this voice which came from heaven when we were with Him on the holy mountain. 2Peter 1:17-18

155

Map 20 - The Life that Glorifies Our Father in Heaven

Glory was given from the Father in a word that identified Christ as His well-pleasing, beloved Son. This happened on the Mount of Transfiguration.

> *Now after six days Jesus took Peter, James, and John his brother, led them up on a high mountain by themselves; and He was transfigured before them. His face shone like the sun, and His clothes became as white as the light.* Matthew 17:1-2

In this incredible moment, the veil of the physical was pulled away for the glory inside to be seen. This was the glory of God – His life lived in His Son. The Greek word translated "transfigured" here is *metamorphoo*. It is used in two other places.

> *And do not be conformed to this world, but be transformed by the renewing of your mind, that you may prove what is that good and acceptable and perfect will of God.* Romans 12:2

> *But we all, with unveiled face, beholding as in a mirror the glory of the Lord, are being transformed into the same image from glory to glory, just as by the Spirit of the Lord.* 2Corinthians 3:18

Transformed is *metamorphoo*. Once created in the image of God, we are now being transformed into the image His Son's glory. We should also note here that the Holy Spirit is responsible for our transformation. He is our "Transformer".

Glory Returned to the Father

> *And whatever you ask in My name, that I will do, that the Father may be glorified in the Son.* John 14:13

> *Jesus spoke these words, lifted up His eyes to heaven, and said: "Father, the hour has come. Glorify Your Son, that Your Son also may glorify You... I have glorified You on the earth. I have finished the work which You have given Me to do.* John 17:1, 4

Jesus' ultimate passion is to glorify His Father. The same must be true of those that follow Him. The ones made into the image of the Son's glory will passionately desire to return that glory to the Father. But, how? Let's go back to our opening verse.

> *Let your light so shine before men, that they may see your good works and glorify your Father in heaven.* Matthew 5:16

The circle of glory is complete as the Father is glorified, not by us, but by others. Here we find the key to the mystery; in the meaning of "your light".

> *In the beginning was the Word, and the Word was with God, and the Word was God. He was in the beginning with God. All things were made through Him, and without Him nothing was made that was made. In Him was life, and the life was the light of men. And the light shines in the darkness, and the darkness did not comprehend it.* John 1:1-5

The light of men is the life of Christ. As we behold His glory, and receive the life that He has given us, we are transformed into the image of His glory. This is the image Peter, James and John saw on the Mount of Transfiguration. That image was the life in Him, the glory of His Father.

> *But You, O LORD, are a shield for me,*
> *My glory and the One who lifts up my head.* Psalm 3:3

The Psalmist's glory is the LORD!! When we let our light shine before men, they will see the life of the Father... in the life of His Son... in the Body of Christ... and they will proclaim the Father's glory. This is the abiding life – "I in them, and You in Me" (John 17:23).

Map 20 - The Life that Glorifies Our Father in Heaven

Conclusion

The life that glorifies our Father in heaven is the normal Christian life. In the next module, we will adventure deeper still into the life that we have been called to live. For now, it is important that we recognize that there is a "greater than" life promised to the followers of Jesus Christ. God is in the process of returning many sons and daughters to glory – and we are not talking about sweet by-and-by life in heaven. He has begun this work in us now.

God's glory came in two ways: In Him identifying Christ as His well-pleasing Son; and in the life that He lived in the Son. We have discovered that we are also, in this way, heirs of God and co-heirs with Christ. God the Father, and Christ His Son, are glorified in the work that They do in us (being transformed) and through us (the good works we have been created to walk in).

Application

Leaders in the Workplace cannot be disciple makers until they have been made into disciples, themselves. Similarly, you cannot be transformation agents until you are being transformed. It is time to get serious about submitting to the Holy Spirit's transforming power. In this humble place, you will find the Life that can live out the normal Christian life in you – and empower you to lead others to do the same.

Reckoning

I am a vessel made to carry and express God's glory.

Assignment

1. Review your notes and the Scripture passages from this week's module. Share the ones that are most meaningful to someone you are discipling.

2. What might your work look like when others see it and glorify your Father in Heaven?

3. What are one or two things in your life (or missing from your life) that inhibit the manifestation of the Father's glory in your work (be specific)? Pray this prayer as often as the Spirit leads you:

    Dear Father, thank you for the promise of Your glory. Though I do not understand it, I believe that the glory You gave to Your Son has been given to me. Therefore, in faith, I choose to take hold of it. I claim it for my own. Please deal with anything in me that is inhibiting this work. I surrender to Your hand in creating a vessel worthy to hold and display the glory I have been given. My desire is that it be for Your glory. I surrender to You. I choose to put to death the deeds of my flesh, and to put on Christ. I trust You to will and to do to Your good pleasure. Amen.

Devotion

Perseverance for Success
TGIF Today God Is First Volume 2 by Os Hillman

> "And we rejoice in the hope of the glory of God. Not only so, but we also rejoice in our sufferings, because we know that suffering produces perseverance; perseverance, character; and character, hope" (Rom. 5:2-4).

Perseverance is the key to every great accomplishment because nothing of lasting value has ever been achieved without it. Industrialist Henry Ford is one of the great success stories of American history, but he failed in business five times before he succeeded. A Ford Motor Company employee once asked his boss the secret of success, and Henry Ford replied, "When you start a thing, don't quit until you finish it."

Map 20 - The Life that Glorifies Our Father in Heaven

Jesus glorified the Father by finishing the work He was given.

The path ahead of you is strewn with obstacles. People will oppose you. There will be financial setbacks, time pressures, illnesses and misfortunes. Some of the biggest obstacles will be inside of you: self-doubt, insecurity, procrastination, and worry. These things are to be overcome through faith, discipline and the Lord's encouragement.

When we persevere through adversity, we win the approval of our Lord Jesus Christ, who told the suffering church at Ephesus, "I know your deeds, your hard work and your perseverance. . . . You have persevered and have endured hardships for my name, and have not grown weary" (Rev. 2:2-3). That, I'm sure, is the same commendation Joseph received from God when he passed the perseverance test.

Perseverance is a refusal to quit. It's falling down 100 times and getting back up 100 times. We need to remember that perseverance is not a matter of forcing doors to open; it's standing in front of the doors as long as it takes before God chooses to open them.

Life is a marathon, not a sprint. The race doesn't go to the swiftest, but to those who don't give up. We need endurance in order to deal with the stress of adversity. We must maintain a balanced diet, exercise regularly, and get plenty of rest. People give up or give out when they feel depleted - when they physically, emotionally and spiritually run out of gas.

When going through adversity, watch out for pessimists, blamers and toxic personalities. Beware of people who try to talk you out of your dreams and goals. Spend time with optimists and encouragers. Seek out people of faith.

Reprinted by permission from the author. Os Hillman is an international speaker and author of more than 10 books on workplace calling. To learn more, visit http://www.MarketplaceLeaders.org

The Map Maker's Guide

Map 21 - The Power of His Life

Spiritual Exercise

Then Moses called Joshua and said to him in the sight of all Israel, "Be strong and of good courage, for you must go with this people to the land which the LORD has sworn to their fathers to give them, and you shall cause them to inherit it. And the LORD, He is the One who goes before you. He will be with you, He will not leave you nor forsake you; do not fear nor be dismayed." Then He inaugurated Joshua the son of Nun, and said, "Be strong and of good courage; for you shall bring the children of Israel into the land of which I swore to them, and I will be with you." Deuteronomy 31:7-8, 23

Be strong and of good courage... Only be strong and very courageous... Have I not commanded you? Be strong and of good courage; do not be afraid, nor be dismayed, for the LORD your God is with you wherever you go. Joshua 1:6-7, 9

Prayer

Dear Father, we love You. We love Your Son. We love Your Holy Spirit. We want to love You more. Our heart's desire is to be strong and of good courage, that we would lead well. We long to hear Your voice of encouragement. Speak to us now. We trust You. In Jesus' name we pray. Amen.

Introduction

In his classic *The Cost of Discipleship,* Dietrich Bonhoeffer said, "Salvation is free, but discipleship will cost you your life." As you might expect, Bonhoeffer was referring to something more than our mortality. Jesus said it this way:

For whoever desires to save his life will lose it, but whoever loses his life for My sake and the gospel's will save it. Mark 8:35

The power to save a life is a great power indeed. For many, this is a decision, a prayer, an event. This is true, of course, but it is far from the whole Truth. There is more here; more than the death of the old man. There is His life; and there is more to His life than most understand. Consequently, there are few that walk in the fullness of It.

Why is the American church not seeing more of His glory? What can Leaders in the Workplace do to begin expressing His glory in the good work that He has prepared for them? These are corporate and personal questions that we must face; and we can, with courage and faith in God's desire and ability to transform us and those within our spheres of influence.

Definition

Grace (*Charis*): Grace (that which affords joy, pleasure, delight, sweetness, charm, loveliness: grace of speech); good will, loving-kindness, favor; of the merciful kindness by which God, exerting His holy influence upon souls, turns them to Christ, keeps, strengthens, increases them in Christian faith, knowledge, affection, and kindles them to the exercise of the Christian virtues; what is due to grace (i.e., the spiritual condition of

Map 21 - The Power of His Life

one governed by the power of divine grace, the token or proof of grace, benefit or gift); thanks (for benefits, services, favors), recompense, reward. *Outline of Biblical Usage, BlueLetterBible.org*

For too many, God's grace has become an excuse for avoiding the pursuit of holiness: "Don't worry about your condition, God has grace for that." Given this definition, "God has grace for that" means something quite the opposite. It means that He is exerting His holy influence upon our souls; turning us to Christ; keeping, strengthening, and increasing our Christian faith, knowledge, affection; and kindling us to the exercise of the Christian virtues. God's grace is the power to overcome our temptations, pursue holiness and live as instruments of righteousness.

Searching Out the Matter
(All Scripture references, but those noted, are NKJV; Thomas Nelson, Inc.; footnotes and headings excluded)

A Short Review (from The Life That Glorifies Our Father in Heaven)

We have been created in the image of the Father, Son and Holy Spirit (Genesis 1:26). He has crowned us with glory and honor (Psalms 8:5). There is glory reserved for the kings that will search out a matter; and He has made us kings (Revelation 1:6). The Psalmist's glory is the LORD (Psalm 3:3)!! This is an important clue to the mystery of God's glory.

All have sinned and fall short of the glory of God (Romans 3:23). Without His redemption and restoration, we will not see, nor partake of, His glory. But there is hope; for He has determined to bring many sons to glory (Hebrews 2:10). Glory and heaven are not the same. There is a glory reserved for us on this earth.

Over 2000 years ago, Christ gave us the glory He had received from His Father, for the purpose of making us one in Them (John 17:22). Christ was transfigured, as the glory of God – His life lived in His Son – was revealed (2Peter 1:17-18; Matthew 17:2). The word here – *metamorphoo* – is also used to describe what God is doing in us (2Corinthians 3:18; Romans 12:2).

The glory is passed back to the Father as we let the life of Christ shine before men so that they glorify the Father (Matthew 5:16; John 1:4). The command is not, "Go and do good works". It is to "let your light shine". That shining releases a demonstration of the power of God that the world will see is not us, but Him. It is the "greater than" life that Jesus promised to all that believe in Him.

The "Greater Than" Life

As the Incarnate Son of God, Jesus lived a life that was greater than any man before Him. How did He do it? As a disciple of His Father, Jesus surrendered Himself to the Father's purpose, sacrificed for His plan, and submitted to His power. On more than one occasion He stressed that it was the Father's work and words that people were seeing and hearing. He has promised that we would do the same... and more!

> *Most assuredly, I say to you, he who believes in Me, the works that I do he will do also; and greater works than these he will do, because I go to My Father. And whatever you ask in My name, that I will do, that the Father may be glorified in the Son. If you ask anything in My name, I will do it.* John 14:12-14

Jesus is continuing to do the work that glorifies the Father. He has invited us to participate with Him. The great mystery is how this is happening. How is it possible for mortal Mankind to do greater things than the anointed and holy God-man? Simply stated, we must also surrender to the Father's purpose, sacrifice for His plan, and submit to His power – that the anointed and holy God-man would do the work. We must exchange our life for His.

Map 21 - The Power of His Life

The Exchanged Life

The key to the power of Christ's life is found in our participation with that life – joining ourselves to Him by faith and transformation. Christ prayed that we would be one with each other, and one with Him and the Father. As we have discussed, this becoming one is a process; a process that begins with our participation in His death. Paul speaks of this exchange:

> I have been crucified with Christ; it is no longer I who live, but Christ lives in me; and the life which I now live in the flesh I live by faith in the Son of God, who loved me and gave Himself for me.
> Galatians 2:20

I want to make a point here about the translation of this verse. Young's Literal Translation recognizes the imperative "the" before "faith". A Greek scholar I know has concurred with this translation, which should then read, "I live by the faith of the Son of God". I believe this is more consistent with the context of this verse and Ephesians 2:8 ("saved through faith, and that not of yourselves"). Our faith is Christ's faith, lived out of His life.

Let me encourage you to meditate on and reckon Galatians 2:20 as truth for yourself; until God does something in you with it. It is too important to put on the shelf until some later day. It is about His life in us. What could be more important?

Others have written on this subject with much greater eloquence. Two books I recommend are *The Normal Christian Life*, by Watchman Nee, and *The Saving Life of Christ*, by Major W. Ian Thomas. For now, let me suggest the following:

1. Though we may not understand the complete mystery of it, Galatians 2:20 is the truth regarding our life in Christ. If you can hear it, faith will come (Romans 10:17).

2. Say this verse, even out loud, focusing on your crucifixion with Christ. Ask God to give you a vision of your death with Christ. Let faith arise.

3. Meditate on this verse regularly, fostering transformation through the renewal of your mind.

4. Invite Christ to prove His life in you, through word and deed. Your experience of His life will encourage you to continue laying hold of that for which Christ Jesus laid hold of you.

5. Recognize that our death in Christ is only the beginning. He has promised us His life – His resurrected life.

This last point brings us to a critical truth about the life that Christ has made available to those that believe on Him. As with all truth, it has the potential to make you free. I feel the need to warn you, it may also challenge your doctrinal paradigm. Remember, the Holy Spirit and the Lord Jesus are our teachers. Listen to them and allow the truth to do whatever the Father has in it for you.

The Life that Saves

Did you know that the effectual work of Christ's death on the cross did not save us? Believe me, you are not alone in your objection. Take a survey. Ask your Christian friends, "What did Christ do to save you?" Most will say, "He died on the cross." Paul had something different to say.

> But God demonstrates His own love toward us, in that while we were still sinners, Christ died for us. Much more then, having now been justified by His blood, we shall be saved from wrath through Him. For if when we were enemies we were reconciled to God through the death of His Son, much more, having been reconciled, we shall be saved by His life. Romans 5:8-10

There is no question that Christ's death was required and effectual. His death justified and reconciled us to God. But, "much more, we shall be saved by His life". Salvation is accomplished by His life, not by His death. Furthermore, there is "much more" to the effectualness of His life. Let me say it a different way:

Map 21 - The Power of His Life

As much as our Savior's death accomplished, His life shall accomplish much more!

One of the greatest deceptions in the American church is that a Christian can live out of Christ's death. We have allowed ourselves to settle for a ticket to heaven, bought by His death. The tragic and sobering truth is that His death will not get us there. Nothing less than His life will save us.

Participating in His Death and His Resurrection

It is the spiritual implications of Christ's death and resurrection that make them of first importance to our faith. Like Christ – and with the exception of those translated directly to heaven – every human being will die a physical death and be physically resurrected at the end of this age. But only those that participate in Christ's spiritual death and resurrection enjoy the benefits of His life.

It is also important to note that there are two spiritual deaths: The death of our old man and the eternal death of those that are lost to God. The former is accomplished through participation in Christ's death. The latter awaits those who will not exchange their life for His.

As we can see in Paul's letter to the Romans, death and resurrection are closely related. Read Romans 6:1-14 to get a full context of the passage; then consider the incredible truths that are found there:

> *How shall we who died to [the] sin live any longer in it? …as many of us as were baptized into Christ Jesus were baptized into His death… [we] were buried with Him through baptism into [the] death, that just as Christ was raised from the dead by the glory of the Father, even so we also should walk in newness of life.* vv. 2-4

There are a few points to make here. First, notice the tense of "died" and "buried". For Paul, and those like him, these are past events.

Second, I have inserted the imperatives where they are found in Young's Literal Translation. As you can see, there is "the sin" and "the death". "The sin" is the original sin – Mankind's rebellion against God's rule over our hearts. "The death" is that of our old man, the child of Adam that was born into rebellion.

Lastly, there is the principle of "baptized" and "baptism". While many have been taught that baptism is a symbol of our death and resurrection in Christ (and the first act of Christian obedience), I suggest to you that it is much more. In fact, baptism is less an act of man than it is a work of God.

Baptism is a sacrament – a sacred moment – that accomplishes the mystery of putting off the old man and putting on Christ. As a preacher once said, "Something supernatural happens when you go down in that water." Baptism does not accomplish salvation, but it is a step in the salvation process.

For those that disagree with this view, I have no controversy with you. For now, let me suggest that something is accomplished "through baptism" that is very important to Paul's teaching here. It may not mean what I say it means, but it must mean something. Search it out and put meaning to it for yourself. Again, Jesus Christ and the Holy Spirit are our teachers. We can trust them for the truth.

Now, back to Romans 6.

> *… just as Christ was raised from the dead by the glory of the Father, even so we also should walk in newness of life. For if we have been united together in the likeness of His death, certainly we also shall be in the likeness of His resurrection…* vv. 4-5

What has happened in the past (i.e., spiritual resurrection), should and shall be accomplished in the newness of life we receive in our subsequent participation in His resurrection. Paul's use of "should" and "shall be" indicate that our participation in His resurrection is a process that begins and continues in the life we live before our physical death.

Map 21 - The Power of His Life

Furthermore, the Greek for "newness" – kainotes – means "life of a new quality; the believer, being a new creation". It is not "newness" in time, but "newness" in creation. This is not something that man can do. It must be a work of God.

> *... our old man was crucified with Him, that the body of sin might be done away with, that we should no longer be slaves of [the] sin. For he who has died has been freed from sin.* vv. 6-7

These two small verses identify one of the most significant powers of the exchanged life – the power of our freedom from "the body of sin" (our old man), "the sin" (our rebellion) and "sin" (in general). This is almost too awesome to consider! But consider it we must. We must ask ourselves, "Do we believe this to be true for those that have been crucified with Him?"

I encourage you – if you believe it – to say so verbally (i.e., out loud). Remember, faith does not come from what we see and experience. Faith comes by hearing, and hearing by the word of God (Romans 10:17). Hear the word of God and faith will rise up in your heart. Then reckon what you believe to be true in your life. The power of this truth will make you free!

> *Now if we died with Christ, we believe that we shall also live with Him, knowing that Christ, having been raised from the dead (resurrected), dies no more. Death no longer has dominion over Him.* vv. 8-9

The power of our participation in Christ's death is to live (and keep on living) with Him; and living in Him, to die no more. The power of His resurrection (and our participation in it) is power over spiritual death.

> *For the death that He died, He died to sin once for all; but the life that He lives, He lives to God. Likewise you also, reckon yourselves to be dead indeed to [the] sin, but alive to God in Christ Jesus our Lord.* vv. 10-11

The power of our life in Christ is a life that is truly alive, and lived to God – in the center of His will and work. It is this life that is eternal and abundant, full of godliness and peace. This is the joyful, Spirit-filled life!

By now, you must be asking, "How do we live such an overcoming life? What am I missing?" Paul anticipated such questions from the faithful in Rome. His answer:

> *Therefore do not let [the] sin reign in your mortal body, that you should obey it in its lusts. And do not present your members as instruments of unrighteousness to sin, but present yourselves to God as being alive from the dead, and your members as instruments of righteousness to God. For sin shall not have dominion over you, for you are not under law but under grace.* vv. 12-14

> *I say then: Walk in the Spirit, and you shall not fulfill the lust of the flesh.* Galatians 5:16

The key to the overcoming exchanged life is our active participation in it. Mature Christians know that our faith walk is a walk... in the Spirit. It is not a standing around. Our life in Christ is also a race and a fight. We must not let "the sin" reign. How? By surrendering to the reign of our Lord Jesus Christ.

We must live like we are alive, with our faculties available as instruments (aka, weapons) for God's use. We must forcefully stand against the temptations that come from the sinful nature of our flesh, the world and Satan's vast army of demons.

It is important to recognize that Satan's power over the believer is a deception. We are overcomers by the blood of the Lamb and the word of our testimony (Revelation 12:11). Our testimony is our participation in the death, burial and resurrection of our Lord and Savior. Satan has been defeated!

Our role in the battle for the kingdom of heaven is enforcement. Our time on this planet is our training ground for the ages to come; when we will co-reign with Christ as His Bride. This will be a physical reality. For now, we participate in the spiritual reality of our life in Christ.

Map 21 - The Power of His Life

Participating in His Ascension

> *But God, who is rich in mercy, because of His great love with which He loved us, even when we were dead in trespasses, made us alive together with Christ (by grace you have been saved), and raised us up together, and made us sit together in the heavenly places in Christ Jesus, that in the ages to come He might show the exceeding riches of His grace in His kindness toward us in Christ Jesus.* Ephesians 2:4-7

We are not only made to be partakers of Christ's death and resurrection, but of His ascension. This is perhaps the most challenging mystery of our participation in Christ's life; and likely the most powerful. As you read this excerpt from F.J. Huegel's *Bone of His Bone*, keep in mind that we are exploring the current spiritual reality of the future physical manifestation of our life with Christ, as His Bride.

> As Paul puts it, we were "made to sit together in the Heavenlies with Christ Jesus" (Eph. 2:6). Jesus states the case in His High Priestly prayer, which had as its supreme object this very union of which we are speaking, in this wise: "I in them and Thou in Me . . . Father I will that they also whom Thou hast given Me be with Me where I am that they may behold My glory." That He had in mind His going to the Father is evident enough, for He had already said: "And now I am no longer in the world. And now I come to Thee." By faith He was already taking His place at the right hand of the Father. He was returning by the way of the Cross, the empty tomb, and ascension to the Throne He had left, and by faith He was taking with Him those who in the foreknowledge of God were to form His mystic body. The Heavenly Bridegroom was placing the Bride at His side on the Throne.

At this point, I come to the end of my abilities to explain what I know to be true: Believers have, in Christ, <u>on this side of heaven</u>, access to the very power of God; seated with Him on the throne, to co-reign with Christ in the spirit realm. It is a truth that Christ and the Holy Spirit must reveal to you. I encourage you to pursue this truth in the books mentioned previously in this lesson.

Conclusion

I am convinced that the life that Jesus lived – filled with the power of God – is possible for every follower of Christ. I am also convinced that it is only in our full participation in His death, burial, resurrection and ascension that we will find the "greater than" life He has promised us. My anticipation is for the exceedingly abundantly above all that we can ask or think, according to the power that works in us (Ephesians 3:20). I hope and pray for the same increase in your anticipation; for all of the work Christ intends to do through you.

Let me remind you not to let go of this, until God does something in you with it. It is too important to put on the shelf until some later day. It is about His life in us. What could be more important? And to that end, I have prayed as Paul did in His prayer to the church at Ephesus:

> *...that the God of our Lord Jesus Christ, the Father of glory, may give to you the spirit of wisdom and revelation in the knowledge of Him, the eyes of your understanding being enlightened; that you may know what is the hope of His calling, what are the riches of the glory of His inheritance in the saints, and what is the exceeding greatness of His power toward us who believe, according to the working of His mighty power which He worked in Christ when He raised Him from the dead and seated Him at His right hand in the heavenly places, far above all principality and power and might and dominion, and every name that is named, not only in this age but also in that which is to come. And He put all things under His feet, and gave Him to be head over all things to the church, which is His body, the fullness of Him who fills all in all.* Ephesians 1:17-23

Application

By this time, it should be clear that the opportunity for leading in the Workplace is much more than we might even imagine. It is also more than even the most intelligent and powerful can accomplish. It is kingdom work.

Map 21 - The Power of His Life

The Workplace Leaders' only hope for kingdom success is through participation in the life of Christ. As someone has said, "Let go and let God."

Reckoning

With Jesus Christ, I have been crucified, buried, resurrected and seated at the Father's right hand.

Assignment

1. Review your notes and the Scripture passages from this week's module. Share the ones that are most meaningful to someone you are discipling.

2. Pray Paul's prayer to the Ephesians over yourself and those you have been commissioned to disciple. Put your name and theirs in the appropriate places and reckon the truth of your (and their) participation in the death, burial, resurrection and ascension of Christ.

Devotion

God Is Not About YOUR Success
TGIF Today God Is First Volume 2 by Os Hillman

> "I tell you the truth, unless a kernel of wheat falls to the ground and dies, it remains only a single seed. But if it dies, it produces many seeds. The man who loves his life will lose it, while the man who hates his life in this world will keep it for eternal life."
>
> John 12:24-26

God is all about your death so that HIS success can be realized through you! This is why the Church is having such little impact - there are too many believers who have not yet died to their old nature so that Christ can live fully through them. When believers come to the end of themselves they will lose their lives to Him and live through the power of the Holy Spirit and begin to see the reality of a living gospel that impacts lives, workplaces, cities and nations.

"Much of modern Christian enterprise is 'Ishmael.' Born not of God, but of an inordinate desire to do God's will in our own way - the one thing our Lord never did," said Oswald Chambers. The psalmist describes what it means to live in our own strength:

"Unless the LORD builds the house, its builders labor in vain. Unless the LORD watches over the city, the watchmen stand guard in vain. In vain you rise early and stay up late, toiling for food to eat - for he grants sleep to those he loves" (Ps 127:1-2).

How does one die so that Christ can be our all and all? It usually takes a crisis of significant proportions for most people to relinquish the control of their lives. It means we come to the end of ourselves and our striving to control the events in our lives and we finally come to the place where we can say, "Lord, I surrender. Please take full control of my life."

Reprinted by permission from the author. Os Hillman is an international speaker and author of more than 10 books on workplace calling. To learn more, visit http://www.MarketplaceLeaders.org

The Map Maker's Guide

Map 22 - The Power of Abiding

Spiritual Exercise

> *Therefore whoever hears these sayings of Mine, and does them, I will liken him to a wise man who built his house on the rock: and the rain descended, the floods came, and the winds blew and beat on that house; and it did not fall, for it was founded on the rock.* Matthew 7:24-25

> *If we confess our sins, He is faithful and just to forgive us our sins and to cleanse us from all unrighteousness.* 1John 1:9

As the days are becoming more evil, trial, tribulation and persecution are increasing. Christ warned that the only people who would stand are those that hear and do what He taught. Great will be the fall for those that hear only. These are sobering thoughts. Who among us understands what Jesus requires? Who then can say they are confident that they are prepared? How desperate must the times get before we get serious about our preparation, and our discipling of those in our spheres of influence?

Prayer

Father God, we confess that we have been poor watchmen. We have wandered from our post, turned a blind eye, or refused to consider the warning signs. We invite your rebuke, chastening and whatever else it takes to make us ready; and make us responsible participants in the Bride's preparation for Your Son's return. Have mercy on us. Forgive us our sin. Deliver us from all unrighteousness. In Jesus' name. Amen.

Introduction

Through our exploration of The Power of His Life, we have discovered the depth and height of our participation in the life of Christ. From our death in Him, through burial and resurrection, and all the way to ascension, the supernatural power of God manifests itself in the transformation of His children. Understandably, you may have come away with the impression that such consideration is "too heavenly minded to be any earthly good". Perhaps you are one of those (like me) that need to know what it looks like and what can be done to lay hold of it.

As we explore further into the life of submission to His power, we will examine the keys and the power of the life that abides in the resurrected and ascended Christ. We will discover and experience the power of His life, by abiding in it. We will uncover the treasure of His precious and great promises for those who will abide.

Definition

Abide (*menō*): To remain; in reference to place, to sojourn, tarry, not to depart (to continue to be present, to be held, kept, continually); in reference to time, to continue to be, not to perish, to last, endure (of persons, to survive, live); in reference to state or condition, to remain as one, not to become another or different; to wait for, await one. *BlueLetterBible.com Outline of Biblical Usage*

Map 22 - The Power of Abiding

"Abide" contains a depth of meaning beyond the capacity of our minds to understand. It references place, time and, perhaps most importantly, state of being. As we will discover, it is one of the greatest mysteries of the kingdom of God.

Like all of the kingdom mysteries, we must first let the truth of it become faith in our hearts. Belief precedes understanding and revelation. It is only then that the truth will make us free, renew our minds and transform us.

So, invite the Holy Spirit to speak the meaning of abide into your heart. The Lord promises that if we seek, we will find. Let Him know you are seeking a deeper revelation as you search out this matter.

Searching Out the Matter
(All Scripture references, but those noted, are NKJV; Thomas Nelson, Inc.; footnotes and headings excluded)

The Importance of Abiding

> *I am the vine, you are the branches. He who abides in Me, and I in him, bears much fruit; for without Me you can do nothing. If anyone does not abide in Me, he is cast out as a branch and is withered; and they gather them and throw them into the fire, and they are burned. If you abide in Me, and My words abide in you, you will ask what you desire, and it shall be done for you. By this My Father is glorified, that you bear much fruit; so you will be My disciples.* John 15:5-8

Every Christian should be familiar with this passage. From it, we know that the life of the vine flows through the branches to produce its fruit. Branches don't produce fruit. They transport the life that produces the fruit. They are blessed in this limited but important function. At least four very important things are promised to those that abide in Christ:

First, "He...bears much fruit... without me you can do nothing" – We are promised to be neither barren nor unfruitful. Our fruitfulness in God's kingdom is dependent on and directly related to our abiding with His Son. There is no other way to be productive in God's kingdom. Christ said the same thing about Himself (John 5:19). He then sent His disciples in the same way that His Father sent Him (John 20:21). It is the abiding life of Christ that does what He did.

Second, "...you will ask what you desire, and it shall be done for you" – The meaning of this verse goes back to Psalm 37:4. It is the will of God to give us the desires of our hearts. As we abide in Christ, we discover those desires, ask for them, and they immediately become the purposes of God that will not be denied Him (Job 42:2).

Third, "My Father is glorified, that you bear much fruit..." – This is the physical manifestation of the power of abiding. The fruit that glorifies the Father are the greater than works of John 14:12; something greater than the works He did through Jesus. These are the good works of Matthew 5:16 – works that others will look at and say, "Isn't God awesome!" As we abide in Christ, God's supernatural work becomes the fruit of our life. This is the life for which we were created: To glorify our Father in heaven.

Lastly, "...you will be My disciples." – This abiding, fruit producing, Father glorifying life is the requirement of every disciple of Christ. A sobering thought: Those that are not abiding, are not producing; and they are not glorifying; and they are not His. Therefore, we must discover how to abide, and how to disciple others into an abiding relationship with Christ.

Keys to Abiding

Now that we understand the gravity of abiding in Christ, let's continue searching to find the keys we need to partake of that life.

Map 22 - The Power of Abiding

But you do not have His word abiding in you, because whom He sent, Him you do not believe. John 5:38

The word of God did not abide in the Jewish leaders because they did not believe that Jesus was the Christ. It is not surprising that our belief in Jesus is the beginning of the abiding life. But it is only the beginning. Don't be like so many who have neglected to go on to fullness in Jesus Christ.

Therefore let that abide in you which you heard from the beginning. If what you heard from the beginning abides in you, you also will abide in the Son and in the Father. 1John 2:24

All that we have heard from God contributes to our abiding in the Son and the Father: Through the teaching, preaching, and reading of God's word; through reading Christian literature; and through the direct words that come from God in prayer, meditation, dreams, godly counsel, etc. This is great news!

But we must remember that anyone who is "a hearer of the word and not a doer, is like a man observing his natural face in a mirror; for he observes himself, goes away, and immediately forgets what kind of man he was." (James 1:23) His faith dies for lack of the work thereof.

My point here is that there is more to the abiding life than just hearing and believing. We must obey what we hear.

But whoever keeps His word, truly the love of God is perfected in him. By this we know that we are in Him. He who says he abides in Him ought himself also to walk just as He walked. 1John 2:5-6

We must walk as Christ walked – in perfect obedience to the Father.

As the Father loved Me, I also have loved you; abide in My love. If you keep My commandments, you will abide in My love, just as I have kept My Father's commandments and abide in His love. John 15:9-10

As Jesus kept His Father's commandments and abides in His love, we must do the same in Jesus. By keeping His commandments, we will abide in His love; and the love of God will be perfected in us. In this we can be confident that we abide in Him.

As you can see, our part in abiding is not complicated: Hear, believe, and obey. It is a blessing to know that our loving Father has made it simple enough for children to understand. The faith of a child, with a heart to respond, is all that is required for us to find the power of abiding.

As we submit to the abiding life, the Father draws us deeper into the mystery. He reveals more of His kingdom, we hear more clearly, and the faith of Christ grows. As we respond in obedience, our abiding is strengthened and the cycle of increased maturity continues (from glory to glory).

The Sacrament of Communion

There is another way – a supernatural way – that we come to abide in Jesus Christ: Through the sacrament of communion. As with all the sacraments, communion is a sacred moment; a moment in God's presence when we have the opportunity for God to do something supernatural in each of us.

Very early in His ministry, Jesus had some profound things to say about communion. Here are a few excerpts from the sixth chapter of John's Gospel:

Do not labor for the food which perishes, but for the food which endures to everlasting life, which the Son of Man will give you, because God the Father has set His seal on Him. v. 27

Jesus is encouraging them to think beyond what they have seen – the feeding of the five thousand.

Then they said to Him, "What shall we do, that we may work the works of God?" v. 28

Still, their minds are stuck on the miracle – the physical evidence of His power. Without chastening (because the works are important), Jesus encourages them again to think beyond that which can be seen.

Map 22 - The Power of Abiding

Jesus answered and said to them, "This is the work of God, that you believe in Him whom He sent."
v. 29

Interestingly, here we see again the first step of abiding: Belief in Jesus.

But their confusion continues, and they ask Him for a greater sign, something like the manna given in the desert (vv. 30-31). In response, He makes this profound statement:

For the bread of God is He who comes down from heaven and gives life to the world. Then they said to Him, "Lord, give us this bread always." And Jesus said to them, "I am the bread of life. He who comes to Me shall never hunger, and he who believes in Me shall never thirst. vv. 33-35

The mystery deepens as Jesus reveals that He will not only give them "the food which endures to everlasting life" (v. 27), but that He is that food. With passion, He encourages them to come and believe. Then, He pushes them beyond their capacity to understand:

Most assuredly, I say to you, unless you eat the flesh of the Son of Man and drink His blood, you have no life in you. Whoever eats My flesh and drinks My blood has eternal life, and I will raise him up at the last day. For My flesh is food indeed, and My blood is drink indeed. He who eats My flesh and drinks My blood abides in Me, and I in him. vv. 53-56

Rather than reject this word of Jesus (as so many did), or pass over it because we cannot grasp its meaning with our natural minds, let's pause to let the Holy Spirit speak. Just to be clear, I am suggesting that stop here until you have asked the Holy Spirit for revelation into this mystery. Don't miss this great opportunity to hear for yourself.

Now, with the limitations of mind and pen, recognizing there is a part I cannot put into words, let me share what these verses mean to me (at this time):

The supernatural work of God in communion is our being abided, by God, in Jesus Christ. When a follower of Jesus takes communion in faithful reverence, God strengthens their abiding in His Son.

This is why it is so important to approach communion in reverence and faith. Nothing less can abide in Jesus Christ. To come any other way is to waste the sacred moment of communion. Paul put it this way:

Therefore, my beloved, as you have always obeyed, not as in my presence only, but now much more in my absence, work out your own salvation with fear and trembling; for it is God who works in you both to will and to do for His good pleasure. Philippians 2:12-13

Do not fear, little flock, for it is your Father's good pleasure to give you the kingdom. Luke 12:32

In response to our working out our salvation with fear and trembling, God works in us for His good pleasure – abiding us in His Son; and thereby giving us His kingdom.

Furthermore, in strengthening our abiding in Christ, the Father also strengthens our fellowship with each other. This is why we take communion with the community of believers. Our communion is with Jesus and with the Jesus in each other. In communion, the power of abiding is also the power of community.

Conclusion

Abiding in Christ is one of the greatest mysteries of the kingdom; and one of the most powerful. Not only does abiding release the power of God in our lives, but it marks us as a disciple of Christ. If we abide, we will be fruitful – and assured of an abundant entrance into the kingdom of God. Abiding requires a "believing into" Christ. It comes by faith, not by mental exercise. Faith comes by hearing and hearing by the word of God (Romans 10:17).

Map 22 - The Power of Abiding

Leaders in the Workplace, our gracious Father has made it simple; and the return on our investment so very great. For the one that will hear and do, searching out the truth of abiding will be the most fruitful adventure of their life.

Application

Searching out the mysteries of God is best done in community. Jesus is with us when we are together; and He always has something to say. Recognize that you do not have to have all the answers to lead others into the mysteries of God. In fact, you will not. Don't let this deter you. Take the lead in humility. Let others know you need them to help you hear from God. This alone will be one of your best disciple-making moments.

Reckoning

The power of abiding is for those who will hear, believe and obey.

Assignment

1. Review your notes and the Scripture passages from this week's module. Share the ones that are most meaningful to someone you are discipling.

2. Search out the matter of abiding by reading and meditating on the definitions and Scripture references found in Vines Expository Dictionary.

Devotion

To Know My Ways
TGIF Today God Is First Volume 2 by Os Hillman

> "That is why I was angry with that generation, and I said, 'Their hearts are always going astray, and they have not known my ways.' So I declared on oath in my anger, 'They shall never enter my rest'".
> Heb 3:10-11

Technology is supposed to make our ability to accomplish things easier and make us more productive. I love the technology gadgets available to us today. In twenty years these will seem as old and archaic as the eight track player. (See, some of you don't know what that is.)

Research reveals that the average person is working much longer hours today because we literally can work from anywhere. Our technology allows us to stay in constant contact with others, which means we are always on call. Unless we intentionally set boundaries, we will never rest from our work.

God got angry with the people of Israel because they did not know His ways. They failed to recognize the boundaries He had set for them that would ensure a spiritual and physically successful life. They chose to disregard His ways. This disobedience led to their inability to enter God's rest.

God's rest means that we can actually do our work and still be refreshed through His Spirit in our inner man. It is the opposite of sweat and toil. It means that the fruit of our work comes as a result of abiding in the vine of His grace and power. Jesus said you can do nothing (worthwhile) unless you are connected to the vine.

In order to do this you and I must do two things. We must understand His ways and we must do His ways. When we follow these two things, we will begin to experience His supernatural rest in all of our endeavors.

Reprinted by permission from the author. Os Hillman is an international speaker and author of more than 10 books on workplace calling. To learn more, visit http://www.MarketplaceLeaders.org

The Map Maker's Guide

Map 23 - The Power of Prayer

Spiritual Exercise

And this is eternal life, that they may know You, the only true God, and Jesus Christ whom You have sent. John 17:3

Our common ideas regarding prayer are not found in the New Testament. We look upon prayer simply as a means of getting things for ourselves, but the biblical purpose of prayer is that we may get to know God Himself. It is the only way we can get in touch with the truth and the reality of God Himself. Oswald Chambers

As we prepare to explore the power of prayer, let us turn our hearts to the One that is the source of all power. Consider His strong desire for each of His children to know Him and His Son; so much so that He has set the condition of eternal life on that knowledge. Invite Him to work the miracle of revelation into your heart, mind, soul and strength.

Prayer

Father God, we want to know You more. We want to know Your Son more. Thank You for Your offer of eternal life. We praise You and trust You as the God of our Lord Jesus Christ. You are the Father of glory. We humbly ask that You give us the spirit of wisdom and revelation in the knowledge of You and Your Son; that we may know what is the exceeding greatness of Your power toward us who believe, according to the working of Your mighty power. This we ask in Jesus' name. Amen.

Introduction

In the lesson on Intimacy with God, we learned that God lost, in mankind's rebellion, the intimate relationship He intended to have with His people. We discovered that the intimacy He desires cannot be found in the asking and demanding prayers that so many in the church practice. There is a better way to know God and His Son; a better way to pray.

We have also learned that God has particular ways for accomplishing His purposes. His ways must become our ways if we are to participate in His restorative work. God's preferred way of prayer is what Larry Crabb calls "relational prayer". Hopefully, you have been strengthening your relationship with our Father in heaven by practicing *The PAPA Prayer*.

In this lesson, we will build on our understanding and practice of prayer by exploring the Biblical promises of "the prayer that avails much". We will discover the power of prayer and the requirements for that power. We will discover, as Paul Billheimer has so eloquently stated in *Destined for the Throne*, that:

Prayer is where the action is!

Map 23 - The Power of Prayer

Definition

Effective (*energeō*): To be operative, be at work, put forth power; to effect; to display one's activity, show one's self operative. *Outline of Biblical Usage, BlueLetterBible.org*

The Greek word *energeō* is used twenty-two times in nineteen New Testament verses. In all but a couple, it describes supernatural operative power in the working of miracles, or the transformation of individuals and groups. *Energeō* is much more than the "energy" we generate from electric or nuclear power plants. Keep this in mind as we explore the power of prayer.

Searching Out the Matter
(All Scripture references, but those noted, are NKJV; Thomas Nelson, Inc.; footnotes and headings excluded)

The Promises of Prayer

John Wesley has been quoted as saying "God does nothing but in answer to prayer." While this is a bit overstated (no one was here to pray creation into existence), when you consider the importance and magnitude of prayer, it is easy to understand the heart behind such a bold statement. Indeed, we must not underestimate the power of prayer.

> *And the prayer of faith will save the sick, and the Lord will raise him up. And if he has committed sins, he will be forgiven. The effective, fervent prayer of a righteous man avails much. Elijah was a man with a nature like ours, and he prayed earnestly that it would not rain; and it did not rain on the land for three years and six months. And he prayed again, and the heaven gave rain, and the earth produced its fruit.* James 5:15-17

The promises of prayer laid out in this passage are enough to motivate any warm-blooded Christian: Healing, forgiveness and power over nature; all from "a man with a nature like ours". Is anything impossible with prayer?

> *Then you will call upon Me and go and pray to Me, and I will listen to you. And you will seek Me and find Me, when you search for Me with all your heart.* Jeremiah 29:12-13

God promises to listen to us and reveal Himself when we call on Him in prayer. Really think about that for a moment. The One who measures the Universe in the span of His hand, and upholds it by the word of His mouth, has condescended to give us His attention.

> *Call to Me, and I will answer you, and show you great and mighty things, which you do not know.* Jeremiah 33:3

Not only will He answer our call, but He will take the opportunity to show us the great and mighty mysteries of His kingdom.

> *Be anxious for nothing, but in everything by prayer and supplication, with thanksgiving, let your requests be made known to God; [7] and the peace of God, which surpasses all understanding, will guard your hearts and minds through Christ Jesus.* Philippians 4:6-7

The cure for anxiety, and the path to supernatural peace, is prayer. Prayer is God's prescription for anxiety attacks. This promise is one of my favorites; primarily because it has been real for me during the most stressful times in my life.

Now for perhaps the greatest promise of all:

Map 23 - The Power of Prayer

If you then, being evil, know how to give good gifts to your children, how much more will your heavenly Father give the Holy Spirit to those who ask Him! Luke 11:13

Another great promise of prayer is the Holy Spirit – given to those that ask the Father for Him. This wonderful truth begs the question: Is the Holy Spirit's power in our lives inhibited by our lack of effectual fervent prayer? If so, then what can we do to engage that power? Searching deeper, we will discover the answer.

Effective Prayer Requires Righteousness

The effective, fervent prayer of a righteous man avails much. James 5:16

James encourages us that the prayer that avails much is the prayer of a righteous man, woman or child. Righteousness is the beginning point of effective prayer. So, where do we get this righteousness; and how do we know we have it?

We begin with faith in the work of God through the obedience of His Son.

For as by one man's disobedience many were made sinners, so also by one Man's obedience many will be made righteous. Romans 5:19

For with the heart one believes unto righteousness… Romans 10:10

Righteousness is a gift of God, given to those that believe on His Son.

But of Him you are in Christ Jesus, who became for us wisdom from God—and righteousness and sanctification and redemption—that, as it is written, "He who glories, let him glory in the Lord." 1Corinthians 1:30-31

Righteousness is our becoming, in Christ, all that God requires us to be – "in Christ" because He is our righteousness.

Likewise you also, reckon yourselves to be dead indeed to sin, but alive to God in Christ Jesus our Lord. Therefore do not let sin reign in your mortal body, that you should obey it in its lusts. And do not present your members as instruments of unrighteousness to sin, but present yourselves to God as being alive from the dead, and your members as instruments of righteousness to God. For sin shall not have dominion over you, for you are not under law but under grace. Romans 6:11-14

Finally, righteousness is a gift that we must reckon to be true in our lives – moving us from believing unto righteousness to the actual presentation of our members as instruments (aka, weapons) of righteousness. This is made possible because Christ has become righteousness for us.

As we learned in the lesson on Renewing the Mind, reckoning is accounting what is true to God, as true for His children. By this accounting, the Holy Spirit renews our minds unto transformation. Reckoning is laying hold of that for which Christ Jesus laid hold of me (Philippians 3:12). This is a great time to practice the power of reckoning God's truth. Stop here and mediate on these passages, and any others to which the Holy Spirit leads you.

Effective Prayer Requires Godly Reverence

We must recognize that becoming righteous is a process. We would be naïve to think that this process has been completed in us on this side of eternity. We must be continuously careful in the way we approach God. This is a critical truth; one that we must return to if the church is to be an effective agent of God in the earth.

Map 23 - The Power of Prayer

It is foolish – even dangerous – to approach God in an unrighteous manner. This includes the whole of our being – thoughts, desires, body, emotions, character, etc. There are things that don't belong – that God won't allow – in His presence.

> *Therefore, brethren, having boldness to enter the Holiest by the blood of Jesus, by a new and living way which He consecrated for us, through the veil, that is, His flesh, and having a High Priest over the house of God, let us draw near with a true heart in full assurance of faith, having our hearts sprinkled from an evil conscience and our bodies washed with pure water.* Hebrews 10:19-22

We are encouraged to enter His presence boldly, but this boldness is wrought out of consecration and a true heart. We must approach Him with a humble heart and contrite spirit (Isaiah 66:2). The closing request of Psalm 139 is a great place to start.

> *Search me, O God, and know my heart;*
> *Try me, and know my anxieties;*
> *And see if there is any wicked way in me,*
> *And lead me in the way everlasting.* Psalm 139:23-24

We can approach God "in Jesus' name" because it is "in Christ" that we are righteous before Him. "In Jesus' name" is an important consideration as we approach God. "On Jesus' behalf" is another way of saying it; or, "with Jesus' agenda as our only agenda". Coming in His name means our time with our Father is only about Him and His agenda. It means coming to pray what He wants prayed – waiting patiently to hear the desires of His heart for the meeting. We are there for Him – submitted to His will and direction in prayer.

Effective Prayer Requires Hearing from God

Every follower of Jesus wants to see their prayers accomplish the things for which they are praying. Most are righteous and many are fervent in their prayers. Yet, there is very little evidence of the outcomes alluded to in the James 5 passage (e.g., healing, weather miracles).

Perhaps it is a matter of praying effectively. Remember from our definition that "effective" prayer is prayer that will "put forth power". It is perfectly normal, and expected, that Christians will pray with power. But How?

> *So Jesus answered and said to them, "Assuredly, I say to you, if you have faith and do not doubt, you will not only do what was done to the fig tree, but also if you say to this mountain, 'Be removed and be cast into the sea,' it will be done. And whatever things you ask in prayer, believing, you will receive."* Matthew 21:21-22

The first prerequisite of effective prayer is "believing". But, how do we believe? Do we work up faith? Do we presume to have it? No, for faith is a gift (Ephesians 2:8); and faith comes by hearing, and hearing by the word of God (Romans 10:17). To believe, we must hear a word from the Lord about the object and objective of our prayer.

> *And whatever we ask we receive from Him, because we keep His commandments and do those things that are pleasing in His sight. And this is His commandment: that we should believe on the name of His Son Jesus Christ and love one another, as He gave us commandment.* 1John 3:22-23

Many like to stop with the first phrase of this passage, treating God like a vending machine. But, as we can see, we must keep His commandments and do those things that are pleasing in His sight. This is the second

Map 23 - The Power of Prayer

prerequisite. How does that happen? It happens when I listen to what He would have me obey AND what will please Him.

> *Now this is the confidence that we have in Him, that if we ask anything according to His will, He hears us. And if we know that He hears us, whatever we ask, we know that we have the petitions that we have asked of Him.* 1John 5:14-15

Thirdly, effective prayer requires our asking "according to His will", and not our own. How do I know His will if it is not in hearing Him express it? Effective prayer requires "ears to hear". This must be developed; and it will include moments of failure. We must remember that He is more interested in our attempts than in our success. He has grace to cover a multitude of mistakes.

The Heart that Hears

Behind every set of "ears to hear", there is a heart that hears. Recently, a dear friend of mine shared that he had come into a new understanding regarding the hearing of God's voice. In the past, he operated as if God was speaking all the time and he just didn't have his spiritual ears tuned in to what God was saying. He believed the issue was with his "hearing", so he employed various means to hear more effectively: Fasting, seeking quiet places, pushing out distractions, etc. None of these are wrong; they just don't get at the heart of the issue.

The revelation my friend has received is that God's words do not return void; they will accomplish what He intends (Isaiah 55:11). They are alive and powerful (Hebrews 4:12). In other words, if God has something to say to us, we will hear it. If we are not hearing, the problem is not with our ears. The problem is with our heart; for God does not waste His words on those that will not respond. The problem is our unwillingness to do what He says. To encourage us in this regard, Jesus said:

> *If anyone wills to do His will, he shall know concerning the doctrine, whether it is from God or whether I speak on My own authority.* John 7:17

In our willingness to do His will (and to pray it), we learn to distinguish God's voice from others (i.e., our flesh, the world, or Satan). Knowing it is His voice and His will, we can begin to pray with the confidence and fervency that avails much.

Effective Prayer Requires Fervency

Last, but not least, the effective prayer of a righteous man is described as fervent. God does not waste words. The Holy Spirit has been careful to include this word as a part of the prayer that avails much. We should be sure to understand its meaning.

Fervent is from the Greek word *zeō*, meaning "to boil with heat". Metaphorically, it means to have "boiling anger, love, or zeal for what is good or bad". This is not the dignified prayer most of us are use to. This is passionate prayer born out of desperation to know and pray the will of our Father.

As I write this, I am convicted that my prayer life lacks the level of fervency described by James. For the most part, I am lacking revelation and understanding about the importance of His will during my time with Him. There also seems to be an issue of pride and self-sufficiency that inhibits the passion of my prayers. God help us all to fight our way out of the apathy, indifference, pride and arrogance that inhibits the power of prayer in our lives.

Map 23 - The Power of Prayer

Conclusion

There is much to consider in this lesson – perhaps more than most. Let me encourage you that it is worth reading through again (and again). In the meantime, the short of it is that power in prayer requires righteousness, humility, a heart willing to respond, and fervency. These are developed in the Holy Spirit's transformational work, coupled with our faithful practice.

Joyful, Spirit-filled ministry is impossible without the effective fervent prayer of a righteous man (woman or child). The difference between ineffective prayer and prayer that avails much is vast. The promises God has attached to prayer are beyond all that we can think or imagine. God does very little in the life of a man who does not pray well. All the "greater than" things are done in and through the righteous one that will fervently pray the Father's will.

Application

Leaders in the Workplace are particularly challenged to pray. We feel that prayer takes time out of our busy schedules. Perhaps we should consider that it's the busy schedules that take time out of our communicating with God Almighty. Prayer should be a strategic imperative for every Leader in the Workplace. For those that believe, it is time to check priorities and calendars. It should not be hard to weed out those things that are less profitable than the effective fervent prayer of a righteous man.

Reckoning

My prayer, in Christ, will avail much.

Assignment

1. Review your notes and the Scripture passages from this week's module. Share the ones that are most meaningful to someone you are discipling.

2. Evaluate your prayer life – how strong is your prayer life relative to each of the following categories (1=don't have a clue, 10=perfect)? Explain the extreme ratings (3 and below; 8 and above).

    i) Disciplined
    ii) Relational
    iii) Fervent
    iv) Effective
    v) Persistent
    vi) Transformational
    vii) Expectant

3. Develop a prayer plan: Some immediate steps you can take to improve your prayer life.

4. Transform your plan to a written covenant with God.

Devotion

Practicing the Presence of God through Prayer
From Rob Streetman; The inLight Adventure Blog

> *Rejoice always, pray without ceasing, in everything give thanks; for this is the will of God in Christ Jesus for you.* 1Thesselonians 5:16-18

Map 23 - The Power of Prayer

Until recently, to "pray without ceasing" has seemed an impossible task. Though I am not there yet, God has given me a practice in prayer that is moving me closer to that wonderful state of being that Brother Lawrence called "Practicing the Presence of God". Here is how it works for me.

As I am sure it is with you, much of my time in prayer has been spent fighting off the interrupting and distracting thoughts. Most of these come from my flesh, the world and the devil. However, I am convinced that some are from God and from my good heart. So, how do I know which ones deserve my attention and which ones don't?

In the past, I have presumed that anything that doesn't sound like God must be pushed out of my mind. There are two problems here. First, this line of thinking exposes a naïveté (or arrogance) that I can always tell them apart. Worse, and more likely still, what are the chances that I am only considering the ones I am interested in? Who's in charge here, anyway?

Second, the battle to push out what I perceive to be the wrong thoughts is regularly the biggest distraction of all. One thought is forced out to be replaced by three others. Before long, I'm only thinking about what I'm thinking about.

Been there? Frustrated? You bet! But there is a better way.

> For the weapons of our warfare are not carnal but mighty in God for pulling down strongholds, casting down arguments and every high thing that exalts itself against the knowledge of God, bringing every thought into captivity to the obedience of Christ, and being ready to punish all disobedience when your obedience is fulfilled. 2Corinthians 10:4-6

God has shown me that the only way to deal with this challenge is to bring "every thought into captivity to the obedience of Christ". Yes, it really is that simple.

Whatever thought comes into my mind, I grab it, hold it up to my King, and ask Him what He wants me to do with it. If He says throw it away, then I do so in His authority. More often than I expected, He has something to say about it (e.g., a correction or insight into a stronghold). Many times, it becomes a point of prayer – like a meeting that I have that day.

The point here is that I submit to His authority over all my prayer life – even those parts that I thought He didn't care about. One thing I have noticed: The thoughts that come from my enemies have reduced significantly. I believe it is because what satan intended for evil, God has turned to good – and satan wants no part of that.

And I have discovered an incredible, unexpected benefit of this new discipline: It has increased my ability to pray without ceasing – practicing His presence – throughout the day. The Holy Spirit's training during my quiet time has prepared me for the more distracting interruptions that inevitably come during the more active times of my day.

Now, when a thought comes, I more naturally capture it for my King's review. The practice has put more in charge of my day, our relationship is growing, I more regularly respond/react "in Christ", and, most importantly, I get to enjoy His presence more.

The Map Maker's Guide

Map 24 - The Power of Unity

Spiritual Exercise

You are my hiding place;
You shall preserve me from trouble;
You shall surround me with songs of deliverance. Selah Psalm 32:7

For in the time of trouble
He shall hide me in His pavilion;
In the secret place of His tabernacle
He shall hide me;
He shall set me high upon a rock. Psalm 27:5

You shall hide them in the secret place of Your presence
From the plots of man;
You shall keep them secretly in a pavilion
From the strife of tongues. Psalm 31:20

He who dwells in the secret place of the Most High
Shall abide under the shadow of the Almighty.
I will say of the Lord, "He is my refuge and my fortress;
My God, in Him I will trust." Psalm 91:1-2

Prayer

Father God, we trust in You as our hiding place. You have been steadfastly faithful. Guide us to the secret place of Your presence. In Jesus' name. Amen.

Introduction

In our lesson on The One Another Fellowship, we discovered that loving one another is a requirement of every follower of Jesus Christ. We have also discussed that the pronoun "you" is plural over 85% of the times it is used in the New Testament. This includes Jesus' command for our work:

> *Let your light so shine before men, that they may see your good works and glorify your Father in heaven. Matthew 5:16*

It is the light of many, in the work of many, that our Father in heaven is glorified. Similarly, the Great Commission was given to the followers of Jesus Christ that together they would make more disciples. Being a disciple that makes disciples means there are no "Lone Rangers" in the kingdom of God.

> *I do not pray for these alone, but also for those who will believe in Me through their word; that they all may be one, as You, Father, are in Me, and I in You; that they also may be one in Us, that the world may believe that You sent Me. John 17:20-21*

Furthermore, the followers of Jesus were not to be a loosely knit disciple making group. Jesus prayed that His disciples, and those that followed them, would be as close as He and His Father. His vision for the church is a "body fitly joined together and compacted" (Ephesians 4:16; KJV). Sounds a bit like a can of sardines; or, if you prefer, a phone booth overflowing with people.

181

Map 24 - The Power of Unity

Clearly, God's intention for the church is a unity beyond our imagination... and our capability. Only He can accomplish it (as Jesus prayed). In this lesson, we will discover that there is a power released in God making us one. It is the power of unity.

Definition

Unity (*henotēs*): Unity, unanimity, agreement; from *heis*, meaning "one" (in contrast to many), and metaphorically, "union" and "concord". *Blue Letter Bible Outline of Biblical Usage* and *Vines Expository Dictionary*

Synergy: The working together of two things to produce a result greater than the sum of their individual effects. The term synergy comes from the Greek word *synergia* meaning "working together". *Wikipedia, the Free Encyclopedia*

Searching Out the Matter
(All Scripture references, but those noted, are NKJV; Thomas Nelson, Inc.; footnotes excluded)

Maturing in Christ is a Group Project

Marketplace Ministry requires the making of disciples God's way; helping others through the transformation process.

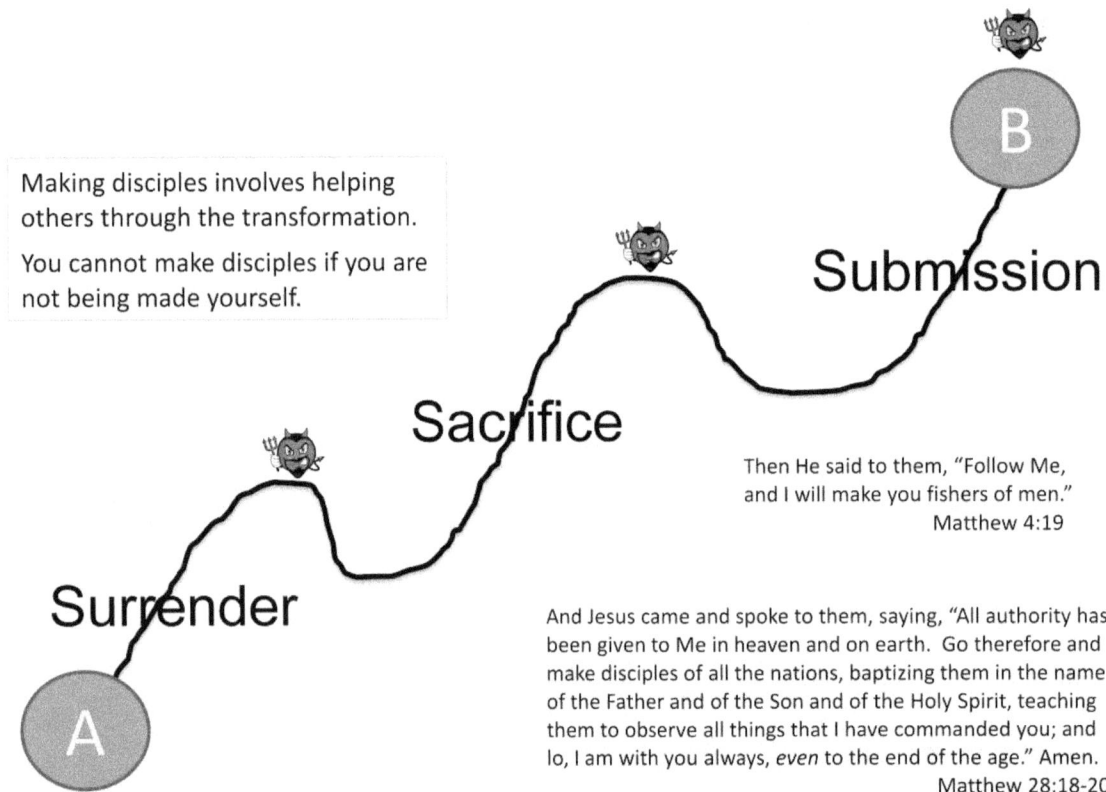

Making disciples involves helping others through the transformation.

You cannot make disciples if you are not being made yourself.

Submission

Sacrifice

Then He said to them, "Follow Me, and I will make you fishers of men." Matthew 4:19

Surrender

And Jesus came and spoke to them, saying, "All authority has been given to Me in heaven and on earth. Go therefore and make disciples of all the nations, baptizing them in the name of the Father and of the Son and of the Holy Spirit, teaching them to observe all things that I have commanded you; and lo, I am with you always, *even* to the end of the age." Amen. Matthew 28:18-20

When we consider the processes of "glory to glory transformation" and "finding joyful, Spirit-filled ministry", we recognize that our maturing as Christians is a ferocious battle. There is a devil at every level. Satan intends to impede our progress. That is why disciple making is so critical. We all need someone to encourage, edify and equip us through the process. And we need to be that for others. Battles are best fought in platoons.

During my career, the teams I worked with were constantly on the lookout for synergistic technology relationships – relationships where the resulting product was greater than the sum of the individual parts;

Map 24 - The Power of Unity

where something extra was produced. The ultimate purpose of these relationships was to provide business value that would "take us to the next level".

The same can be said for unity in the Body of Christ... with two significant exceptions. First, the "something extra" is the supernatural presence and empowerment of God. God is answering His Son's prayer with the power necessary to overcome our predilection for independence, suspicion, competition, etc. Second, God's purpose in unity is much greater than most have considered. Consequently, unity is woven into the whole fabric of our participation in God's work.

The Purpose of Unity

Unity is a fundamental component of God's story. In fact, He has made our unity a prerequisite for the restoration of two things that were lost in the Garden: His intimacy with us, as we become His Son's wife; and His habitation in us, in the New Jerusalem "prepared as a bride adorned for her husband". Unity in the Body of Christ is the proof and expression of our belonging to our Heavenly Father and His Son. Additionally, it is:

1. The Product of the Church's Glory.

   And the glory which You gave Me I have given them, that they may be one just as We are one…
   John 17:22

   Our unity is so important to Christ that, to accomplish it, He has given us the glory He received from the Father. We must ask ourselves, would He give His glory to those that will not use it to accomplish its intended result?

2. The Prescription for Evangelism.

   I in them, and You in Me; that they may be made perfect in one, and that the world may know that You have sent Me, and have loved them as You have loved Me. John 17:23

   Our unity will convince the world of the Father's love in sending His Son. It is the only prescription for evangelism in the New Testament. Our Lord and Savior has been praying this prayer to His Father for over 2000 years. We must not give up hope that He will succeed. Instead, we must agree with Him in this prayer; and surrender to the Father's response in us. I

3. The Promise of His Return.

   …till we all come to the unity of the faith and of the knowledge of the Son of God, to a perfect man, to the measure of the stature of the fullness of Christ… Ephesians 4:13

   Let us be glad and rejoice and give Him glory, for the marriage of the Lamb has come, and His wife has made herself ready. Revelation 19:7

   The wife made ready is the Church unified in the faith and the knowledge of the Son of God. Having "made herself ready" is the next great milestone of the church; ushering in Christ's Second Coming and the beginning of His Millennial Reign.

4. The Proof of Our Love for One Another.

   But above all these things put on love, which is the bond of perfection. And let the peace of God rule in your hearts, to which also you were called in one body; and be thankful. Colossians 3:14-15

   A new commandment I give to you, that you love one another; as I have loved you, that you also love one another. By this all will know that you are My disciples, if you have love for one another. John 13:34-35

Map 24 - The Power of Unity

The holy, beloved elect of God have been given the bond of perfection: Sacrificial love for one another. And we have been called in one body – a joined and knit together many-membered body, not a dismembered one.

5. The Power that Abides Us in Jesus Christ and Our Heavenly Father.

    ...that they all may be one, as You, Father, are in Me, and I in You; that they also may be one in Us... John 17:21

    Our unity with Christ and our Father in Heaven is dependent on, and proportional to, our unity with one another.

The purpose of unity to the God-head cannot be over-estimated. It should be no surprise that God exercises His power to accomplish so great a purpose. As we will see, our participation in His purpose for our unity yields more power; that the world would be drawn to, and glorify, our Father in heaven.

An Expression of His Presence

The manifestation of the power of God is not like turning on a light switch, as some have suggested. The power of God is an expression of His presence. If we are not practicing His presence, then we will not know His power. Only when we are participating in what He is doing will we experience His power to do exceedingly abundantly above all we can ask or think.

Therefore, the more we participate in Him making us one, the more power we will experience. The following are a few of His very special promises, found in the power that flows out of unity.

1. Unity prepares us for the release of the fear of God and His power.

    And they continued steadfastly in the apostles' doctrine and fellowship, in the breaking of bread, and in prayers. Then fear came upon every soul, and many wonders and signs were done through the apostles. Acts 2:42-43

    The closeness of the early church created an environment for the supernatural. God showed up! And His power was released through the leaders of this close community.

2. Unity empowers Jesus Christ's vision for the church.

    ... till we all come to the unity of the faith and of the knowledge of the Son of God, to a perfect man... that we should no longer be children, tossed to and fro and carried about with every wind of doctrine, by the trickery of men, in the cunning craftiness of deceitful plotting, but, speaking the truth in love... may grow up in all things into Him... according to the effective working by which every part does its share, causes growth of the body for the edifying of itself in love. Ephesians 4:13-16

    All that the church can be – maturity unto perfection, protection from deception, the liberty to speak the truth in love, effective working (operative power), and progressive growth of the body – comes from unity. Not one of these, much less the whole, is possible in the natural. Yet, the power for all of it is promised in our unity.

3. Unity establishes the environment for Pentecost – the baptism of the Holy Spirit.

    ... they were all with one accord in one place... and they were all filled with the Holy Spirit... Acts 2:1,4

    The desire for First Century power in the church is growing. It will not come through great speakers or energetic worship services. Pentecostal power is a product of unity.

4. Unity is the source of God's blessing of life forevermore.

Map 24 - The Power of Unity

Behold, how good and how pleasant it is
For brethren to dwell together in unity!
It is like the precious oil upon the head,
Running down on the beard,
The beard of Aaron,
Running down on the edge of his garments.
It is like the dew of Hermon,
Descending upon the mountains of Zion;
For there the LORD commanded the blessing—
Life forevermore. Psalm 133

Dwelling together in unity is like the priestly anointing (think Holy Spirit) and the LORD's blessing for eternal fruit-bearing life. Can we have either without unity?

The supernatural presence of God is promised for those that will earnestly pursue unity with all followers of Jesus Christ. As we examine our hearts for the things that separate us from each other, we should ask ourselves, "Are those things worth it?"

Conclusion

In conclusion, let us remember that the call to unity is not a higher bar that we must strive to reach. Quite the contrary, it is a gift that the Lord and the Father have given us to enjoy. The power that God has made available for those that will agree with, and pursue, Christ's prayer for unity is beyond estimation. To lay hold of it, we must let go of the attitudes and agendas that divide us.

Application

Building the kingdom is about cooperation, not competition. This is an accepted business principle. In the Workplace, a follower of Jesus Christ can pursue fellowship with the brethren without the constraints of doctrine and denomination – and work in unity for the glory of the Father without engaging in divisive sectarianism. In the process, God will honor our agreement with His Son's prayer by showing up in the work. And others will be drawn to Him there.

Leaders in the Workplace have been strategically positioned to be agents of God's answer to Jesus' prayer for unity. Please, please, please, don't miss the opportunity. The Body of Christ is depending on you.

Reckoning

Christ is passionate and intentional about His wife's preparation.

Assignment

1. Review your notes and the Scripture passages from this week's module. Share the ones that are most meaningful to someone you are discipling.

2. Invite the Lord to examine your heart. What are the attitudes and agendas that are separating you from the Body of Christ? Confess your sin and commit to walk in unity with the whole Body.

3. Meditate on Christ's prayer for unity in John 17:20-23. Ask Him how He wants you to agree with Him in word and deed.

Devotion

Just How Close Were They?
From Rob Streetman; The inLight Adventure Blog

Map 24 - The Power of Unity

It is amazing to think that the Father is making us one as He and His Son are one. It is one of the great mysteries of the kingdom. As you consider the following, I hope you will remember that we believe to understand (not vice-versa). I pray that you will find the Lord's faith, and the Spirit's wisdom and revelation.

> *My sheep hear My voice, and I know them, and they follow Me. And I give them eternal life, and they shall never perish; neither shall anyone snatch them out of My hand. My Father, who has given them to Me, is greater than all; and no one is able to snatch them out of My Father's hand. I and My Father are one.* John 10:27-30

So Who's hand are the sheep in? Can a sheep be in more than one place? What, are they throwing them back and forth like a hot potato? Or two circus jugglers? Of course not! They are the same hand.

And here we finally learn the truth: Jesus and His Father are one. Not, "We will be one when I go back to Him." No, this Jesus – who made Himself of no reputation – is somehow, mysteriously, one with His Father.

> *For unto us a Child is born,*
> *Unto us a Son is given;*
> *And the government will be upon His shoulder.*
> *And His name will be called*
> *Wonderful, Counselor, Mighty God,*
> *Everlasting Father, Prince of Peace.* Isaiah 9:6

This verse has always troubled me – until now. The Father and Son are so much "one", that they share titles.

> *In the beginning was the Word, and the Word was with God, and the Word was God. He was in the beginning with God. All things were made through Him, and without Him nothing was made that was made.* John 1:1-3

Interestingly, though God did all the work when Jesus was on the Earth, none of the work of creation was done without Him, nor through Him.

> *Now to the King eternal, immortal, invisible, to God who alone is wise, be honor and glory forever and ever. Amen.* 1Timothy 1:17

Who is this King? Not Jesus, but the invisible God (the Father). More title sharing.

> *When Jesus heard that, He said, "This sickness is not unto death, but for the glory of God, that the Son of God may be glorified through it."* John 11:4

> *So, when he had gone out, Jesus said, "Now the Son of Man is glorified, and God is glorified in Him. If God is glorified in Him, God will also glorify Him in Himself, and glorify Him immediately.* John 13:31-32

And so, glory passes between the Father and Son freely and intimately. Of course, this is something we already knew – the Father and Son are perfectly united. What is amazing is the claims of Christ that we would be as united with each other and Them. It is the Father's intention that His Son's Bride be perfect, without spot or wrinkle. So...

The oneness that Jesus speaks of includes the Father, His Son, and His human sons and daughters. This is a mystery that will never make sense to our limited minds. However, we can know it in our heart, soul and strength. It can be reality to us if we desire and pursue it.

Humbly yours and forever His,

Rob

The Map Maker's Guide

Map 25 - God's Mighty Force

Spiritual Exercise

Now to Him who is able to do exceedingly abundantly above all that we ask or think, according to the power that works in us, to Him be glory in the church by Christ Jesus to all generations, forever and ever. Amen. Ephesians 3:20-21

… it is God who works in you both to will and to do for His good pleasure. Philippians 2:13

Do not fear, little flock, for it is your Father's good pleasure to give you the kingdom. Luke 12:32

Prayer

Heavenly Father, to You be glory in the church by Christ Jesus. Thank you for working in us to accomplish Your good pleasure; including the promise of Your kingdom. Like Joshua, we commit ourselves to be strong and of good courage. So much of Your kingdom is beyond our imagination… and our experience. Our hearts desire is to know You and Your Son, for this is eternal life. Give us the spirit of wisdom and revelation in the knowledge of You. We surrender to Your purpose, we chose to sacrifice for Your plan, and we submit to Your power. We do this because we love You and desire that the world would see Your glory; even now in our lives. We trust You in this. Amen.

Introduction

Mature followers of Jesus Christ recognize that there is a fierce battle being waged for the souls of mankind, both in and outside of the church. The Scriptures hold great encouragement in regards to the battle preparations that have already been made, as well as the weapons that have been provided for our participation. The Workplace Leader's responsibility is to carry truth and faith into the battle, so that others will be encouraged to become more engaged. Those that answer the call to war will discover that David's Mighty Men are but a shadow of what God has empowered us to be as His Mighty Men, Women and Children.

Definition

Mighty (*dynatos*): Able, powerful, mighty, strong; mighty in wealth and influence; strong in soul (i.e., to bear calamities and trials with fortitude and patience, strong in Christian virtue); to be able (to do something, excelling in something, having power for something). *Outline of Biblical Usage, BlueLetterBible.org*

Searching Out the Matter
(All Scripture references, but those noted, are NKJV; Thomas Nelson, Inc.; footnotes and headings excluded)

"Be Strong and of Good Courage"

Seven times before the nation of Israel entered the Promised Land, God told Joshua to be "strong and of good courage". The time had come for God to give them what He had promised – the desire of their hearts. We need the same encouragement today; for, whether we like it or not, we are in a battle of our own. We have been promised a kingdom, but it is a kingdom we must fight for. Jesus made this clear.

Map 25 - God's Mighty Force

And from the days of John the Baptist until now the kingdom of heaven suffers violence, and the violent take it by force. Matthew 11:12

John, in his Revelation of Jesus Christ, was given a vision of the veracity of this epic battle.

And war broke out in heaven: Michael and his angels fought with the dragon; and the dragon and his angels fought, but they did not prevail, nor was a place found for them in heaven any longer. So the great dragon was cast out, that serpent of old, called the Devil and Satan, who deceives the whole world; he was cast to the earth, and his angels were cast out with him. And the dragon was enraged with the woman, and he went to make war with the rest of her offspring, who keep the commandments of God and have the testimony of Jesus Christ. Revelation 12:7-9,17

Those "who keep the commandments of God and have the testimony of Jesus Christ" are us. There is no escaping the battle of the Ages. Satan has brought the fight to us. Paul put it this way:

For we do not wrestle against flesh and blood, but against principalities, against powers, against the rulers of the darkness of this age, against spiritual hosts of wickedness in the heavenly places. Ephesians 6:12

There is no getting around it: The battle is too much for mere mortals. Perhaps this is why so many Leaders in the Workplace have decided to stand by and watch the kingdom be taken from them. So, how are we, mere humans, to stand in such a violent battle?

Finally, my brethren, be strong in the Lord and in the power of His might. Ephesians 6:10

In that day the LORD of hosts will be
For a crown of glory and a diadem of beauty
To the remnant of His people,
For a spirit of justice to him who sits in judgment,
And for strength to those who turn back the battle at the gate. Isaiah 28:5-6

Now is the time to reckon that "in the Lord and in the power of His might" we are more than mere humans. We are God's Mighty Men, Women and Children. The LORD of hosts will be our strength!

The Mighty Force of God

The images of war in the Old Testament are a foreshadowing of the battles that Christians face in the new. My favorite warriors are those mighty men that served under King David. Here are a few of their exploits (from 2Samuel 23:8-12, 18-23):

- Adino killed eight hundred men at one time.

- Eleazar was one of four that defied the Philistines when the men of Israel had retreated. He arose and attacked the Philistines until his hand stuck to the sword. The people returned after him only to plunder.

- Shammah killed a troop (300) of Philistines in a lentil field. So the LORD brought about a great victory.

- Abishai lifted his spear against three hundred men and killed them.

- Benaiah killed two lion-like heroes of Moab, went down and killed a lion in the midst of a pit on a snowy day, and killed an Egyptian, a spectacular man.

These men knew that the LORD was with them; that their feats were beyond human ability. David knew it, too. He had no worries when it came to His army. When the call to war was given, his men waded into the battle, full of faith and courage. By just being in the presence of David's Mighty Men, the remainder of David's army (including green recruits) learned both how to fight and how to have faith in their God.

Map 25 - God's Mighty Force

The same must be true for us today! God is raising up many mighty men, women and children to fight for His Kingdom. His Son is our Captain.

> For it was fitting for Him, for whom are all things and by whom are all things, in bringing many sons to glory, to make the captain of their salvation perfect through sufferings. Hebrews 2:10

> Now I saw heaven opened, and behold, a white horse. And He who sat on him was called Faithful and True, and in righteousness He judges and makes war. His eyes were like a flame of fire, and on His head were many crowns. He had a name written that no one knew except Himself. He was clothed with a robe dipped in blood, and His name is called The Word of God. And the armies in heaven, clothed in fine linen, white and clean, followed Him on white horses. Revelation 19:11-14

His victory is sure. We are blessed to participate. While we all may have different assignments, His mission is clear.

His Mission = Our Marching Orders

King Jesus was sent by His Father with a mission that was unlike that of any king this world has ever seen (or will ever see). He was not interested in conquering nations. He had a much greater, and more difficult, mission in mind. Listen carefully to His inauguration address.

> And He was handed the book of the prophet Isaiah. And when He had opened the book, He found the place where it was written:

>> " The Spirit of the LORD is upon Me,
>> Because He has anointed Me
>> To preach the gospel to the poor;
>> He has sent Me to heal the brokenhearted,
>> To proclaim liberty to the captives
>> And recovery of sight to the blind,
>> To set at liberty those who are oppressed;
>> To proclaim the acceptable year of the LORD."

> Then He closed the book, and gave it back to the attendant and sat down. And the eyes of all who were in the synagogue were fixed on Him. And He began to say to them, "Today this Scripture is fulfilled in your hearing." Luke 4:17-21

Jesus came to establish the kingdom of God, heal the brokenhearted, and make men free. This freedom is salvation (*sozo*). It includes the healing of heart, soul, mind and strength. We are to be His instruments and weapons of righteousness. As the Father sent Him, in the same way, He sends us. His mission has become our marching orders.

As a foreshadowing prophecy to the Luke 4 passage, the 58th chapter of the book of Isaiah has more to say about our marching orders:

> Is this not the fast that I have chosen:
> To loose the bonds of wickedness,
> To undo the heavy burdens,
> To let the oppressed go free,
> And that you break every yoke?

> Is it not to share your bread with the hungry,
> And that you bring to your house the poor who are cast out;
> When you see the naked, that you cover him,
> And not hide yourself from your own flesh?
> Then your light shall break forth like the morning,
> Your healing shall spring forth speedily,

Map 25 - God's Mighty Force

And your righteousness shall go before you;
The glory of the LORD shall be your rear guard. Isaiah 58:6-8

As Christ's kingdom representatives, we are to be agents of deliverance, transformation and sacrificial love ministry. For this purpose, the King has armed us with powerful weaponry.

Our Weapons

Much has been said regarding the weapons and God's way for our warfare, recorded in the sixth chapter of Ephesians. There are three points I would like to make, that you may not have considered; points that I believe will further empower you for the battle. First, there is the opening of Paul's encouragement.

> *Finally, my brethren, be strong in the Lord and in the power of His might.* Ephesians 6:10

Being strong in the Lord is bringing to bear the Holy Spirit's gifts and fruit, through submission to the life of Christ. The gifts of the Spirit are available to every believer as the Spirit determines – for the benefit of all (1Corinthians 12:7-11). We should be careful not to constrain the Spirit in this. The power of God must be received in the package that is offered. Otherwise we run the risk of accepting a counterfeit gift, offered by Satan.

The fruit of the Spirit (love, joy, peace, longsuffering, kindness, goodness, faithfulness, gentleness, self-control) is present and fully available in every believer. For example, the impatient believer does not need to pray for patience, but for the impatience to be removed. The same is true for love and the judgmental spirit that inhibits the manifestation of unconditional love.

The power of His might is the force that only He can bring to bear on our behalf. The Greek word for "power" here is *kratos* – the power of God's authority; His power to reign. Our strength in that power is found in our prayer, "Your kingdom come".

When we are strong in the authoritative power of God, we are calling on Him to establish His Kingdom in the places He has called us to invade – from the alley way to the board room. As God establishes His kingdom in a place or situation, the atmosphere is changed and we are able to enter in, clothed in the armor of God, wielding the sword of the Spirit.

My second point is about this very thing: How we wield the word of God. Sadly, many in the church – even leaders – have determined that the word of God is best used against their brethren. Many mean well; and many do not. In any case, certainly there are better uses for a sword than inflicting wounds to your own body. How about using it to make the church free from the wiles of the devil?

> *Then Jesus said to those Jews who believed Him, "If you abide in My word, you are My disciples indeed. And you shall know the truth, and the truth shall make you free."* John 8:31-32

> *For the word of God is living and powerful, and sharper than any two-edged sword, piercing even to the division of soul and spirit, and of joints and marrow, and is a discerner of the thoughts and intents of the heart.* Hebrew 4:12

God's word is the Spirit's sword for making the captives free. This is what our Captain came to accomplish; and what He commissioned us to do on His behalf. He has commanded us to courageously face the enemy, participating with the Spirit, as God's weapons of righteousness. Together we will experience greater success in the spirit realm than David's Mighty Men did in the physical.

Lastly, a word about prayer. Understandably, some consider it a weapon; for it has been used to defeat the enemy on many fronts. I suggest that it is something more; more than a weapon; even more than a part of our spiritual armor.

Map 25 - God's Mighty Force

Prayer is nothing less than God's way for our engaging in the battle and the purpose for which we are armed. To put on the armor of God is to prepare for battle. Prayer is the battle itself; with God's word being our chief weapon employed against our enemies during the conflict.

Knowing Our Enemy

The enemies of God must be our enemies. As we know, Satan is our arch enemy. But there are two others that Satan has allied himself with – to manipulate and defeat the army of God.

> For those who live according to the flesh set their minds on the things of the flesh... For to be carnally minded is death... [7] Because the carnal mind is enmity against God... Romans 8:5-7

> Adulterers and adulteresses! Do you not know that friendship with the world is enmity with God? Whoever therefore wants to be a friend of the world makes himself an enemy of God. James 4:4

Satan, our flesh and the world (systems, not people): These are our enemies. It is good to understand they mean our destruction. It's also good to know who our enemies are not. We must have our minds renewed in the knowledge that even our worst human enemy is simply a captive agent of the enemy we have been called to fight. This begs a very important question: How do we engage the captives (even those that act on behalf of our real enemies)?

> But I say to you who hear: Love your enemies, do good to those who hate you, bless those who curse you, and pray for those who spitefully use you. To him who strikes you on the one cheek, offer the other also. And from him who takes away your cloak, do not withhold your tunic either. Give to everyone who asks of you. And from him who takes away your goods do not ask them back. But love your enemies, do good, and lend, hoping for nothing in return; and your reward will be great, and you will be sons of the Most High. For He is kind to the unthankful and evil. Therefore be merciful, just as your Father also is merciful. Luke 6:27-30,35-36

What an incredible battle plan!! Who but God would have known that the most successful strategy would be to fight the evil in others with the weapons (of the kingdom) that we have been given: Love, blessing, humility, forgiveness, generosity, kindness and mercy. The Power behind these cannot be over stated.

A Soldier's Focus

Lastly, as soldiers of God's kingdom, we are called to focus on pleasing our Commander. This seems obvious, but it certainly doesn't hurt to be reminded; as Paul reminded Timothy.

> You therefore must endure hardship as a good soldier of Jesus Christ. No one engaged in warfare entangles himself with the affairs of this life, that he may please him who enlisted him as a soldier. 2Timothy 2:3-4

We must be careful not to entangle ourselves in the affairs of this life. These will be different things for each of us. It is up to each one to hear from the Lord regarding the things that should be removed and avoided.

> Therefore Jesus also, that He might sanctify the people with His own blood, suffered outside the gate. Therefore let us go forth to Him, outside the camp, bearing His reproach. For here we have no continuing city, but we seek the one to come. Hebrews 13:12-16

As Christ said, we must take up our cross and follow after Him. He is outside the camp. What does that mean to you? What is the camp that you must leave behind? Is it your concentration camp? Are you a captive? The King is calling you out to freedom – to join Him in making others free.

Map 25 - God's Mighty Force

Conclusion

God has made it clear that we are to be soldiers engaged in a violent battle for His kingdom. His ways and thoughts in battle are above our own. He has commanded us to resist the temptation to fight with the captives, and join Him in the battle against our true enemies.

Many are unintentionally aiding the enemy by battling against the wrong foe. Others are ignorant victims, thinking they can be safe on the sidelines. Those that are putting up a fight are weakened by division in the ranks. If we are to enjoy the victories of our King, we must fight this war, His way. As we do, He will empower us to enjoy the victories with Him.

One final concluding reminder: We must remember that we are "instruments of righteousness". We are not given power and authority to exercise them as independent agents. It is His power, not our own. We are merely instruments and weapons. We are the light of the world only as we live out of His life.

Application

If Jesus Christ is our King and we are Leaders in the Workplace, then we are His captains – the Mighty Men, Women and Children of God. There is still time to sound the battle cry and rally the troops. This is the privilege and responsibility of the Workplace Leader. For the Father's name, glory and kingdom, gird up your loins for battle and wade into it with faith and boldness. Become God's Mighty Force!

Reckoning

I am a violent one that will take the kingdom of heaven by force.

Assignment

1. Review your notes and the Scripture passages from this week's module. Share the ones that are most meaningful to someone you are discipling.

2. Ask God to reveal those things that stand between the Spirit's fruit and those around you.

3. Meditate on the meaning of the Kingdom suffering violence, your place in the battle, and the weapons God has given you to be a member of His mighty force.

Devotion

Speaking Against the Inhibitors
From 40 Days of Fasting and Prayer Devotion; New River Community Church

The last week or so, I have had a growing concerned for those that might not "go outside the camp". I have wondered about what would inhibit them, and what I could do to help them "trust and obey" Christ's call to come out to Him. In fact, I have been casually surveying those I meet to see what they think.

Before we get to the list, I want to assure you that my motives are selfish. I have an agenda here. Simply put, I don't want to go anywhere without all of you (and some that have already found the road less traveled too hard for their liking). In my response to each inhibitor, I intend to arm you with the sword of the Spirit, the word of God, so that you might be able to stand against the wiles of the Enemy yourself, and encourage others to do the same. So here goes:

Inhibitor #1 – The perceived cost in finances, time, and all other comforts of this world:

My first suggestion is to change the word "cost" to "investment"; see the parables of the pearl, and the hidden treasure (Matthew 13: 44-46). Secondly, let's keep in mind that this investment is guaranteed, by the promises of God, to produce off-the-chart returns (Malachi 3:10,11 and Matthew 19: 29). Lastly, let's be careful not to allow the Enemy to paint worse case scenarios, when our Provider is, above all, a lover of our souls.

Map 25 - God's Mighty Force

Inhibitor #2 – A lack of vision or understanding of where we are going:

As before, let's change the language. For God's people, "vision" is really "promise". With this in mind, review Joshua 1: 3-9 and 24: 12-14. Secondly, as much as we want to know where we are going before we commit to go there, it is simply not God's way to distract us with unnecessary details. With Him, it is always a question of "Who". Is it not enough that He is where we are headed?

Inhibitor #3 – A lack of faith, generally in Him being with us in the journey:

In business, it is a requirement to have a good end-to-end plan before you begin a major change. We have been trained by the world to expect the same from God. However, in His Kingdom, we are only shown enough to require our trust and obedience. Satan will try to discredit our LORD by suggesting He is unfair in not revealing it all. But the One Who is Greater has promised not to forsake us (Joshua 1: 5).

We must recognize that it is for our good that we are called to walk in faith with Him. The journey is, in itself, a test of our faith. Its exercise creates strength and relationship with the Most High God. The best advice I can give is to cry out, "Lord, I believe, help my unbelief." It is in His faith that we walk. He is eager and able to answer our cry.

Inhibitor #4 – Not knowing Him:

As it turns out, this is the most truthful of all the inhibitors. We simply do not know the LORD well enough to run out to Him. It is like a toddler whose Father has been at war or on the mission field for the last two years. This little one will hide and cry before he will be picked up, much less run to meet this perceived stranger. The obvious answer is getting to know Him. That is the purpose of these 40 days of fasting and prayer. Take full advantage of the season. You will be amazed at His love, gentleness, power and encouragement. He is all we need for every step. He yearns for us to join Him.

One last point in closing: It has been suggested that we actively seek out those that need an encouraging word. If you have been encouraged, then you cannot dismiss yourself from this critical responsibility. Helping others find their way is perhaps the most important "out of the camp" act we are called to at this time. Don't get distracted by fear or doubt. Be bold in your love for your brother and sister in Christ.

The Map Maker's Guide

Map 26 - The Church He is Building - Model

Spiritual Exercise

For the word of God is living and powerful, and sharper than any two-edged sword, piercing even to the division of soul and spirit, and of joints and marrow, and is a discerner of the thoughts and intents of the heart. Hebrews 4:12

So shall My word be that goes forth from My mouth;
It shall not return to Me void,
But it shall accomplish what I please,
And it shall prosper in the thing for which I sent it. Isaiah 55:11

Prayer

Father in Heaven, we surrender our will to You. We long to hear and know Your voice. We commit to do what we hear. With the psalmist we pray, "Search me, O God, and know my heart; try me, and know my anxieties; and see if there is any wicked way in me, and lead me in the way everlasting." We anticipate Your word accomplishing what You please. We pray that it would make us free. In Jesus' name. Amen.

Introduction

As we've previously discussed, Jesus Christ's vision for the church He is building is a unified body of believers that share the truth in love, create operative energy in working together, and build up the body by their love for one another (Ephesians 4:11-16). This fellowship will be manifested, at the end of this Age, as the wife of Christ and the New Jerusalem – the restored habitation of the Father, Son and Holy Spirit.

Hear, O Israel: The Lord our God, the Lord is one! You shall love the Lord your God with all your heart, with all your soul, and with all your strength. And these words which I command you today shall be in your heart. Deuteronomy 6:4-6

For we are His workmanship, created in Christ Jesus for good works, which God prepared beforehand that we should walk in them. Ephesians 2:10

Loving the Lord with all our strength involves practical action in accordance with the ways of God. We must put into action what we have heard (being doers of the word), and we must lead others into the loving and knowing of God that comes through the good works that we have been called to walk in.

Therefore whoever hears these sayings of Mine, and does them, I will liken him to a wise man who built his house on the rock: and the rain descended, the floods came, and the winds blew and beat on that house; and it did not fall, for it was founded on the rock. But everyone who hears these sayings of Mine, and does not do them, will be like a foolish man who built his house on the sand: and the rain descended, the floods came, and the winds blew and beat on that house; and it fell. And great was its fall. Matthew 7:24-27

But be doers of the word, and not hearers only, deceiving yourselves. For if anyone is a hearer of the word and not a doer, he is like a man observing his natural face in a mirror; for he observes himself, goes away, and immediately forgets what kind of man he was. James 1:22-24

Map 26 - The Church He is Building - Model

As Jesus and James have admonished, being a hearer of the word only, and not a doer of the work, leaves us vulnerable and deceived. In this lesson, we will briefly review Christ's vision for His church and then move on to explore how His vision should be worked out in this age and season.

Definition

Church (*ekklesia*): From *ek*, "out of," and *klesis*, "a calling", was used among the Greeks of a body of citizens "gathered" to discuss the affairs of State; a gathering of citizens called out from their homes; an assembly. *Vine's Expository Dictionary*

Fellowship (*koinōnia*): Fellowship, association, community, communion, joint participation, intercourse; intimacy; a gift jointly contributed, a collection, a contribution, as exhibiting an embodiment and proof of fellowship. *BlueLetterBible.org Outline of Biblical Usage*

The church – our Savior King's wife – has been called out of something; and called into something. We've spoken of this often; it's time to do more than talk. As Leaders in the Workplace, we must decide: Will we go out to Him, or will we continue to compromise ourselves, our families, our fellowships and our communities?

I am praying that the grace of God, the faith of Jesus Christ, and the power of the Holy Spirit will propel you into your destiny for the called out fellowship of the kingdom.

Searching Out the Matter

(All Scripture references, but those noted, are NKJV; Thomas Nelson, Inc.; footnotes excluded)

Review from "The Church He is Building – Vision"

Before the beginning of time, God intended to have a people that He would inhabit. That which was lost in the Garden will be restored in the New Jerusalem.

> Then I, John, saw the holy city, New Jerusalem, coming down out of heaven from God, prepared as a bride adorned for her husband. And I heard a loud voice from heaven saying, "Behold, the tabernacle of God is with men, and He will dwell with them, and they shall be His people. God Himself will be with them and be their God. Revelation 21:2-3

As we discovered in Ephesians 4:11, Christ gave gifts to the church for her restoration. In the following verses (vv. 12-16), His vision for the church is described in amazing detail:

- Equipped – meaning repaired for its intended use (like a broken bone or tattered net).

- Unity of both the faith and the knowledge of the Son of God, even unto perfection.

- No longer deceived by our enemies.

- Speaking the truth to one another in love.

- Maturing in all things, into Him.

- Knit tightly together (loosely knit bodies won't survive).

- Effectively working – creating the operative energy of ministry.

- Every part doing its share (for the profit of all).

- A fellowship building itself up in sacrificial love.

Map 26 - The Church He is Building - Model

This is the church that will become His wife. This is His passion; the subject of His intercession. Her perfection is a prerequisite for His coming back to establish His Father's eternal kingdom.

> And I heard, as it were, the voice of a great multitude, as the sound of many waters and as the sound of mighty thunderings, saying, "Alleluia! For the Lord God Omnipotent reigns! Let us be glad and rejoice and give Him glory, for the marriage of the Lamb has come, and His wife has made herself ready." Revelation 19:6-7

Imagine yourself in this setting. Go ahead; close your eyes and imagine. This is our destiny: To marry the King of kings; to be given His name for eternity; to co-reign with Him.

So how do we pursue this wonder of God's creation? Always, always, it must be God's way.

God's Desire for His Church

At this point, we are so far from Christ's vision for the church, it may seem impossible to get there. But nothing is impossible for God. It would be easy to throw in the towel – to admit defeat. But that would be to admit a lie, for God has the victory in hand. Christ will have His wife.

To be a participant in that victory, we need only submit to the way He is building His church. I suggest we begin by looking at the most successful building program in the history of the church – a building program imbued with power. It's also happens to be the beginning of the one in which we are a part. Let's take a quick look at its creation and character.

> ... and that day about three thousand souls were added to them. Acts 2:41

> And the Lord added to the church daily those who were being saved. Acts 2:47

> However, many of those who heard the word believed; and the number of the men came to be about five thousand. Acts 4:4

> Now the multitude of those who believed were of one heart and one soul... Acts 4:32

> And believers were increasingly added to the Lord, multitudes of both men and women... Acts 5:14

It is no wonder that, throughout the history of Christendom, there has been much said about going back to the original church model. And this talk seems to be increasing as we draw closer to the end of the Church Age. In fact, there are many groups that are pursuing this example of healthy community living.

Is it any wonder? Just look at the results. Thousands being added at a time! The Lord adding to the church daily! When was the last time any fellowship could claim such Great Commission results?

It is time we dismissed the manmade church growth programs, and embraced God's way – demonstrated in the "First" church. Those that will buck the prevailing trends will discover the power that Jesus Christ exercises in building His church.

One word of caution: While it is true that God has given us a prescription for building His church, we must avoid the temptation to turn it into another church growth program. God's ways and thoughts are far above our own. The minute we try to codify and control His way is the minute we lose the power that His dynamic life brings to it. The Workplace Leader should consider this process as a framework that allows for liberty in response to the guidance of the Holy Spirit.

Map 26 - The Church He is Building - Model

God's Way in Building the "First" Church

As we explore the way Jesus built the "First" church, I remind you that He has not limited His building to our church facilities and campuses. He is also building His church in the Workplace. The following prescription for church building applies there as well.

Secondly, we must recognize that God is a process oriented problem solver. The "First" church didn't grow up in a day. They didn't immediately start sharing their belongings. Expecting that at the onset is getting ahead of ourselves and God; and creates an unnecessary and fearful distraction. So, let's carefully explore just what happened at the beginning, in the second chapter of Acts. Read the full chapter, start to end; then read each referenced verse as you consider the following steps:

1. Those that would be the core of the church were waiting with one accord and in one place (v.1). God has placed a core group of dedicated believers within your sphere of influence. Begin by gathering together.

2. They waited expectantly for the Lord's anointing (vv. 2-12). Your experience may or may not be as dramatic as that first outpouring of the Holy Spirit, but it will be noticeable by you, and by others.

3. They were mocked (v. 13). Do not be surprised that some mock you and your group. In fact, it is a good sign; even a blessing (Matthew 5:11).

4. They were bold in their response, sharing the Gospel of the kingdom as the Holy Spirit directed (vv. 14-36). It is important to note that your group may have the opportunity to share with unsaved individuals, those that claim to be saved, and those that are what they claim.

5. They asked, "What shall we do?" (v. 37). This is always the pivotal question.

6. The answer, "Repent", is always the best first response (v.38). It was the first thing commanded by John the Baptist, Jesus and Peter. Why should it be any different with us? What we must remember is that repentance begins with "the sin". It requires getting off the throne of our hearts; that Christ might dwell there. It is a continual and progressive process, not just a onetime decision.

7. They were baptized (v. 38). As we've discussed, baptism is a work of God that has importance in the process of salvation. The implications are too important to minimize. This, too, was commanded by John the Baptist, Jesus and Peter.

8. After repentance and baptism, they received the promised Holy Spirit (vv. 39). The order and emphasis is critically important. God's promises are incredible... and conditional. The church in America has minimized the conditions and oversold the promises. We have compromised the Gospel, confused and frustrated many, and weakened the church in the process.

9. Being "saved from this perverse generation" (v. 40) is required for the church to be true to itself – the called out ones. Christ is outside the camp. In Revelation 18:4, He cries out, "Come out of her, my people, lest you share in her sins, and lest you receive of her plagues." Compromise with the world is a death wish.

10. Verse 42 contains the first description of Christ's "First" Church. Should we be doing anything else until we are doing these things well? We have covered each of these in detail in other parts of this curriculum. Each one is important; practiced together, they set the stage for God to show up.

11. What must it have been like for fear to come upon every soul (v. 43)! This of course is the fear of the LORD. In other words, God showed up!! And it was then, and only then, that many signs and wonders were done. Of course, the "then" means "after these things". The order is important. It will do no good to begin in the middle; or at the end. God has a way of doing things. We must conform to His way if we hope to do things in the power of His kingdom.

Map 26 - The Church He is Building - Model

For many, thoughts of the "First Church" go immediately to their sharing everything (v. 44-47). As we have now discovered, there is much that must happen before such a vibrant community is possible. Isn't it time we got started? It's really quite simple: Go back to step one; and BEGIN!

The Power of the Church

Some may ask, "Why should we take such a radical approach?" First and foremost, because it is God's way, our obedience is required. Secondly, doing things God's way is the best way to position ourselves for the release of God's power in the work.

There is no doubt that the church Christ is building is a church filled with, and operating in, the power of God. Luke was careful to record this for our encouragement.

> *Then fear came upon every soul, and many wonders and signs were done through the apostles.* Acts 2:43

> *And with great power the apostles gave witness to the resurrection of the Lord Jesus. And great grace was upon them all.* Acts 4:33

> *And through the hands of the apostles many signs and wonders were done among the people.* Acts 5:12

> *Also a multitude gathered from the surrounding cities to Jerusalem, bringing sick people and those who were tormented by unclean spirits, and they were all healed.* Acts 5:16

This looks a lot like Jesus' promise that those who believed in Him would do what He was doing, and even greater things (John 14:12). This is His promise for the church today. Powerful moves of God have not been limited to the first century church. Just since the founding of America, there have been two Great Awakenings, the Azusa Outpouring and other less documented "revivals".

Even now, God is moving powerfully in other parts of the world. There is no limit – in time or geography – to the One that is building His church. He has commanded us to join Him in this great and mighty work. So, what are we waiting for?

Conclusion

Christ is building His church. His vision is becoming reality. The evidence of the church He is building is the manifestation of great power and grace, signs and wonders, and incredible growth. Keep in mind that the growth you see may not be an increase in "new" believers, but in "true" believers – those truly surrendered to the King. Participation with Christ in building His church in the Workplace is an adventure. Adventures are initially a mixture of excitement and fear. Deal with the fear and it all becomes a life of exciting adventure!

Application

As Albert Einstein said, "Insanity is doing the same thing over and over again and expecting different results." If anyone understands the need and dynamics of change, it is Leaders in the Workplace. It is no coincidence that you have been elevated in this season of great challenge for the church. The need is not for invention, but for a return to the ways that work best – the ways that draw on the resources of God. If you are one of those whose heart is loyal to Him, He will show Himself strong on your behalf (2Chronicles 16:9).

Reckoning

I have been intentionally positioned to participate in Christ's building program.

Map 26 - The Church He is Building - Model

Assignment

1. Review your notes and the Scripture passages from this week's module. Share the ones that are most meaningful to someone you are discipling.

2. How do you define church? Do you believe that your fellowship includes every area of church life? What if your paradigm was such that your activities in the institution were a subset of church done God's way?

3. Why do we call our congregations, denominations and institutions "churches"? How is this potentially confusing to those outside (and some inside) the *ekklesia*?

4. Make the following devotion a spiritual exercise for your group.

Devotion – Duplicated in Map 7

From John Eldredge: Waking the Dead (pp. 190, 191)

When he left Rivendell, Frodo didn't head out with a thousand Elves. He had eight companions. Jesus didn't march around backed by legions of angels, either. He had twelve men – knuckleheads, every last one of them, but they were a band of brothers. This is the way of the kingdom of God. Though we are part of a great company, we are meant to live in little platoons. The little companies we form must be small enough for each of the members to know one another as friends and allies.

Who will fight for your heart?

How can we offer the stream of counseling to one another, unless we actually know one another, know each other's stories? The reason counseling became a hired relationship between two people was largely because we couldn't find it anywhere else; we haven't formed the sort of small fellowships that would allow the stream to flow quite naturally. Is it possible to offer rich and penetrating words to someone you barely know, in the lobby of your church, as you dash to pick up the kids?

Where will you find the Four Streams?

The Four Streams [discipleship, counseling, healing and warfare] are something we learn, and grow into, and offer one another, within a small fellowship. We hear each other's stories. We discover each other's glories. We learn to walk with God together. We pray for each other's healing. We cover each other's back. This small core fellowship is the essential ingredient for the Christian life. Jesus modeled it for us *for a reason*. Sure, he spoke to the masses. But he lived in a little platoon, a small fellowship of friends and allies. His followers took his example and lived this way, too. "They broke bread in their homes and ate together with glad and sincere hearts" (2:46). "Aquila and Priscilla greet you warmly in the Lord, and so does the church that meets at their house" (1 Cor 16:19). "Give my greetings to the brothers at Laodicea, and to Nympha and the church in her house" (Col 4:15).

The Map Maker's Guide

Epilogue - For Your Assignment

"As you have learned, this is My way for getting back what We lost in mankind's rebellion. It is the way My children become a part of Our restoration work. This Age is drawing to a close much faster than you think. It will happen with or without your participation. However, and this is very important, much is depending on you."

"I will do my best", said Somebody, feeling both small for the task and encouraged that the Mapmaker would trust him with the assignment. "I know I will not be alone."

"Yes, We will be with you. I, My Son, and the Holy Spirit have come to abide with you, and in you. As a branch abides in the vine, you now abide in My Son; and through Him, you abide in Me. You will never be alone. Trust and obey... there is no other way."

"One last word, Somebody."

"Yes, Mapmaker?"

"I love you, Somebody; like I love My Son, I love you."

"I love you too, Father; and I love Jesus and the Spirit. I truly want to love each of You more."

"You will, Somebody; you will."

And so we have come to the end of The Map Maker's Guide. If you have made it this far, you are truly a Somebody. Not a Somebody the world will respect, but a Somebody that God will honor and use for His glory and kingdom.

If you have made it this far, you also should have a bit more understanding about the desires of your heart, your assignment, and what it takes to be transformed from one to the other. My desire and prayer has been that God would use The Map Maker's Guide to encourage, edify and equip you, as a Leader in the Workplace, to be a disciple maker and transformation agent in your community. If it has done this work in you, then my work is done... and yours is just beginning.

Ministry in the Workplace may be the last hope for the church. God has a desire to do something extraordinary in the Workplace – in your particular spheres of influence. Through this study you have been called out and prepared to participate in His restorative work.

Your next decisions will be critical in your walk before the Lord. Much has been invested in you; and much is now expected. As the Angel of the Lord said to Joshua, "Be strong and of good courage." As a final gift of encouragement, I offer these passages for your meditation, and some recommendations for your consideration.

Workplace Leaders in the Making

Therefore we also, since we are surrounded by so great a cloud of witnesses, let us lay aside every weight, and the sin which so easily ensnares us, and let us run with endurance the race that is set before us, looking unto Jesus, the author and finisher of our faith, who for the joy that was set before Him endured the cross, despising the shame, and has sat down at the right hand of the throne of God. Hebrews 12:1-2

Delight yourself also in the Lord,
And He shall give you the desires of your heart. Psalms 37:4

But we all, with unveiled face, beholding as in a mirror the glory of the Lord, are being transformed into the same image from glory to glory, just as by the Spirit of the Lord. 2Corinthians 3:18

Now to Him who is able to do exceedingly abundantly above all that we ask or think, according to the power that works in us, to Him be glory in the church by Christ Jesus to all generations, forever and ever. Amen. Ephesians 3:20-21

Therefore, my beloved, as you have always obeyed, not as in my presence only, but now much more in my absence, work out your own salvation with fear and trembling; for it is God who works in you both to will and to do for His good pleasure. Philippians 2:12-13

You are the light of the world. A city that is set on a hill cannot be hidden. Nor do they light a lamp and put it under a basket, but on a lampstand, and it gives light to all who are in the house. Let your light so shine before men, that they may see your good works and glorify your Father in heaven. Matthew 5:14-16

So Jesus said to them again, "Peace to you! As the Father has sent Me, I also send you." John 20:21

Even as you are being used to make disciples in your spheres of influence, you are being made yourself. This is the joy of making disciples: Experiencing the Holy Spirit transforming you, as Jesus uses you to transform others. There is no greater adventure.

Focus and Perseverance

As I write these final words, my heart goes out to all that will hear and do what the Lord is saying. You have been exposed to many of the kingdom's mysteries. You may have forgotten more than you remember. No worries there; for the word is alive and powerful, and the Holy Spirit will bring to your remembrance what you need. The following are a few keys to the kingdom that I have found useful in my adventure:

1. Surrender, sacrifice and submit your life – every day. Your future assignments, and the "exceedingly abundantly more than you can ask or think", are only possible if you exchange your life for His. It is by His life that we are being saved; to be partakers of the divine nature, and to live in the adventure of joyful, Spirit-filled ministry.

2. Live for eternity like you are dying today. You will find more joy and peace in the adventure by focusing on God's bigger plan. You will have more impact for His kingdom if you will live each day with purpose, as if it were your last. This is a mindset that you must fight to obtain and protect.

3. Keep your eyes focused on the glory of the Lord – the primary condition for transformation. Your focus will cause others to look to Him, as well. Be aware that your enemies will attempt to distract you. Establish safeguards to protect yourself and others. Practice turning to Him in the morning, and regularly during the day.

4. Find your platoon; those that have your back in the spiritual battles you will face. In response to His Son's prayer, God has provided you with a community of believers for the adventure. You will need them as much as they need you.

5. On a regular basis, spend time with the Lord reviewing the desires of your heart, the people in your spheres of influence, His gifts for your assignment, and the three or four truths He has given you for the renewing of your mind.

6. Practice what you have learned; and teach it to others. Invest in twelve, and focus most of your time, attention and prayer on the three that are most passionate about the adventure. Make disciples who will make disciples, who will make disciples, etc.

7. Make the most of your chaos moments (don't waste the pain). When moments and seasons of chaos come, ask God what He is up to and join Him in the work. It will also be important for you to help others through their chaos moments and seasons. This is the mark of a true disciple maker.

8. Do not allow the enemy to discourage you in your adventure. Remember, your journey and your assignment are born out of the very purpose of God; and no purpose will be denied Him.

God bless you with His grace for the adventurous life.

Humbly yours and His forever,

Rob

The Map Maker's Guide

Bibliography

Bonhoeffer, Dietrich; *The Cost of Discipleship* (New York; SCM Press), 1959.

Chambers, Oswald; *My Utmost for His Highest* (Grand Rapids; Discovery House); 1992.

Colson, Chuck; *How Now Shall We Live?* (Wheaton; Tyndale House); 1999.

Crabb, Larry; *The PAPA Prayer* (Brentwood, Integrity); 2006.

Eldredge, John; *Waking the Dead* (Nashville; Thomas Nelson, Inc.); 2003.

Eldredge, John; *Wild at Heart* (Nashville; Thomas Nelson, Inc.); 2001.

Hayford, Jack (Executive Editor); *New Spirit-filled Life Bible* (Nashville, Nelson), 2002.

Hillman, Os; *Today God is First – Volumes 1 & 2;* http://www.MarketplaceLeaders.org.

Huegel, F.J.; *Bone of His Bone* (Jacksonville; Seedsowers Christian Books); 1997.

Roberts, Frances; *Come Away My Beloved* (Uhrichville, Barbour); 1973.

Streetman, Rob; *Marketplace Ministry Tips; Chapel Hill News and Views;* September, 2013.

Streetman, Rob; *The inLight Adventure Blog;* http://inlight.wordpress.com.

Streetman, Rob; *The Small Group Bible Study Series;* http://www.inlightconsulting.com/Small_Group_Study.html.

Unknown; *Outline of Biblical Usage;* http://www.blueletterbible.org/.

Unknown; *The Free Dictionary;* http://www.thefreedictionary.com/.

Unknown; *The Google Dictionary;* http://www.google.com.

Unknown; *The Merriam-Webster Dictionary;* http://www.merriam-webster.com.

Various; *Wikipedia, the Free Encyclopedia;* http://en.wikipedia.org.

Vine, William Edwy; *Vine's Expository Dictionary* (Nashville; Thomas Nelson, Inc.); 1985.

Vineyard Music; *I Surrender All;* http://www.youtube.com/watch?v=7x2IpLSfqp8.

The Map Maker's Guide

Recommended Reading

Section One – Preparation

The Dream Giver; Bruce Wilkinson

Wild at Heart; John Eldredge

Why You Think the Way You Do; Glenn Sunshine

Culture Making; Andy Crouch

The Fear of the Lord; John Bevere

Section Two – Surrendering to His Purpose

Crazy Love; Francis Chan

The PAPA Prayer; Larry Crabb

Spiritual Authority; Watchman Nee

Rees Howells – Intercessor; Norman Grubb

Humility and Absolute Surrender (combined set); Andrew Murray

Section Three – Sacrificing for His Plan

The Normal Christian Life; Watchman Nee

Radical; David Platt

The Treasure Principle; Randy Alcorn

Humility; Andrew Murray

The Cost of Discipleship; Dietrich Bonhoeffer

Section Four – Submitting to His Power

Destined for the Throne; Paul Billheimer

The Word and Power Church; Doug Banister

The Normal Christian Birth; David Pawson

They Found the Secret; V. Raymond Edman

They Shall Expel Demons; Derek Prince

The Saving Life of Christ; Major W. Ian Thomas

Devotionals

My Utmost for His Highest; Oswald Chambers

Come Away My Beloved; Frances J. Roberts

With Christ in the School of Prayer; Andrew Murray

The Hidden Treasure; John Brown

www.ingramcontent.com/pod-product-compliance
Lightning Source LLC
LaVergne TN
LVHW081345060426
835508LV00017B/1426

* 9 7 8 0 9 9 6 2 2 7 4 1 4 *